STUDIES IN SLAVE AND POST-SLAVE SOCIETIES AND CULTURES

Series Editors: Gad Heuman and James Walvin

FROM SLAVERY TO EMANCIPATION
IN THE ATLANTIC WORLD

STUDIES IN SLAVE AND POST-SLAVE SOCIETIES AND CULTURES

Series Editors: Gad Heuman and James Walvin

ISSN 1462-1770

FROM SLAVERY TO EMANCIPATION IN THE ATLANTIC WORLD

Editors

SYLVIA R. FREY

Tulane University

and

BETTY WOOD

University of Cambridge

FRANK CASS
LONDON • PORTLAND, OR

First published in 1999 in Great Britain by
FRANK CASS PUBLISHERS
Newbury House, 900 Eastern Avenue
London, IG2 7HH

and in the United States of America by
FRANK CASS PUBLISHERS
5804 N.E. Hassalo Street
Portland, Oregon 97213-3644

Copyright © 1999 Frank Cass Publishers

Website: www.frankcass.com

British Library Cataloguing in Publication Data

From slavery to emancipation in the Atlantic world. –
(Studies in slave and post-slave societies and cultures)
1. Slavery – United States – History 2. Slave-trade – History
3. Slaves – Emancipation
I. Frey, Sylvia R., 1935– II. Wood, Betty, 1945–
306.3′62′09

ISBN 0-7146-4964-3 (cloth)
ISBN 0-7146-8025-7 (paper)
ISSN 1462-1770

Library of Congress Cataloging-in-Publication Data

A catalog record for this book is available
from the Library of Congress

This group of studies first appeared as a special issue of *Slavery and Abolition*,
Vol.20, No.1, April 1999 (ISSN 0144-039X), published by Frank Cass.

Printed in Great Britain by Antony Rowe Ltd.

Contents

List of Illustrations

Introduction

SYLVIA R. FREY and BETTY WOOD

In recent years a number of studies have created a surge of new interest in the Atlantic dimensions of Western history: in migration and settlement patterns, family organization and social structures, demography and politics, agriculture and religion, economic development and consumer behaviour. The burden of these investigations suggests that the modern world has been shaped by a complex series of dialectics that link together the histories of many different and distinct cultures in a vast global system. It also suggests that the intricate societies that made up the Atlantic world shared certain common characteristics as well as marked differences and points to the possibilities for exploring a whole host of historical issues and for making explicit intertopical comparisons.

It was these possibilities which inspired the formation in 1995 of the Tulane–Cambridge Atlantic Studies group, a long-term collaborative project of the Faculties of History of Tulane University and the University of Cambridge. Our intention was to create a unique forum for international and inter-disciplinary dialogue for the purpose of exploring the interconnections between economic, political, moral, and cultural realms as an Atlantic World experience. To that end we brought together in a conference setting a group of eminent scholars from Europe, the Caribbean, Canada, and the United States to focus on the differential aspects of two broad structural changes that were common to many societies of the Atlantic world – the establishment of slavery and emancipation – on race, class, and gender. The geographic context for the project was the American South, the Caribbean, Latin America, and West Africa. The papers in this volume were presented at the inaugural conference held at Tulane University in November 1996.

Ours is a deliberately complex approach, dealing as it does with different groups of people in scattered and vastly different geographic regions and societies. It is precisely this complexity that we expected would shed light on certain critical questions: what can be learned by examining slavery in the Americas and in the African context about patterns of adjustment and change? To what extent did enslaved peoples succeed in creating a dynamic world of interaction within the Americas; across the Atlantic? What was the reaction of Africans to Europeans (and vice versa) outside the context of slavery? Did the common history of slavery produce a generic black identity or identities or did slaves develop a 'double consciousness' as a result of intimate contact with whites?[1] How did such factors as social geography and spatial organization affect the experiences of different groups of enslaved peoples? How, specifically, were experiences gendered?

The experience of emancipation raised a different set of questions, the principal one being the question of freedom. Who defined freedom and for what purposes? Did emancipation produce a shift in attitudes toward slavery among the enslavers; toward former enslaved peoples? Did different labour regimes of emancipation change patterns of labour usage and relationships between workers as well as between workers and their former owners? To what extent were the work experiences of liberated slaves similar to and different from those of enslaved peoples? What can we say of the creative and political work of enslaved and free peoples? Viewed both from the African and the American side how is slavery remembered? What is the link between remembering and forgetting the experiences of slavery and identity formation? What are the theoretical and methodological implications of the conference's findings?

The papers included in this collection form a representative sample of those presented to the inaugural conference. They address some but by no means all of the issues raised by the Tulane–Cambridge Atlantic Studies Group. They illuminate certain spatial and temporal conjunctions and contrasts, but reveal no definitive narrative. Nor did we expect them to. Viewed in relationship to one another and in the context of existing scholarship they cast interesting light on three broad subjects: the moral as well as the political dimensions of slavery and emancipation; the role of ritual and memory in the process of politicization; and the role of memory in the construction of identity. We present these essays with editorial comments in the hope that they will generate discussion and encourage further exploration of the many links that connected and continue to connect human beings on both sides of the Atlantic as well as the various linkages between internal and external developments.

Linda Heywood's paper sets out what is a recurring theme in the history of slavery and emancipation, the interaction of European and African peoples in the same cultural, economic, and political fields. Whether in African or New World slave societies, African and European ideologies and practices existed concurrently, at times complementing, at times testing one another. The continuing dialogue produced new ideologies and practices that transcended and transformed their antecedents. In a major conceptual breakthrough, Heywood describes a complicated transcultural process that evolved through three stages: the transformation of West Central African culture in Portugal; Luso-African tranculturization in Kongo and Angola;

and the evolution of a more complex form of Luso-African culture in Brazil. Central to her thesis is the paramount role of Roman Catholicism in every stage of this process.

The extent to which religion informed the behaviour of Africans in New World slave societies is a theme that runs through several of the conference papers and through much of the recent historiography on slavery.[2] Heywood's work in particular demonstrates the way in which religious ideology and practice functioned both as a form of political expression and as memory. The example she provides of the São Tomé confraternity in 1526 claiming secular freedom for all members of a Christian community resonates throughout the black Atlantic world, in Catholic and Protestant societies alike, throughout the history of slavery. The insistence of enslaved peoples that baptism made one free forced New World enslavers and their European supporters to construct political, legal, and religious defences to protect against the moral force of this argument.

In the Atlantic world, regardless of time and place, enslaved people, like European peasants and dispossessed people in revolutionary societies, drew on a wide array of religious rituals to assert cultural autonomy and to articulate their political demands. Religious rituals and festivals evolved over time into a rich tradition of performance culture that married tradition to innovation and took on a more explicitly political form. The broad outlines of this performance culture can be traced through the New England election-day rituals described by William Piersen, to the John Canoe carnivals that spread throughout the hemisphere,[3] to the militaristic parades described by Julie Saville in her paper on post-emancipation South Carolina and Louisiana.

Part of the ancestral memory of Africans, militaristic parades were the mediums through which African American men defined and expressed their identity and the principal means for the reformation of political identities of New World Africans. Military service in the American Revolution, in the Haitian Revolution, and in the American Civil War built on that tradition. In the American South the experience African American men gained as soldiers was part of their political transformation, a transformation that began in the American Revolution and reached a new level of maturity during the years of Civil War and Reconstruction. Saville's comparison of freed people's political ideology and organizations with the first national freedom struggle of African Americans in the American Revolutionary war era clearly demonstrates the importance of an evolutionary process which conjoined traditional African patterns with a greatly expanded European definition of rights. The spontaneous and frequently individual actions that characterized the black Revolutionary role were replaced by organized, collective, public demonstrations at the heart of which was a catalogue of rights that defined a growing list of corporate rights rooted in an expanding sphere of political culture.[4]

If, as Saville shows us, the process of Westernization gave black men a political agenda and a political voice to express it, that same process produced decidedly ambivalent results for black women. Seen in conjunction with Rebecca Scott's conference paper, Saville's work shows how far black men had travelled down the road to political maturity and how much black women had lost as a consequence of the assimilation of western political ideas. With emancipation, many black women benefited by being relieved of hard labour in the fields but confinement to the home, whether by choice or cultural proscription, denied them access to the institutional forums necessary for the development of ideas that were available to black men through service in the military and secular clubs and organizations. The civic rituals created by African Americans during the Civil War era celebrated a masculine, militarized ideal that roughly corresponded to a white gendered model of citizenship which limited the public political conduct of black women to pre-industrial forms. There were to be sure forums where the voices of women could still be heard, the two most important of which were their churches and their workplaces. The reaction to the feminization of religion in the nineteenth century forced black women and white women alike to relinquish public leadership roles and muted, if it did not still, their message of spiritual equality.[5] Black women did, however, continue to enjoy a measure of economic autonomy roughly equal to that of men.

The reformation of an African-American economic identity or identities seems to have followed a similar course throughout the hemisphere. As in the forging of their religious and political identities, the evolving economic identities of enslaved people involved a complex process of adapting 'European' institutions whose central features were already familiar to them in ways that satisfied their own cultural and material needs. Everywhere, and with varying degrees of success, enslaved people struggled to secure for themselves economic rights and economic autonomy in the interstices of the 'overlapping and sometimes clashing interests' (Usner, p.29) of slave owners and political authorities.

Dan Usner and Mary Turner's papers add to the growing volume of scholarship that delineates the ways in which this political struggle was played out in the overlapping world of work and local trade.[6] Everywhere in the Americas owners defined the various tasks associated with the 'formal' economy but enslaved people negotiated conditions of work. Issues differed significantly through time and across space, but the fundamental purpose of slave negotiations and slave protest was the same throughout the Americas: to limit the power of owners and to establish the principle of workers' rights. Both Usner and Turner point to the relationship between the prominent role of African women in Atlantic economies and their need to reclaim the independent status they had enjoyed as petty traders in West African societies. In all New World slave societies African-American women dominated local exchange and market activities, a right they continued to defend against the tightening restrictions on slaves' economic activities that Usner describes as a common pattern by the early nineteenth century. Turner's discussion of the role played by enslaved women in Berbice in the negotiation of economic rights highlights their importance in the development of a catalogue of economic rights that had profound political implications.

The political and the economic merged in another way. As Mary Turner and Rosanne Adderley remind us, both during slavery and after emancipation, negotiations over types and conditions of work, as well as over degrees of freedom, could involve interested third parties with agendas of their own. There was a complex interplay of moral and commercial imperatives in early nineteenth-century imperial legislation aimed at ending the Atlantic slave trade and, subsequently, dismantling the slave system, which collided with local and metropolitan European sugar interests. The 1826 Berbice code regulated and sought to 'modernize' labour discipline and established 'wage slavery' and basic civil rights for enslaved people but left patterns of labour and the work experience essentially unchanged.

The question of moral versus commercial interests takes a different form in Rosanne Adderley's work on Africans illegally enslaved following the passage by the British Parliament in 1807 of an act outlawing the African slave trade and the 1833 Emancipation Act. The issue in Trinidad and the Bahamas was whether resettlement should benefit Africans alone or satisfy the needs of both liberated Africans and British commercial interests. In the end, despite differences in staple crop agriculture between these two colonies, liberated Africans became menial agricultural labourers in the sugar economy of Trinidad and performed the same range of occupations as the rest of the black labouring population in the Bahamas. As such they became 'an integral yet free component of the slave society' (Adderley, p.71). This demonstrates both the limitations and the possibilities of emancipation policies. As Adderley emphasizes, and as Turner's paper corroborates, emancipation was 'an experimental process that was fraught with practical and cultural difficulties' (Adderley, p.68).

The various labour experiments embarked upon in very distinctive landscapes and social and political environments demonstrate above all what Saville calls 'the instability of slavery and freedom' and links the two conditions 'in inseparable and ongoing tension' (Saville, p.82). The patterns that began to emerge in Berbice as the ending of the slave system came into view, and took shape in Trinidad and the Bahamas as described by Adderley, became more or less fixed in Louisiana and South Carolina as described by Julie Saville. Menial agricultural labour continued to be performed by gangs of African American wage workers. In that sense little had changed from the late eighteenth century. What had changed were patterns of black mobilization and of black male leadership. The sight of hundreds of black men marching to the polls in the South Carolina Lowcountry and in the Louisiana sugar and cotton parishes described by Rebecca Scott, was a visible representation of how far the process of politicization had advanced. The marches, which heralded the rise of an organized black labour movement, also point to the continuing interplay between the political and economic agendas of African Americans.

Rebecca Scott's paper leads us forward in the evolutionary process from political activism to the emergence of a black labour movement in the late nineteenth century and simultaneously takes us backward to what Larry Powell calls the 'retreat from Reconstruction' (Powell, p.129). One of the fundamental questions that Scott's essay raises is what can be learned about the 'politics of freedom' (Scott, p.104) by looking at the decades that separated the ending of chattel slavery from the events at Thibodaux in 1887. By 1868 a free labour system had emerged in the Louisiana sugar industry but the economic omnipotence of the white growers remained intact. Less than twenty years later, the full implications of the sense of solidarity and consciousness of group interests that had been developing within the African-American community manifested itself in an organized strike.

The defining moment in Louisiana was the launching of massive workers' strike for better wages, overtime pay for night work, and the elimination of payment in scrip. Scott's powerful narration of the details of the strike points not only to progress in the process of politicization but also to the limits of freedom. When black men resorted to the use of armed defence to restructure the relations of labour and redistribute its material rewards, the massive power of the state was deployed to preserve the power imbalance between black worker and white employer. State-sponsored coercive power such as that employed to break the Thibodaux strike demonstrates clearly and unequivocally a point powerfully made by the conference papers. Although slavery was transformative for all parties, necessitating adjustments and adaptations on all sides, in the end, as Michael Gomez has recently observed, whites 'retained all the prerogatives of power'.[7] The appalling example of the Thibodaux massacre graphically illustrates that they did not hesitate to use it.

Whatever freedom eventually came to mean, enslavers and enslaved alike and their progeny everywhere in the Atlantic world were ultimately forced to re-examine their individual and collective memories of that ignominious and traumatic experience and to use it to redefine themselves. Larry Powell and Theresa Singleton's papers form an interesting and useful contrast between forgetting and remembering in the construction of the terrible past of slavery and the long and difficult road to freedom. Singleton's deeply nuanced analysis of the places where the memory of the slave trade resides in Ghana and the Republic of Benin reveals the interconnections between memory and social identity. The deeply charged relationship between African-American residents and visitors, who insist that Ghanaian castles be preserved as memorials to the slave trade so as to create a diasporist African nationalism, and Ghanaian museum staff, who prefer to express a more complex heritage that celebrates Ghanaian national identity, contrasts sharply with the remarkable openness of the Beninois in acknowledging their role in the slave trade. The Beninois celebrate themselves and their national identity by seizing the mantle of a diasporic hero, Toussaint Louverture, as a symbol of Beninois independence from France. The two examples together speak volumes about the multiple meanings and uses of historical memory.

Larry Powell tells a different story but in so doing illuminates another side of Theresa Singleton's argument. The 'invention' of Liberty Place was not so much a question of preserving knowledge of what happened during this Reconstruction conflict as an 'invention' of memory for use as a political tool. Powell points to the same standardizing processes noted by other conference participants, the deployment of the military in the expression and formation of masculine identities – both black and white – and the manipulation of religious and cultural symbols by different groups for a variety of purposes. The recent effort by supporters of David Duke to co-opt the memory of the event that Liberty Place represents, and the eagerness of the old white New Orleans elite to disavow the monument and the memory it contains, vividly illustrates Singleton's point that places as well as objects have 'multiple and sometimes contradictory meanings', which change according to the context and purpose of the creators. Interpreting memory, Singleton reminds us, is not so much a lens through which to examine the past but a window through which to view living reality.

NOTES

1. The concept of 'double consciousness' was formulated by W.E.B. Du Bois in *Souls of Black Folk* (Chicago, 1903). For a recent elaboration see Michael A. Gomez, *Exchanging Our Country Marks. The Transformation of African Indentities in the Colonial and Antebellum South* (Chapel Hill, University of North Carolina Press, 1998).

2. For recent examples of studies which pursue this theme in the North American and Anglophone Caribbean context see Mechal Sobel, *Trabelin' On: The Slave Journey to an Afro-Baptist Faith* (Westport, Greenwood Press, 1979); Margaret Washington Creel, '*A Peculiar People': Slave Religion and Community-Culture Among the Gullahs* (New York, 1988); Charles Joyner, *Down by the Riverside: A South Carolina Slave Community* (Urbana, University of Illinois Press, 1984), and Sylvia R. Frey and Betty Wood, *Come Shouting to Zion. African American Protestantism in the American South and British Caribbean to 1830* (Chapel Hill, University of North Carolina Press, 1998).

3. William D. Piersen, *The Development of an Afro-American Subculture in Eighteenth-Century New England* (Amherst, University of Massachusetts Press, 1988). For the John Canoe festivals see Ira De A. Reid, 'The John Canoe Festival: A New World Africanism', *Phylon*, Vol.3 (1942), pp.349–70 and H. S. Ames, 'African Institutions in America', *Journal of American Folk-Lore*, Vol.18 (1905), pp.15–32.

4. See Benjamin Quarles, *The Negro in the American Revolution* (Chapel Hill, University of North Carolina Press, 1961) and Sylvia R. Frey, *Water from the Rock. Black Resistance in a Revolutionary Age* (Princeton, Princeton University Press, 1991).

5. For recent discussions of this theme see, Christine Leigh Heyrman, *Southern Cross: The Beginnings of a Bible Belt* (New York, A.A.Knopf, 1997) and Susan Juster, *Disorderly Women: Sexual Politics and Evangelicalism in Revolutionary New England* (Ithaca, Cornell University Press, 1994).

6. For recent contributions to this scholarship see Ira Berlin and Philip D. Morgan (eds.), *Cultivation and Culture. Labor and the Shaping of Slave Life in the Americas* (Charlottesville, University Press of Virginia, 1993); Roderick A. McDonald, *Economy and Material Culture of Slaves. Goods and Chattels on the Sugar Plantations of Jamaica and Louisiana* (Baton Rouge, Louisiana State University Press, 1993) and Betty Wood, *Women's Work, Men's Work. The Informal Slave Economies of Lowcountry Georgia, 1750–1830* (Athens, The University of Georgia Press, 1996).

7. Gomez, *Exchanging Our Country Marks*, p.177.

The Angolan–Afro-Brazilian Cultural Connections

LINDA M. HEYWOOD

More than three decades ago in an article on the Portuguese roots of Brazilian spiritism, Donald Warren cautioned scholars and the Brazilian public against over-emphasizing the Amerindian and African roots of Brazilian popular culture to the neglect of the Portuguese background. He argued that the spiritism which Brazil's white middle class practised had 'deep roots in historical and contemporary sources in Portugal'.[1] Since then Brazilian scholarly and popular works have filled many of the gaps Warren pointed out at the time. Yet there is still a lot we need to know about the roots of Brazil's popular culture. This is especially the case of Brazil's African roots, where studies have yet to delineate clearly the links between Brazil's popular culture and its Portuguese and African roots.[2] Indeed, most of the works available on Afro-Brazilian culture focus on the nineteenth-century West African (Yoruba/Dahomey) roots of contemporary Afro-Brazilian folk culture, and rarely on its earlier Portuguese/Kongo-Angolan roots.[3]

This study takes up the challenge that Warren posed. It contends that a knowledge of the African diaspora to Portugal and the nature of Portuguese relations with the Kingdom of Kongo and Angola from the sixteenth to the eighteenth centuries can provide invaluable insights into the transcultural process that took place in Brazil from the sixteenth to the early nineteenth century. It also argues that such an approach must examine the role played by the Catholic Church in Portugal, Kongo-Angola, and Brazil in articulating elite and popular culture. Without this Portuguese and Kongo-Angolan background, any discussion of the African contribution to Afro-Brazilian and Brazilian culture would be incomplete. The paper also challenges studies that highlight developments in Africa and the Americas with only cursory background references to Europe when studying the formation of the Atlantic world up to 1800. Like Paul Gilroy, it calls for widening the conversation on the Black Atlantic to include Europe, Africa and America.[4]

The roots of Afro-Brazilian culture lay deep in the history of Afro-Portuguese relations, especially as it was mediated through the Catholic

Church. Since early medieval times, the Catholic Church had been the articulator of both elite and popular culture in Portugal. Although best known for the Inquisition and the forced conversion of Jews and Muslims in Portugal and Spain, the religious brotherhoods and pagentries honouring various saints which the church sponsored also allowed a folk Catholicism to flourish alongside an orthodox Catholicism in medieval Portugal, and permitted thousands of persecuted Jews and defeated Muslims to join the church.[5] This same process would lead to the conversion of hundreds of thousands of west and west-central Africans who came to Portugal from the mid 1400s onwards. These Africans, as Portuguese peasants and other converts had done earlier, were attracted more to the folk Catholicism of the church than to the orthodox Christianity of the priests and members of the elite. Here an African folk Catholicism would arise alongside the Portuguese folk Catholicism.

The main reason why an African folk Christianity thrived in Portugal stemmed from the church's practice of honouring saints, including non-white ones. The church's structure allowed for the establishment of confraternities or brotherhoods in their names, and their feast days honouring saints with public festivities were also crucial. For black Portuguese, among the most important saints and the confraternities (brotherhoods) established in their names and which came to be associated with Africans were St. Ephigenia, Our Lady of the Rosary, Saint Benedict, Saint Anthony of Catagerona, and Saint Gonçalo.

As Portugal became the centre of an expanding Empire it imported larger and larger numbers of African slaves. By 1505 the country had imported between 136, 000 and 151,000 enslaved Africans. This increase was a major factor for the growing popularity of the Lady of Our Rosary and the black saints among Portugal's black population. At the time Africans were especially identified with the chapel of the church of Nossa Senhora de Rosario of São Domingo in Lisbon and with the brotherhood established in her honour. The church's chapel became a special place where blacks congregated, possibly because the sanctuary also contained a statute of St. George and an image of the three magi, including the black Balthazar with whom the converts identified.[6]

Although no extant document is available that recorded the event, sometime before 1496, blacks associated with the white-dominated Brotherhood were sufficiently numerous to separate from the white Brotherhood. In 1496, for example, the Brotherhood of the Most Holy Rosary of Our Lady of the Black men of São Salvador da Matta which was situated in the monastery of São Domingos of Lisbon received royal permission in the form of an *Alvara*, giving its members permission to give out candles and collect alms in the caravels which went to 'Mina and the rivers of Guiné.[7] The permission to work in these particular caravels obviously reinforced the special ties between the members of the brotherhood and Africa.

The brotherhood was most likely established to meet the complaints of the many law-abiding black churchgoers who were married to interpreters and seamen, and whose homes were often broken into by officials seeking runaway slaves. Black Portuguese suffered these harassments because officials suspected them of hiding runaway slaves.[8] After the brotherhood received its first *compromisso* in 1565, it became the official channel between the courts and the black population.[9]

The brotherhoods became an important network for Lisbon's black population during the sixteenth century. They functioned in other cities as well, and during the seventeenth century they obtained royal charters to hold their own public celebrations. The special devotional services the Lisbon chapter held in São Domingos chapel, and mutual aid and burial services the organization offered members were mainly responsible for its popularity.[10] Although by the beginning of the eighteenth century blacks joined other brotherhoods, Nossa Senhora came to be associated almost exclusively with Lisbon's African and mixed population. The brotherhood became so identified with blacks that between 1707 and 1721 whites abandoned her devotion. At the same time its members set up a fund for purchasing the freedom of members of the brotherhood who were still slaves. The brotherhood also continued to be accused of hiding runaway slaves.[11]

When blacks in Portugal became free after the publication of the 1761 law which banned the further importation of slaves into Portugal, and the later 1773 law, black brotherhoods became quite independent.[12] A 1779 law, which made it legal for the black confraternity of Santo Benedito to purchase slaves who were members of the brotherhood but who were being mistreated by their owners, allowed their membership to grow.[13]

Africans in Portugal not only used the brotherhoods for religious and welfare purposes, but they also became the venues for preserving and transforming African culture. Although the earthquake and fire of 1755, which destroyed all the papers of the Lisbon brotherhood, have made it difficult for historians to reconstruct the range of cultural activities which its members promoted, some of its activities certainly helped in the transformation of African culture in Portugal. Historians are divided on this question, some believing that the brotherhoods were no more than a screen for the practice of 'pagan rituals', as some contemporaries charged. In any event, the brotherhoods gained notoriety for the public dramas that its members promoted.[14] One of these, which highlighted the theme of Portuguese/Kongo-Angola/Brazil linkages, involved a ceremony in which

Africans dramatized the conversion and crowning of the Christian king of the Kongo. Announcements from 1730 show that the Africans involved in planning the celebration were writing to participants in the 'lingua do preto', in this case a Portuguese/African orthography which contained a significant number of Bantu terms – such as Zambiampum, Catambala, and Zuambala – and which was interspersed with Bantu linguistic conventions.[15]

The roots of the celebration of the crowning of the Kongo king were certainly linked to the special relationship which developed between the Lisbon and Kongolese monarchs, especially during the long reign of Kongo's King Afonso (1509–42). The presence of a number of Kongolese nobles (the first one arrived in Portugal in 1483) as well as the increase in the number of Kongolese and Angolan slaves in Portugal from the early sixteenth century (the first boat load of Kongo slaves arrived in Portugal in 1513) must certainly have attracted the attention of the members of the brotherhoods.[16] Historian Tinhorão has argued that the dramatization of the crowning of a Kongo king during the 'Congo ceremony', which eyewitness recorded was still taking place in Lisbon and Porto in the nineteenth century, and which records from the Rosario brotherhood suggest had a long history, was the way that Portugal's black members of the brotherhood sought to link themselves to the prestige of the Kongo court. By the nineteenth century blacks who had official roles in the performance inherited those positions, and carried on the tradition of staging elaborate embassies with impressive dramatization, music and dance which recalled the real prestige that Kongo kingdom held from the sixteenth to eighteenth centuries.[17] One 1730 document described the African and mulatto participants of the Feast of Rosario of the blacks of the Church of Rosario in Lisbon as carrying and playing a whole range of African musical instruments including 'three marimbas, four fifes, 300 harps, tambourines, congos and cangáz'. The participants also danced the *cumbi* (*nkumbi*), a Kongo word referring to a drum used in ceremonies honouring great hunters and which in Brazil referred to a dance of Kongolese origin.[18]

The cultural presence of Africans, and especially the Kongo-Angola links to Portugal, was not only confined to the church and the brotherhoods but was evident in other parts of Portuguese society as well. For example, by the early sixteenth century Portuguese courtly and popular writers and artists recorded the African cultural presence in Portugal. Here also a Kongo-Angola input was evident. Famous Portuguese cultural icons such as Camões, Gil Vincente, and Garcia de Resende provide the first evidence, many based on mere fantasy, of the growing presence of Africa in Portugal. Resende, for example, included in his famous *Miscellanae* a verse which referred to barbarous customs of 'Guinee & Manicõo' as well as to the conversion of the Manicongo, who

vijmos christão ser tornado (we came to make them Christians)
& con elle grande copia (and with the king a great multitude)
de gente de seu reynado (of the people of his kingdom)
mamdou por religiosos (sent for religions)
& por frades virtuosos (and virtuous friars)
q lhe el rey de caa mãdaua (which our king sent from here)
& elle mesmo préguau (and he himself asked)
nosse fee a hos duuidosos (for our faith for his unbelievers).[19]

Not only did Portuguese men of letters incorporate into their writings the important events regarding Portugal's relations with Africa, but they also satirized the emerging Luso-African culture that was evolving in Portugal. Gil Vincente, who, as Warren points out, vigorously represented 'lower class culture in the popular idiom',[20] went a long way in giving voice to this Afro-Luso culture. In 1520 when he published his first plays, he utilized black characters who spoke in a distinctly Afro-Lusitanian dialect. Although his intention was to use the language spoken by Portugal's black population to evince comedic relief and amusement in his plays (much as later American literati used the speech of black characters to stereotype African Americans), the adoption of the language by later writers popularized Afro-Creole among the Portuguese.[21] As one writer noted, in these early Portuguese plays 'Africans sing in it, make love in it, and philosophize in it'.[22] Some of the black characters who appeared in Gil Vincente's and later plays dealing with life at court were undoubtedly fashioned after Kongo nobles at the court of the Portuguese kings or slaves in the country with whom they were familiar.[23]

The changing relationship between Portugal, Kongo-Angola and Brazil during this period carried this transculturation process even further, and led to new and different cultural manifestations in Portugal, Kongo and Brazil. There were several reasons for this. Among the most significant were Portuguese territorial advances in the Kongo-Angola region from the sixteenth century onwards, the activities of Catholic missionaries in Kongo-Angola and Brazil, and the migration of Portuguese slaves and freemen from Portugal and converts from central Africa to Brazil, who brought various elements of Luso-African culture with them. Furthermore, the forced migration of thousands of Kongo-Angolan slaves from Africa to Brazil helped contribute to a more complex transcultural process there than had occurred in either Portugal or Kongo Angola.

As in Portugal, the Catholic Church was again in the forefront of facilitating Luso-African tranculturalization in Kongo and Angola. Although the church had some success with the leadership and population of the kingdom of Warri and a few of the small chiefdoms in the region of

Sierra Leone, the missionaries made great headway in Kongo and Angola. From their base in São Tomé they developed close ties with Kongolese rulers on the African mainland. After Portugal created the colony of Angola in the Kimbundu region to the south, they also made many converts among that population as well.

The missionaries' greatest success was in the kingdom of the Kongo where between 1509 and 1542 King Afonso made Catholicism a state religion. Kongo was also one of the first places outside the Portuguese empire where an Afro-Catholic religion emerged. Capuchin, Jesuit and Dominican missionaries who came to the country during the 16th and 17th centuries brought all the various tenets of Catholicism present in Catholic Europe.[24]

Black Catholic brotherhoods which appeared in São Tomé, in Kongo, and in Portuguese Angola were at the centre of the transculturation process. Indeed, the seventeenth-century Capuchin missionary, Cavazzi, claimed that the creation of brotherhoods in Kongo and Soyo, with their strict code of discipline and religious behaviour, was instrumental in enabling Catholicism to penetrate into the region.[25] The earliest black brotherhood in the area was the Rosary brotherhood established in São Tomé in 1526. The São Tomé chapter gained some of the same privileges enjoyed by the Lisbon chapter, especially the right of members to demand that masters free slaves who were members of the brotherhood. The members also gained the privilege of helping slaves who had been manumitted at the death of their masters but who faced legal barriers in obtaining their freedom by the heirs of the deceased.[26]

The first reference to a brotherhood dedicated to the Virgin Mary in Kongo was noted in 1548 in the capital of São Salvador. This confraternity, however, was for Portuguese only.[27] A little more than a decade later Dominicans, who first came to Kongo in the 1560s, seemed to have introduced the festival connected to Our Lady of the Rosary and might also have been responsible for the later popularity of this festival among slaves of Angolan origin in Brazil.[28] A 1595 report noted that there were six brotherhoods in the Kongolese capital, including the Brotherhood of the Rosary. The Angola brotherhood was well established by 1658.[29] Whereas the membership of the brotherhoods in the Kongo were from drawn from the upper class, the membership of the Confraternity of Our Lady of the Rosary in Luanda, where most of the Portuguese community resided, seemed to have replicated the Lisbon practice of drawing its members from the free Kimbundu and slave population of the city.[30]

The creole society that emerged in Kongo and Angola had strong links with the Portuguese and this allowed for the transculturation process to continue. Unlike Portugal where African-born or people of African descent played a central role in the transformation of African culture, in Kongo, creoles, the offspring of Portuguese men and African women, and members of the Kongolese ruling lineages dominated the membership of the Catholic brotherhoods and were responsible for giving them a public face. One late sixteenth-century source referred to the degree of race mixing which was occurring in the Kongo and noted that 'the children of white Portuguese, born in these lands, of Congolese women, are *negros* or white or *pardos*, whom the Spaniards call *mulatos*'.[31] Indeed, some sources at the time referred to the Kongo as a 'ladino' society.

As in Portugal, the transculturalization that was underway was visible in a range of cultural markers, including creole languages, further religious syncretism, dress, food, music and social practices. John Thornton's work on African Catholicism in Kongo and Angola has delineated the process in the religious sphere. There, he notes, early catechisms in Kikongo and Kimbundu, prayers, schisms, burnings at the stake, and inquisition visits all characterized the depth of transculturalization in central Africa from the sixteenth to the eighteenth centuries.[32] Although some of these developments had their roots in Portugal, others were the result of the unique relationships that developed between Portugal, Kongo and Angola from the fifteenth century onwards. These would further influence the Luso-African culture in Portugal as well as the transformation that was occurring in Brazil.[33] For example, some of the Portuguese residents in Angola continued the custom that had developed among the dominant class not to make public appearances without the spectacle of a train of clients, slaves, servants and other hangers on. As Charles Boxer noted for seventeenth-century Luanda, 'a noble Portuguese who does not take with him many negroes and negresses [mucamas] for the service of his household ... and other household servants such as cooks. washerwomen, and others who get water and firewood from the bush, with many musical instruments such as marimbas, chicalhos, bagpipes, native violins, etc ... they may not respect him in the least'.[34]

The transculturalization process was also evident in many of the cultural practices of the population. In 1620 an eyewitness recorded the Jesuit-sponsored Luanda carnival that was held in honour of the canonization of the feast of St. Francis Xavier. The celebration, with its floats, caricatures of recent political events between Europeans and Portuguese, and incorporation of local African motifs, was yet another demonstration of the dynamism of the transculturalization process underway. As David Birmingham has concluded, 'the procession represented a complete syncretism of pagan rituals from the Mediterranean pantheon, of Christian rituals from the Iberian church, and of Mbundu and Kongo rituals'.[35] Such festivals were regular features of Angola's Luso-African heritage and have survived into the post-independence period.

This mix of Portuguese and African was not limited to religiously inspired celebrations dominated by whites, mulattos and urban Africans but penetrated into other aspects of the central African environment as well. For example, in 1699 a visiting missionary expressed amazement when the king of Mbwela, a region located between Kongo and Angola, entertained him in a style which he noted made him think that he was 'no longer in Congo but in some European country by the exquisiteness of the foods with the abundance of bread, wine, and other things of our homeland'.[36]

Many factors led to the continuation of the evolution of this Afro-Luso culture in Brazil. The make-up of the early settlers certainly played a role. In areas such as São Paulo, for example, the fact that the first blacks arriving in the region came not from Africa but from Portugal as part of the population that made up the 1530 *donatário* of Martim Afonso da Sousa meant that many of the cultural adaptations that had already taken place in Portugal, Kongo and Angola came with the slaves to Brazil.[37] Although many of these Portuguese slaves would not have been members of the brotherhoods because of royal protection which made it illegal to sell slaves who were members of the brotherhood overseas, some masters disregarded the law and sold slave members to slave holders in Minas. This was especially the case among masters who suspected that their slaves joined the brotherhood to gain this protection. These slaves would have brought to Brazil some of the cultural practices of the brotherhoods.[38]

Furthermore, the Portuguese male practice of fathering children with African women continued in Brazil as it had in Kongo and Angola. By the 1690s an Italian visitor to Bahia estimated the city's mulatto or *pardo* population to be between 8,000 to 10,000 with whites numbering only 20,000 people and enslaved Africans accounting for 50,000 people.[39] This population bias towards Africans and Luso-Africans certainly guaranteed an overwhelmingly African element in the Brazilian folk culture that was emerging.

By far Kongo-Angola provided a significant majority of the early Brazilian slave population. In São Paulo, for example, African slaves entering the region originated exclusively from the Kongo-Angola region. An early population reference to a black African presence in Brazil comes from 1583 when the chroniclers listed 14,000 slaves as against 25,000 whites and 18,000 'civilized' Indians. The estimated number of 'none-civilized' native Americans in the region that became Brazil would have numbered nearly one million. By 1776 the total population estimate was about 1.5 million and according to the estimates of Stuart Schwartz the free people of colour were the most rapidly growing segment of the population during the colonial period. They, along with the slaves, accounted for approximately two-thirds of the population of colonial Brazil. This predominantly black, mulatto, and cabuclo/mestiço population was bound to have a significant impact on the formation of Brazilian civilization at this time.

Recent scholarship by David Eltis and Joseph Miller has suggested that more than half the number of slaves – 15,000 a year by the 1790s – who reached Brazil's southern region between 1595 to the 1800s came from west central Africa.[40] Africans who came to Brazil did not carry a uniform culture, of course, nor did they come from a great variety of places. Certainly one could find at least some slaves from virtually every trading port in Africa, but to play on this diversity would be to underestimate the fact that statistically most slaves arrived in the eighteenth century and came from just two points, the 'Costa da Mina' (virtually entirely from Dahomey and its neighbours) and 'Angola'. Thanks to careful control by the Portuguese state, and the fact that Portuguese slavers went to few other places, these two regions supplied Brazil with well over 90 per cent of its African slaves before 1750. Angola, however, made up about nine-tenths of the slaves entering Brazil. It was only in the latter part of the eighteenth century that slaves from Dahomey and Nigeria (the Slave Coast) came to supply the Yoruba west African contingent of the Afro-Brazilian population.

Angolan slaves comprised three peoples who spoke three distinct languages – Kimbundu, Mbundu, and Kikongo – and lived in different states, the most important being the Kingdom of the Kongo, the Kimbundu states of Ndongo, Matamba, Njinga and Kasanje, and the Ovimbundu states of the central highlands. Today the Kimbundus, Kongos and Ovimbundus still comprise the overwhelming majority of the Angolan population. The rulers and peoples from this region who supplied slaves to the Portuguese had several common cultural characteristics, including closely related languages, religious beliefs and practices, similar customs, including dances, initiation rights and musical instruments. Their political ideologies had many similarities, among them basic ideas about who should rule, the obligation of kings, procedures for exercising power, and common religious rituals in politics. Furthermore, they all had highly formalized public rituals that allowed the socialization of young people and membership in various religious and secular organizations.

Not only did Kongo-Angola provide Brazil with many of its slaves, but Africans moved between the two regions. For example, in 1620 some Kongolese captives, among whom were members of the Kongolese nobility (*fidalgos*), were sold to Brazilian slavers, but by 1624 a number of them were allowed to return to Africa following complaints made by the Kongolese to the king of Portugal.[41] The movement of Africans between

Kongo-Angola and Brazil continued, for in 1642 a former Angolan slave who had become a *pombeiro* (bush trader), informed the newly installed Dutch authority in Loango that he had travelled with his master to the Kongo and Kimbundu region and had also made two voyages to Brazil. He also noted that his master, as was the case generally among the Portuguese, did not buy and sell slaves except those who came from Queen Njinga's territory and from the Kimbundu region because they believed that they made better slaves.[42] Another example of the kind of relations which existed between Kongo and Brazil comes from a 1643 report from The Hague which noted that two Kongolese ambassadors had travelled with a ship from Brazil to request the help of the Dutch in their war against Queen Njinga.[43] The presence of Kongo-Angolan slaves, some of them nobles and warriors from wars between the Kongo kings and the Kimbundu, particularly during the reign of Queen Njinga, as well as between Portugal and Kongo-Angolans, guaranteed that central African slaves would have kept alive the stirring events of Kongo and Angola's history in Brazil.

These Kongo-Angolan slaves, although constituting a minority of the population during the formative years in Rio de Janeiro, would have reinforced the culture among the creole slaves who originated from Portugal.[44] Indeed, both the number of slaves coming from Portugal and Kongo-Angola rose significantly during the early eighteenth century after the discovery of gold and diamond in Minas Gerais, Goais, and Mato Grosso. After the 1758 decree abolishing slavery in Portugal, slave imports directly from Africa brought in an African population who made up the bulk of the labouring and agricultural workers in the region.

As in Portugal and Africa, the Catholic Church provided the means for these central Africans and their Angolan descendants to become part of Brazilian society. For example, African slaves, who along with Indians lived in Jesuit missions in the coastal settlements, had numerous opportunities to participate in the many festivals and public functions the church sponsored. Thus it was not surprising to find that Africans were present at most seventeenth- and eighteenth-century public religious festivities such as church dedications and festivals of saints. One author, in describing the dedication of the eighteenth-century church of Nossa Senhora do Pilar do Ouro Preto, noted that the public procession not only included 'Turks and Christians' who sang and played their instruments, but also 'eight blacks on foot playing shawns'.[45]

Even more than in Portugal, creole slaves from Portugal or those who had been familiar with black saints in Kongo-Angola used their association with the church as a way to create a unique Afro-Brazilian cultural legacy. As Roger Bastide has argued, the attachment which the black population had to black saints led some parishes in Brazil to establish and celebrate feasts days for Saint Benedict as early as 1711, although this saint was not officially recognized by Rome until 1743 nor canonized until 1807. Similarly, blacks who came from Angola and Kongo who were familiar with the veneration of Our Lady of the Rosary in Africa, which had been introduced by Dominican missionaries, were instrumental in popularizing her feast among Brazil's colonial population.[46] Bastide's observations about the popularity of these saints and Our Lady of the Rosary among the African and creole population who not only celebrated them publicly but also built churches in Brazil certainly resonate with the process which had occurred in the Kongo. There the apparitions of saints, who often intervened in local wars, were accepted, and the dedication of churches to saints was quite common.[47] The growth of a Brazilian African-Catholic (folk) religion with its Angolan flavour was also possible because of the fact that after 1701 the Catholic Churches in Angola and Brazil were linked administratively when the suffragen diocese of Bahia was expanded to include not only Rio de Janeiro and Pernambuco, but Angola and São Tomé as well. For example, although a Brazilian-born mulatto needed papal authorization before he could take orders, thus limiting their numbers, the Brazilian church regularly brought over coloured priests from Angola with a knowledge of Kimbundu and Kikongo to work among the slaves at their monasteries and convents. The practice undoubtedly allowed for the continued growth of the Afro-Catholicism which had emerged at least in the Kongo and Kimbundu region by the middle of sixteenth century, and which had its tenets as contained in the catechism written in Kikongo and Kimbundu and widely used since 1624 and 1642. It also had its own spiritual vocabulary. The priests and captives (some of whom were already converts in Angola and Kongo) helped to spread this Afro-Catholic religion among Brazil's black population. Their use of Bantu vocabulary also undergirded the creole language that became the lingua franca of many of Brazil's African and creole population by the eighteenth century.[48]

In Brazil, as in Portugal and Kongo-Angola, the charters the brotherhoods obtained permitted the confraternity to purchase the freedom of its enslaved members as well as to sponsor a whole range of religious and secular activities. These activities allowed the brotherhoods to play a crucial role in the transformations these African and Luso-African practices into a genuine Afro-Brazilian culture. In Bahia and in the Rio de Janeiro regions during the early days of the colony, the brotherhoods served as social clubs for the creole and Kongo and Angolan populations, although a few opened their doors to 'everybody, even captive blacks and natives of the Guinea coast'.[49]

The impact of Angolan-Kongo culture was particularly noticeable, as Patricia Mulvey has argued, in Our Lady of the Rosary, St. Benedict, Our

Lady of Mercy and Bon Jesus brotherhoods, which 'played a vital function in integrating and assimilating African peoples to Portuguese-American life'.[50] Indeed, Mulvey noted that in early eighteenth-century Pelourinho the membership of the Rosary brotherhoods was predominantly Kongos and Angolans, and that these Africans did not 'dabble in the African cults' nor did they plot rebellions.[51] At the beginning of the colonial period the Brotherhood of Our Lady of the Rosary in Bahia allowed only Angolans to be members, while in Pelourinho between 1703 and 1726 Africans from Kongo and Angola joined creoles to build their own church.[52] Kongos and Angolans may have found it easier to enter into the mainstream of Brazilian life because of their prior familiarity with the Portuguese language and culture and Catholic rituals. Indeed, Bantus were prized in some quarters because of the belief that they were more tractable than Sudanese (Guinea) slaves. By the end of the eighteenth century certain areas were almost exclusively ethnically Kongo-Angolan, as was the case in Minas Gerais and Pernambuco where the majority of the slaves were of Kongolese origin. Slave purchasers also continued to identify certain slaves with various occupations. For example, in Bahia slaves originating from Benguela and Cabinda were preferred for fieldwork because of their docility while the Angolans were 'the most able and useful for service in the city'.[53]

In the brotherhoods, election of officers such as kings and queens, princesses, royal slaves, *feiticeiros* (a religious functionary) and the like allowed Africans from Angola and Kongo to maintain in the diaspora some of the hierarchical social ordering that was the norm in the regions from which they had been taken captive. Perhaps because these customs became part of the public festivals meant to entertain whites on feast days, they were incorporated into the popular culture of the colonial period and allowed Bantu languages, songs and dances to become part of Brazilian culture.

This Kongo-Angolan presence accounted for the widespread popularity of the conga dances, *cumcumbis* and the *congoadas* with the crowning of the king of the Kongo and Queen Njinga which creole and African members of the various brotherhoods performed on the feast days dedicated to the saints and to the Lady of the Rosary. Again the church played a role in promoting Angolan culture by integrating into church celebrations the custom of crowning Africans kings and queens –specifically the King of the Kongo, especially King Dom Henrique and Queen Njinga, two of the most famous leaders in central Africa, and thus allowed the slaves to dramatize actual historical events which occurred between Kongolese rulers, the rulers of the Ndongo Kingdom, and the Portuguese.[54]

Some of the songs that later entered into Brazilian folk culture recalled this religious legacy. In one song 'Queen Jingo of Mozambique' is linked with 'Our Lady of the Rosary', while another goes 'I am Queen Njinga's brother, Godson of the Virgin Mary'. Another, which recalled the wars of Queen Njinga, recreates the time of the slave trade as one of turmoil when Njinga 'ordered me to kill my king'.[55]

Africans had grown so accustomed to performing these historico-religious dramas that in 1786 when members of the Rosario brotherhood petitioned Dona Maria for permission to perform their songs and dances on the feast day of Our Lady of the Rosary, they proudly recalled its Angolan roots, noting that from 'olden times' they had been permitted to have masquerades and dances 'in the language of Angola with instruments involving spiritual songs and praises'.[56] The growing popularity of these festivals after 1700 was doubtless due to the fact that the Angolan-born slaves who were so prominent in the plays were familiar with the history that they were dramatizing. Furthermore, although the priests manipulated the history for the purpose of facilitating conversion, the fact remains that many Kongos and not a few Angolans had been Christians before their enslavement in Brazil. Thus they would have been familiar with the brotherhoods in Luanda, Soyo, and Kongo, and the central role they played in the creole society of Kongo, Angola and São Tomé. Although the brotherhoods in Kongo were associated with the nobles, they attracted popular attention during the public celebrations they staged. No doubt the dramatization of specific events in Angolan and Kongolese history during the religious festivals in Brazil provided many ordinary enslaved Angolans and Kongos the opportunity to play a central a role in the celebrations.

The Kongo-Angolan input was not limited to religious and political themes under the direction of church officials, but these provided slaves with the opportunity to integrate African musical instruments and language into the festivities. Thus the speech, rituals, songs and language of the Angolan and Kongo slaves in time accounted for the core of early Afro-Brazilian religion and culture.

As was the case in Portugal during Gil Vincent's time, Portuguese and Brazilian-born men of letters recorded these dances, songs, language, and other cultural manifestations that Africans from Angola and the Kongo were so instrumental in promoting. Grégorio de Matos (1633–96) was perhaps the earliest Brazilian writer to leave descriptions of the central African elements that were to form Afro-Brazilian culture. He was the first writer to describe *macumba* ceremonies, which he called *quilombo*. Less than a century later Nuno Marques Pereira, in his *Compêndido Narrativo do Perigrino na America*, which had five printings between 1728 and 1765, also described the central African dances called *Calunda*, with its music which he associated with witchcraft and fortune telling. Furthermore, Tomás António Gonzaga (1744–1807) also described the *lundu* dance of Angolan slaves, which he witnessed in Minas Gerais.[57]

This study of the Portuguese and the Kongo-Angolan roots of Afro-Brazilian culture provides a more complex picture of cultural change during the period of the Atlantic slave trade. It should encourage scholars working on slave societies in the Americas to shift their research focus from a preoccupation with cultural change only in the slave societies of the Americas and examine the range of Euro-African interactions both in Europe and in Africa. Such a study would not only enhance and enrich the study of the African diaspora, but also engage scholars in the fields of European, American, and Latin-American history. Such a refocus would advance significantly the teaching of Atlantic history.

NOTES

1. Donald Warren, 'Portuguese Roots of Brazilian Spiritism', *Luso-Brazilian Review*, Vol.V, No.2 (December 1968), pp.3–32.
2. Joe Miller's *Way of Death* (Madison, University of Wisconsin Press, 1988) and John Thornton's more general study, *Africa and Africans in the Making of the Atlantic World* (New York, Cambridge University Press, 2nd edition, 1998) are the exceptions.
3. For the major works on the West African contribution to Afro-Brazilian culture see Roger Bastide, *The African Religions of Brazil* (Baltimore, Johns Hopkins University Press, 1978). See also Patricia Mulvey, 'Black Brothers and Sisters: Membership in· the Black Brotherhoods of Colonial Brazil', *Luso-Brazilian Review*, Vol.17, No.2 (1980), pp.253–79.
4. Paul Gilroy, *The Black Atlantic World: Modernity and Double Consciousness* (Cambridge, MA, Harvard University Press, 1993), pp.1–40.
5. For a discussion of this see Warren, 'Portuguese Roots of Brazilian Spiritism'.
6. José Ramos Tinhorão, *Os Negros em Portugal, Uma Presença Silenciosa* (Lisbon, Editorial Caminho, SA, 1988), pp.80 and 128-9.
7. Maria Luísa Oliviera Esteves (ed.), *Portugaliae Monumenta Africana* (Lisbon, 1995–), Vol.II, pp.260, doc. 152; Charles Boxer, 'Negro Slavery in Brazil', *Race*, Vol.5, No.3 (January 1964), p.45.
8. Antonio Brásio, *Os Pretos em Portugal* (Lisbon, Agência Geral das Colónias, 1944), p.111.
9. A.C. de C.M. Saunders, *A Social History of Black Slaves and Freedmen in Portugal, 1441–1555* (Cambridge, 1982), Ch.8.
10. Saunders, *A Social History*, p.155.
11. Tinhorão, *Os Negros*, p.132.
12. Robin Blackburn, *The Overthrow of Colonial Slavery, 1776–1804* (London, Verso, 1988), p.62.
13. Rodrigues de Carvalho, *Aspéctos da Influéncia Africana Na Formação Social do Brasil* (Brazil, Prensa Universitária da Paraíba, 1967), p.21.
14. Saunders, *Social History*, p.152. See also Tinharão, *Os Negros*, pp.144–5.
15. Tinhorão, *Os Negros*, p.191.
16. Antonio Brásio, *Monumenta Missionaria Africana*, Seria 1, 15 Vols. (Lisbon, Agência Geral das Colónias, 1952–88), Vol.1, 33–4; 279.
17. Tinhorão, *Os Negros*, pp.134-46.
18. Tinhorão, *Os Negros*, pp.190–1. The term *nkumbi* is found in modern dictionaries of Kikongo, such as Karl Laman, *Dictionnaire Kikongo-Français* (Brussels, 1936, reprinted Gregg Press, Ridgewood, NJ, 1964) and W. Holman Bentley, *A Dictionary and Grammar of the Kongo Language* (London, Trübner, 1887).
19. As quoted in Waldeloi Rego, *Coperia Angola: Ensaio Sócio-Etnográfico* (Rio de Janeiro, Graf, 1968), pp.3, 6.
20. Warren, 'Portuguese Roots of Brazilian Spiritism', p.31.
21. Raymond S. Sayers, *The Negro in Brazilian Literature* (New York: Hispanic Institute in the United States, 1956), p.19.

22. Ibid., p.19.
23. Tinhorão, *Os Negros*, pp.233–47.
24. See John Thornton, 'The Development of an African Catholic Church in the Kingdom of the Kongo', *Journal of African History*, Vol.25 (1984), pp.147–67.
25. For a more detailed discussion see Richard Gray, *Black Christians and White Missionaries* (New Haven, Yale University Press, 1990), pp.34–56.
26. Saunders, *A Social History*, p.155.
27. Antonio Brásio, *Missionaria Monumenta Africana*, Vol.15, p.162.
28. Antonio Brásio, *Monumenta Missionaria Africana*, Vol.5, pp.607–14.
29. Antonio Brásio, *Monumenta Missionaria*, Vol.3, p.502. See also Vol.5, p.78 for further references.
30. Gray, *Black Christians*, p.14.
31. As quoted in Jack D. Forbes, *Africans and Native Americans: The Language of Race and the Evolution of Red-Black Peoples* (Urbana, University of Illinois Press, 1993), p.117.
32. John Thornton, *Africa and Africans in the Making of the Atlantic World*.
33. Ibid.
34. C.R. Boxer, 'Race Relations in the Portuguese Colonial Empire, 1415–1825', p.30.
35. David Birmingham, 'Carnival at Luanda', *Journal of African History*, Vol.29 (1988), p.97.
36. Marcellino d'Atri, 'Giornate apostoliche fatte da me...' (1702) in Carlo Toso (ed.), *L'anarchia congolese nel secolo XVII. La Relazione inedita di Marcellino d'Atri* (Genoa, 1984), p.205.
37. Roger Bastide and Florestan Fernandes, *Brancos e Negros em São Paula: Ensaio Sociológico sôbre Aspectos Na Formação, Manifestaçoes Atuais e Efeitos do Preconceito de Côr Na Sociedade Paulistana* (São Paulo, Companhia Editora Nacional, 1971), p.21.
38. Boxer, 'Negro Slavery in Brazil', pp.38–47.
39. Forbes, *Africans and Native Americans*, p.118.
40. David Eltis, D. Richardson and Stephen Behrendt, 'The Structure of the Transatlantic Slave Trade, 1662–1867: Some Preliminary Indications of African Origins of Slaves Arriving in the Americas', Paper given to the Collegium of African American Research Conference, Tenirife, February, 1995; Joseph C. Miller, 'The Numbers, Origins, and Destinations of Slaves in the Eighteenth-Century Angolan Slave Trade', in Joseph E. Inokori and Stanley L. Engerman (eds.), *The Atlantic Slave Trade: Effects on Economies, Societies and Peoples in Africa, the American and Europe* (Durham, 1992), pp.77–116.
41. Antonio Brásio, *Monumenta Missionaria Africana*, Vol.15, pp.508–9; Vol.7, pp.17–24, 64–6, 79–80, 116–17, 119–20,
42. Louis Jaden, *L'Ancien Congo et L'Angola, 1639–1655*, Vol.1 (Brussels, Institute Historique Belge de Rome, 3 vols., 1975), p.352.
43. Antonio Brásio, *Monumenta Missionaria Africana*, Vol.9, p.64.
44. Indian slaves outnumbered Kongo-Angolan slaves by 34 to 1.
45. David P. Appleby, *The Music of Brazil* (Austin, University of Texas Press, 1983), p.19.
46. Bastide, *The African Religions of Brazil*, p.113.
47. John Thornton, 'Perspectives on African Christianity', in Vera Hyatt and Rex Nettleford, *Race, Discourse and the Origin of the Americas: A New World View* (Washington, DC, Smithsonian Institution Press, 1995), pp.169–98.
48. Bastide, *The African Religions of Brazil*, pp.126 and 430. John Thornton, 'Afro-Christian Syncretism in Central Africa', *Plantation Society* (forthcoming).
49. Bastide, *The African Religions of Brazil*, p.431.
50. Patricia Mulvey, 'The Black Lay Brotherhoods of Colonial Brazil: A History (PhD dissertation, City University of New York, 1976).
51. Patricia Mulvey, 'Black Brothers and Sisters', *Luso-Brazilian Review*, Vol.17, No.2, pp.267–69.
52. Ibid., pp.262–67.
53. Rodrigues de Carvalho, *Aspéctos da Influéncia Africana na Formação Social do Brasil* (Brazil, Prensa Universitária da Paraíba, 1967), p.13.
54. For a discussion of these festivals see Roger Bastide, *African Religions*, pp.114–25.
55. Norton F. Corrêa, 'O Quicombi de Rio Pardo', *Correio do Povo*, 11 February, 1978.
56. Patricia Mulvey, 'The Black Lay Brotherhoods'.
57. Maria Luisa Nunes, 'The Presentation of African Culture in Brazilian Literature: The Novels of Jorge Armado', *Luso-Brazilian Review*, Vol.X, No.1 (June 1973), p.87.

Frontier Exchange and Cotton Production: The Slave Economy in Mississippi, 1798–1836

DANIEL H. USNER, JR.

The expansion of cotton production in the Lower Mississippi Valley during the early nineteenth century drastically altered the landscape of economic relations among American Indians, European settlers, and African-American slaves. As a plantation economy based on cotton agriculture spread along the major rivers and even in the backcountry of the region, means of livelihood practised by generations of inhabitants underwent severe pressure. Newcomers who migrated into the Lower Mississippi Valley, meanwhile, found their habits and expectations changing in an unfamiliar environment undergoing rapid commercial development. Under the pressures of an expanding cotton agriculture, forms of production and exchange shared by many people across the boundary between slavery and freedom became more restricted. As more land and labour were committed to new commercial crops, exchange relations between African-American slaves and free people of various backgrounds slipped into a more marginalized position in the regional economy.

As we learn more about the internal economy of slave communities, variation through time and across space has become an important consideration. The combination of activities that African-American slaves developed into quasi-autonomous networks of production and exchange, as well as the relationship of these internal or informal economies with the trans-Atlantic economy, depended on a variety of circumstances. The organization of work hinging on specific commercial crops, the natural environments in which particular plantation economies developed, and the demographic profile of slave and free populations sharing a certain location are just a few of the major variables that influenced the degree and form of economic independence secured at different times by African-American slaves in different regions of the Western Hemisphere.[1]

The temporal dimensions of the internal economy of slavery, however, tend to be overshadowed by scholarship's emphasis on its structural features. We understand how measured independence in production and exchange actually worked on a day-to-day basis, serving the antithetical goals of both slaves and slave-owners in many settings, but we still know too little about the origins and evolution of these activities in particular places. This is partly due to earlier historians'preoccupation with the antebellum South, encompassing a relatively brief period. It also reflects the difficulty that colonial historians of slavery face when trying to trace subtle changes in livelihood over a long span of time. But without better knowledge of how earlier generations of slaves acquired and developed some economic flexibility and autonomy, it is impossible to explain fully how slavery's internal economy was affected by the introduction of new staple crops, work routines, and social pressures.

The territory of the Lower Mississippi Valley that became the state of Mississippi in 1817 is a promising field for studying the evolution of an informal economy among slaves in the formative years of the Cotton South. During the early eighteenth century American Indians, European settlers, and African slaves had created a limited sphere of mutually beneficial relations in spite of the groups' wider oppositional stakes in this colonial region. Small-scale production, face-to-face marketing, and prosaic features of livelihood constituted a frontier exchange economy, in which slaves performed a diversity of economic roles and traded informally with both Indians and colonists. Changes in economic activities and relations occurred gradually and piecemeal over most of the eighteenth century, but by the 1780s the frontier exchange economy began to unravel. Spain and England implemented stronger immigration, commercial, and slavery policies, setting in motion a pattern of change that drastically accelerated once the United States acquired the Lower Mississippi Valley. The rapid migration of slave-owners and slaves from the upper South, the expanding slave trade, and the spread of plantation agriculture into the region transformed livelihood under slavery. The fluidity and openness of exchange relations previously available to slaves, Indians, and settlers became increasingly intolerable to private and public interests now principally committed to producing cotton or sugar. As laws heightened racial barriers and thickened social boundaries during the territorial and early statehood years, the frontier exchange economy in Mississippi could only survive by being refashioned into a form more internal to the growing slave population.[2]

Efforts by Mississippi slaves to maintain production and exchange practices separate from their owners' cotton-driven economy now faced obstacles and tensions similarly encountered by other informal slave economies. Gardening, hunting, gathering, and trading activities had to be adapted to the formal work schedule imposed by owners. Government officials legislated against open trade with Indians and whites and against free movement between fields and forests, reducing an already narrow opportunity for independent production and exchange. In order to secure a modicum of autonomous control over their livelihood, slaves resorted to hidden spaces and illegal transactions in which they interacted with marginalized exchange partners as well as with each other. American Indians were drastically reduced in number with the removal of the Choctaw and Chickasaw nations by the 1830s, while poor and transient whites were stigmatized for their participation in frontier exchange activities considered backward and even subversive.

The small-scale production and exchange activities pursued by enslaved African Americans to mitigate their subordinate and dependent relationship with slave-owners have, until recently, been greatly undervalued by historians. This neglect derived mainly from the value judgements imposed by many contemporary observers of the economic behaviour of slaves. An understanding of the informal strategies of adaptation and resistance that went into the making of the slaves' own internal economy, however, requires that historians carefully disentangle them from the antagonistic observations that prevail in most of our sources. As the slave population rapidly expanded in places like early nineteenth-century Mississippi, apprehension over slave interaction with non-slave-owners seriously escalated among members of the planter class. Contributing to disparaging commentary about slaves' independent economic activity was a growing concern over how to control enslaved workers, who could readily participate in a shadow economy of production and exchange. Many whites, free blacks, and Indians were subjected to the same fear and contempt because of their willingness to engage in economic transactions with slaves.

Investigation of this erosion of customary slave practices in territorial and early statehood Mississippi invites a quick visit to the historiographical debate over differences between Latin and Anglo forms of slavery in the Western hemisphere. The Tannenbaum thesis is no longer as credible as it once was, but the familiar typology attributing various degrees of brutality and prejudice suffered by slaves to the different cultural traditions brought by Europeans still influences some scholarship. Since the Lower Mississippi Valley had been colonized by France and then Spain over the eighteenth century, there is a temptation to portray those nations' supposedly milder types of slavery being replaced by a more repressive type as the United States imposed its slave laws on the region. Cultural dimensions of Americanization are highlighted to explain social and economic change in what became the states of Louisiana and Mississippi. Our understanding of differences and similarities among slave societies, however, has shifted to another line of comparative analysis. The various legal frameworks that Europeans constructed around slavery are no longer measured by degrees of severity and humanity. The timing of a region's trans-Atlantic connections, the relative size of slave and free populations, and the means of staple production are among several variables proving to be as important as, if not more important than, the national origins of slave-owners in determining divergent or convergent forms of slavery. The rapid expansion of cotton agriculture across the lower Mississippi Valley and the rush of slave and free migrants into the region were more instrumental than the cultural and legal traditions introduced by Anglo-Americans in reshaping slavery in Mississippi. The tightening of restrictions around the informal economy of slaves that occurred there during the early nineteenth century was a common pattern wherever the production of an export crop grew in importance.[3]

At the beginning of the nineteenth century, trade and travel in American-Indian nations still provided African Americans in the Lower Mississippi Valley with various opportunities for employment and movement beyond the plantation. Slaves owned by traders and Indians in Mississippi served as interpreters of the Choctaw and Chickasaw languages. Their labour also helped transport merchandise by land and water, process and package furs for exportation, and maintain livestock, buildings, and boats necessary for this commerce. Sailing southward from Chickasaw Bluffs in April 1798, Richard Butler passed 'a perogue loaded with peltry, man'd with negroes and Spaniards, bound for lance "le" grass'.[4] Some slaves working for Indian trade operations were hired out by their owners. The United States factor at St. Stephens, for example, paid Thomas Malone on 31 March 1809 'for 3 months service rendered the Trading House by his negro man Dave in Splitting rails, making fences around the public buildings, handling skins, etc. at $15 per month'.[5] This kind of activity allowed slaves a significant degree of autonomy and even influence as they took advantage of opportunities to trade for themselves. Some even escaped into the territory of Mississippi's Indians, although ownership of slaves by an emerging class within the Choctaw and Chickasaw nations reduced the likelihood of their freedom lasting for long.[6]

The frontier exchange economy that developed across the Lower Mississippi Valley over the eighteenth century included other avenues of autonomous production and exchange for the slave population, French and then Spanish authorities had repeatedly attempted to restrict and regulate trade with slaves, but as in other colonial regions laws against such action had limited effect.[7] Slaves produced food from their own gardening, foraging, and farming activities and traded freely with neighbours, travellers and a growing number of peddlers. 'They are often allowed to raise hogs for themselves', planter William Dunbar reported in 1800, 'and every thrifty slave has his pig pen and poultry house'. Each slave family also 'is allowed a lot of ground and the use of a team, for melons, potatoes, etc'.[8] Towns provided slaves with plenty of opportunity to market goods and services for themselves. In Natchez on the morning of 25 August 1808 traveller Fortescue Cuming 'sauntered to the market-house on a common in front of the town, where meat, fish, and vegetables were sold by a motley mixture of Americans, French and Spanish creoles, Mulattoes and negroes'.[9] Among the people frequenting the Natchez market at that time were Ibrahima and Isabella, a married couple owned by cotton planter Thomas Foster. Born in Timbuktu to a Fulbe king, the recently enslaved African and his wife regularly sold garden produce, Spanish moss, and other items in the Mississippi port town for their benefit.[10]

When United States officials responsible for governing the Mississippi territory first arrived in the region, they expressed dismay over the openness of slaves' independent interaction with Indians and whites alike. Many newcomers worried about the assertiveness and influence that some slaves demonstrated in their frontier roles. Governor Winthrop Sargent called Natchez 'a most Abominable place' because of 'the Ebriety of Indians and negroes on Sundays', among other reasons. The Grand Jury of Adams County complained in June 1799 about Natchez residents permitting slaves to gamble on the outskirts of town. Sundays had become the customary day for slaves to sell their goods in Natchez and then to entertain themselves with food, drink, and sport. The territorial government's dependence on 'a negro slave' as interpreter for the Choctaws was the object of 'very great grievance', according to the grand jury, because it shamed 'free and independent people'. This slave was named Cesar and was owned by Stephen Minor. The 15 dollars per month plus rations that Cesar received from the governor in 1799 was the highest known wage then being earned by a slave in Mississippi, and some citizens believed that only a white man should serve as the government's Indian interpreter.[11]

Early laws in the Mississippi Territory attempted to tighten control over both production and exchange activities of slaves. Governor Sargent observed that 'the Law for regulating Slaves within the Territory, is most Shamefully violated, particularly upon Sundays, and the nights of that, and the preceding day, and in a very notorious manner, at, or in the Vicinity of the Town of Natchez, *where* Slaves are said to assemble in Considerable numbers from distant Plantations, Committing great excesses, and Carrying on an illicit Traffic with the aid and Connivance of the ill disposed'. So in October 1799 he directed county patrols to vigilantly examine 'Passports and Permits to the Slaves for the Sale or Purchase of any Articles, or Commodities whatsoever'. The following May Sargent informed territorial judges of the need to prohibit slaves from 'raising or Vending' cotton in order to prevent theft. Some planters permitted their slaves to produce and sell their own cotton, but the governor argued that this jeopardized the property of most planters. He further called for a prohibition against slave ownership of horses and a penalty against owners who permitted it in order to thwart 'improper intercourse between the Negroes and those who may be disposed to engage with them in illicit traffic'.[12]

A law of 27 May 1800 issued penalties against slaves, owners, overseers and buyers who participated in or permitted slave production and marketing of cotton or slave ownership of horses. Slaves would suffer public whipping, and the others would pay fines that included payment to informants.[13] According to an act of 6 March 1805, 'no person whatsoever shall buy, sell, or receive of, to or from a slave, any commodity whatsoever without the leave or consent of the master, owner or overseer of such slave, expressive of the article so permitted to be bought, sold or bartered'. Owners who licensed a slave 'to go at large and trade as a freeman' would pay a $50 fine. In 1810 sheriffs, coroners, constables, and justices of the peace were authorized to confiscate any article being carried by a slave without his or her owner's written consent and to punish the offender with as many as ten lashes, while any citizen could lawfully apprehend a slave suspected of carrying goods without permissions.[14] Other economic activities of slaves were also restricted by laws that limited hunting with fire to certain areas and prohibited them from keeping dogs and livestock. A law passed in 1803 declared that 'no person whosoever shall send or permit any slave or Indian to go into any of the woods or ranges in the territory, to brand or mark any horse, mare, colt, mule, ass, cattle, hog, sheep, under any pretense whatsoever; unless the slave be in company, and under the direction of some reputable white person'.[15]

Although legal restrictions against independent production and exchange by slaves escalated with the incorporation of Mississippi into the cotton economy of the United States, local conditions continued to encourage informal economic activity. Clearing forestlands for commercial agriculture and labouring intensively over cotton fields consumed a great deal of slaves' time and energy. Yet proximity to still bountiful woods and waters made their access to plant and animal wildlife relatively easy. Their owners' preoccupation with planting more and more cotton made vegetable gardens and poultry yards belonging to slaves a desirable, and in some cases even necessary, source of food supplies for the plantation populace.[16] Growing towns and busy rivers in Mississippi also provided slaves with independent marketing opportunities. Each of these spheres of autonomous economic activity involved negotiations and conflicts at different levels of society as slaves and slave-owners, citizens and officials, residents and travellers pursued sometime overlapping and sometimes clashing interests. Behind all negotiations and conflicts lay African-American determination to secure some control over their livelihood. Production and exchange in the shadow of the plantation constituted an enduring strategy of resistance for slaves attempting to protect household needs and values against the destructive pressures of cotton agriculture.[17]

Joseph Ingraham observed for the 1830s that 'it is customary for planters in the neighbourhood [of Natchez] to give their slaves a small piece of land to cultivate for their own use, by which, those who are industrious, generally make enough to keep themselves and their wives in extra finery and spending money throughout the year'. Twenty years later, Frederick Law Olmsted visited a Mississippi plantation where slaves 'had gardens, and raised a good deal for themselves; they also had fowls, and usually plenty of eggs'. Food from these sources supplemented a weekly allowance, according to the overseer, of a peck of corn and four pounds of pork. At a larger estate of four adjoining plantations, Olmsted learned that each slave family possessed its own fowl-house, hog-sty, and vegetable garden. Slaves fed their hogs during the summer on weeds and fattened them in autumn 'on corn *stolen* (this was mentioned to me by the overseers as if it were a matter of course from their master's corn-fields)'. They frequently sold vegetables, eggs, chickens, and bacon not used to supplement their regular food allowance.[18] State laws continued to prohibit slaves from owning their own horses, cattle, sheep, or hogs and from cultivating their own cotton in order to reduce their competition in marketing these commercial products. But many planters allowed slaves to raise their own swine, and some even permitted them to produce their own cotton at the risk of paying a fine of 50 dollars.[19]

Slaves also found time to procure foodstuffs and other resources away from plantation fields and quarters. After their day's work for the owner was done and on Saturdays or Sundays, slaves gathered wood in nearby forests for sale to others as well as for their household use. Olmsted heard of a slave who earned up to 50 dollars one year by going into the swamps on Sunday and making boards to sell. Slaves who hunted and fished likewise produced items for their own consumption and for buyers. Apprehension over slave ownership of firearms persisted, however, so government authorities attempted to prohibit slaves from possessing weapons. Many slave-owners nonetheless trusted their own slaves who provided game to plantation-house and slave-quarter kitchens, so an 1822 law authorized justices of the peace to grant year-long permits to a slave 'on the application of his master, employer or overseers, to carry and use a gun and ammunition, within the limits of the land or plantation'.[20]

The internal economy of Mississippi slaves overlapped in intricate ways with the plantation economy of their owners. The operation of a profitable plantation depended on a wide range of activities performed by its enslaved residents, including work away from the cotton fields. Cutting timber and herding livestock for the owners' interest kept many slaves in bottomland or upland forests, where the opportunity to hunt provided an independent source of subsistence and trade. The pursuit of these activities, however, could jeopardize plantation routine and order, explaining why managers and overseers expressed so much frustration over slaves' internal economy. Olmsted's account of hunting at one location effectively captured this dilemma:

> The negroes also obtain a good deal of game. They set traps for raccoons, rabbits and turkeys, and I once heard the stock-tender complaining that he had detected one of the vagabond whites stealing a turkey which had been caught in his pen. I several times partook of game while on the plantation that had been purchased of the negroes. The stock-tender, an old negro whose business it was to ride about the woods and keep an eye on the stock cattle that were pastured in them, and who was thus likely to know where the deer ran, had an ingenious way of supplying himself with venison. He lashed a scythe blade or butcher's knife to the end of a pole so that it formed a lance; this he set near a fence or fallen tree which obstructed a path in which the deer habitually ran, and the deer in leaping over the obstacle would leap directly on the knife. In this manner he had killed two deer in the week before my visit.
>
> The manager had sent to him for some of this venison for his own use, and justified himself to me for not paying for it on the ground that the stock-tender had undoubtedly taken time which really belonged to his owner to set his spear. Game taken by the field-hands was not looked upon in the same light, because it must have been got at night when they were excused from labor for their owner.[21]

Slaves found a variety of markets for the produce of their independent farming, gathering, and hunting activities. Many slave-owners purchased goods from slaves as a means of stocking their own households and monitoring the exchange process. Enslaved producers of these goods, in turn, took as much advantage as they could of such a convenient point of trade. Slaves on John Quitman's plantations in Adams and Warren counties were paid cash for chopping wood on Sundays and selling chickens to his Natchez home. They demanded prompt payment and spent their earnings on extra clothing and shoes.[22] Slaves owned by Joseph Davis sold chickens and eggs to his family and to the plantation store. They also sold poultry, garden vegetables, and wood to passing steamboats. In perhaps the most extraordinary example of entrepreneureship practised by a Mississippi slave, the store at Hurricane Plantation beginning in 1842 was actually owned and operated by Benjamin Montgomery, a Virginia-born slave purchased by Davis in Natchez 12 years earlier who quickly became an office clerk, levee planner, architect, and mechanic for his owner. At the plantation store independently run by Montgomery, he accepted wood, chickens, eggs, and vegetables from fellow slaves for dry goods. With a line of credit from New Orleans wholesalers, local whites also visited Montgomery's store.[23]

For slaves living close enough to Mobile, Natchez, and Vicksburg, expanding urban marketplaces offered an important locus for trade even though their independent exchange elicited nervous vigilance from town officials. 'They have the Sabbath given them as a holiday', reported Joseph Ingraham, 'when they are permitted to leave their plantations and come into town to dispose of their produce, and lay in their own little luxuries and private stores'. Although disturbed by such customary violation of the Sabbath, this transplanted New Englander was somewhat amazed by the streams of 'chatting, laughing negroes, arrayed in their Sunday's best' who moved along various roads to Natchez. Some people balanced 'heavily loaded baskets on their heads', while others rode mules and plough horses, 'burthened with the marketable commodities', or pushed 'market carts to and from the city'.[24] Mississippi state law required all slaves travelling off their owners' property to carry permits. By 1822 any citizen could apprehend a slave found without a written pass and bring him or her to local authorities for punishment. Forgery of such permits sometimes occurred, and a penalty of as many as 39 lashes was aimed at any free black or slave who furnished a pass to someone without the owner's consent. A person buying or selling to or from a slave any commodity not specified in the owner's permit was fined $20, while the slave forfeited the articles and was whipped up to ten lashes. Sheriffs, coroners, constables, and justices of the peace were entitled to keep the forfeited goods, but if neglecting to enforce this law they could be charged with a misdemeanour in office. An owner who permitted a slave to 'go at large, and trade as a free man' would pay a $50 fine, while the owner of a ferry or bridge could be fined $25 for allowing a slave to cross without a pass.[25]

The freedom with which slaves seemed to market goods and socialize in Mississippi towns, despite laws intending to circumscribe their activity, caused local officials serious concern. In 1836 Woodville enacted a law banning slaves from visiting town on Sunday unless accompanied by a supervising white. Three years later the penalty for violating this prohibition was increased in severity and a fine was imposed on owners who permitted their slaves to travel to Woodville alone. The town council was still complaining in 1845 about 'the intolerable pest of having our streets filled up with trading carts and noises and drunken negroes on the Sabbath'.[26] Laws against selling alcohol to slaves were generally ineffective, since taverns and grogshops served as lively points of exchange for black, white, and Indian Mississippians at places like the Natchez landing. In addition to the disorderly conduct that municipal authorities associated with slaves who congregated for marketing, were economic advantages held by slave vendors in particular markets. Some slaves who lived in towns operated as middlemen, buying foodstuffs from rural slaves *en route* to the marketplace and selling them from door to door. Other vendors in town markets objected to slaves who actually controlled the price of fish and fowl. Throughout Mississippi in 1831 it became 'unlawful to employ or hire, or cause to be employed or hired, any slave, free negro, or mulatto, to vend or hawk goods, wares, or merchandise within the limits of the several incorporated towns of this state'.[27]

As in the marketplaces of larger southern cities, African-American women played a prominent role in buying and selling goods at Natchez, Vicksburg, and other Mississippi towns. Slave women generally produced most of the garden crops on plantations and preferred to market the produce for themselves. The internal slave economy provided important space for women to secure some control over family and community life, as slave households sought access to foodstuffs and merchandise that were otherwise unavailable in slave-owners' meagre provisions. Women owned by town residents were also responsible for supplying their kitchens, which further increased the visibility of black women at the markets. Since white authorities seemed more nervous about the informal economic activities of slave men, slave women were able to take advantage of townspeople's apparent preference for their presence in marketplaces. This did not spare them, however, from disparaging commentary by observers who self-servingly represented shrewd and aggressive peddling as evidence of African-American women's moral inferiority.[28]

Across the countryside as well as in towns, certain groups of whites acquired a reputation for their social and economic relations with slaves. Men who cut wood for sale to steamboats were commonly accused of hiring, and therefore also harbouring runaway slaves. A planter in 1836 discovered that one of his slaves had been employed for two months by a wood-chopper about five miles below Fort Adams.[29] Boatmen who traded with slaves along riverbanks were always held under suspicion, 'These boats', reported a Mobile newspaper in 1841, 'are small, manned by two, three or four men, and have on board whiskey, brandy, dry goods, etc. which are sold to the negroes in open violation of the law. The goods are sold at half their value and frequently less, which, of itself shows they are not procured honestly.' Individuals who worked on boats as well as passengers also occasionally bartered with slaves. A German traveller heading southward on the Mississippi River to New Orleans in 1817 noted that 'several negroes came to trade' when his boat landed at Tunica Bend.[30] Soldiers stationed at Natchez in the 1830s did not escape the ire of Joseph Ingraham, who heard sounds of 'bestial revelry' coming from the fort one evening. He detected the character of this rendezvous in the voice of 'a little half-tipsy, dapper man in a gray doublet' who was 'expatiating to a gaping crowd of grinning Africans – night-capped or bare-headed white females, in slattern apparel and uncombed locks – two or three straight, blanketed, silent Indians – noisy boys and ragged boatmen – upon the glories of a soldier's life'.[31] Poor whites in general traded once in a while with slaves and were frequently condemned by local authorities for selling liquor and encouraging them to steal. Prominent citizens of Pontotoc County complained in 1841 about 'evil disposed persons ... too much in the habit of trading with negroes'. Olmsted observed in the 1850s that 'there were many poor whites within a few miles who would always sell liquor to the negroes, and encourage them to steal, to obtain the means to buy it of them'.[32]

Mississippi River towns, especially Natchez and Vicksburg, were visited every fall by hundreds of men manning the flatboats that brought crops and goods downriver. Gambling and drinking behaviour among these visitors worried town officials and merchants, particularly because many slaves also participated in the revelry. Spokesmen for law and order complained repeatedly about the moral corruption of both poor whites and slaves being caused by flatboatmen's interaction with them. Selling liquor to slaves, in exchange for goods allegedly stolen from slave-owning households, remained the focus of town leaders' outrage. But mounting suspicion that many flatboatmen from the Ohio Valley also bore 'a secret hatred' toward slavery further fuelled local animosity in Mississippi River towns. By the 1830s efforts to tax and restrict flatboats docking at public wharves sparked some angry confrontations between townspeople and boatmen.[33]

Animus toward groups engaged in regular exchange with slaves rushed violently to the surface in a panic that swept through Madison and Hinds counties in the summer of 1835. Rumours of a slave revolt, plotted by certain whites living or moving on the margins of established communities, exposed an anxiety that had been intensifying over the years. Petty trade and work association between bonded and free people marked fissures in the racial system upon which the cotton economy rested. So when fear of impending rebellion struck, people who encouraged or participated in the internal economy of slaves were suspected of abolitionism or slave kidnapping. In addition to the more than 12 African-American slaves killed, six white were hanged for allegedly conspiring with slaves in west central Mississippi. They included a Kentucky boatman-trader, two steam doctors, and a carpenter-cotton gin builder. The latter owned six slaves in

Livingston, but was believed to be too lenient and familiar with them. A couple of poor farmers who picked cotton alongside slaves on a Hinds County plantation for wages were also arrested and nearly lynched.[34] In the aftermath of this panic, government officials and prominent citizens escalated suppression of loose interaction with slaves by enforcing pass and patrol laws more vigilantly. The ubiquitous presence of informal economic activities, however, eventually restored some of the laxness and fluidity accompanying independent production and exchange among slaves.[35]

Over Mississippi's territorial and early statehood years, forms of production and exchange once central to the regional economy became marginalized and even criminalized. Informal economic practices, nonetheless, remained important to most African Americans and to many whites. When the cotton economy fastened its grip on the Lower Mississippi Valley, frontier livelihood fragmented into more scattered spheres of activity circumscribed by prohibitive laws. Negotiating with slave-owners and overseers and evading patrols and sheriffs, slaves struggled to reshape independent subsistence and trade into an internal economy. Plantation gardens, adjacent forest, town markets, and riverbanks were constricted spaces for an informal economy, but frontier exchange nevertheless persisted on the margins of Mississippi's plantation economy.

NOTES

1. Ira Berlin and Philip D. Morgan (eds.), *The Slaves' Economy: Independent Production by Slaves in the Americas* (London, 1991); Mary Turner (ed.), *From Chattel Slaves to Wage Slaves: The Dynamics of Labour Bargaining in the Americas* (Bloomington, 1995): Roderick A. McDonald, *The Economy and Material Culture of Slaves: Goods and Chattels on the Sugar Plantations of Jamaica and Louisiana* (Baton Rouge, 1993); Betty Wood, *Women's Work, Men's Work: The Informal Slave Economies of Lowcountry Georgia* (Athens, 1995).

2. For examination of exchange relations in the region over the eighteenth century, see Gwendolyn Midlo Hall, *Africans in Colonial Louisiana: The Development of Afro-Creole Culture in the Eighteenth Century* (Baton Rouge, 1992); and Daniel H. Usner, Jr., *Indians, Settlers and Slaves: The Lower Mississippi Valley before 1783* (Chapel Hill, 1992). For comparison with other colonial regions in North America, see Peter H. Wood, *Black Majority: Negroes in Colonial South Carolina from 1670 through the Stono Rebellion* (New York, 1974), pp.95–130, 195–217; and Philip D. Morgan, *Slave Counterpoint: Black Culture in the Eighteenth-Century Chesapeake and Lowcountry* (Chapel Hill, 1998), pp.318–76.

3. Important contributions to this debate for the Lower Mississippi Valley include David C. Rankin, 'The Tannenbaum Thesis Reconsidered: Slavery and Race Relations in Antebellum Louisiana', *Southern Studies*, Vol.18 (1979), pp.5–31; Jerah Johnson, 'Colonial New Orleans: A Fragment of the Eighteenth-Century French Ethos', in Arnold R. Hirsch and Joseph Logsdon (eds.), *Creole New Orleans: Race and Americanization* (Baton Rouge, 1992), pp.12–57; and Judith Kelleher Schafer, *Slavery, the Civil Law, and the Supreme Court of Louisiana* (Baton Rouge, 1994), pp.1–10.

4. Dawson A. Phelps (ed.), 'Excerpts from the Journal of the Reverend Joseph Bullen, 1799 and 1800', *Journal of Mississippi History*, Vol.17 (1955), pp.262, 273; Diary, April–July 1798, Richard Butler Papers, 1795–1825 (Louisiana and Lower Mississippi Valley Collections,

Louisiana State University, Baton Rouge).

5. Choctaw Factory Miscellaneous Accounts, 1803–1825, Records of the Office of Indian Trade (National Archives, Washington, DC).

6. Natchez, *Weekly Chronicle*, 29 March 1809.

7. Lawrence Kinnaird (trans. and ed.), *Spain in the Mississippi Valley, 1765–1794* (3 vols. Washington, DC, 1946–49), Vol.II, pp.15051, Vol.III, pp.42–3; James S. Robertson (ed.), 'A Decree for Louisiana Issued by the Baron of Carondelet, June 1, 1795', *Louisiana Historical Quarterly*, Vol.20 (1937), pp.590–605.

8. J.F.H. Claiborne, *Mississippi as a Province, Territory, and State, with Biographical Notices of Eminent Citizens* (Jackson, 1880), pp.144–5.

9. Reuben Gold Thwaites (ed.), *Early Western Travels, 1748–1846*, Vol.IV: *Cumings Tour to the Western Country* (Cleveland, 1904), pp.320–1.

10. Terry Alford, *Prince among Slaves* (New York, 1977), pp.60–1, 68, 85.

11. Dunbar Rowland (ed.), *The Mississippi Territorial Archives 1798–1803: Executive Journals of Governor Winthrop Sargent and Governor William Charles Dole Claiborne* (Nashville, 1905), Vol.1, pp.82, 164–5, 233–4; Clarence Edwin Carter (ed.), *The Territorial Papers of the United States*, Vol.V: *The Territory of Mississippi, 1798–1817* (Washington, DC, 1937), pp.63–4.

12. Mississippi Territorial Archives, Vol.1, pp.176–7, 232.

13. William D. McCain (ed.), *Laws of the Mississippi Territory, May 27, 1800* (Beauvoir Community, MI, 1948), pp.237–40.

14. *Statutes of the Mississippi Territory* (Natchez, 1816), pp.384, 388–9.

15. Ibid, pp.308–9, 359, 385–6, 393; A. Hutchinson, *Code of Mississippi* (Jackson, 1848), pp.282–3, 287–8.

16. Steven F. Miller, 'Plantation Labor Organization and Slave Life on the Cotton Frontier: The Alabama-Mississippi Black Belt, 1815–1840', in Ira Berlin and Philip D. Morgan (eds.), *Cultivation and Culture: Labor and the Shaping of Slave Life in the Americas* (Charlottesville, 1993), pp.155–84.

17. For other approaches to this struggle, see Alex Lichtenstein, '"That Disposition To Theft, With Which They Have Been Branded": Moral Economy, Slave Management, and the Law', *Journal of Social History*, Vol.22 (1988), pp.413–40 and John Campbell, 'As "A Kind of Freeman"? Slaves' Market-Related Activities in the South Carolina Upcountry, 1800–1860', *Slavery and Abolition*, Vol.12 (1991), pp.131–69.

18. Joseph Holt Ingraham, *The Southwest. By a Yankee* (2 vols., New York, 1835), pp.54–5; Frederick Law Olmsted, *A Journey in the Back Country* (New York, 1860), pp.50–1, 74–5.

19. *Code of Mississippi*, p.519; Charles S. Sydnor, *Slavery in Mississippi* (Washington, DC, 1933), pp.97–8.

20. Olmsted, *Journey in the Back Country*, p.75; *Code of Mississippi*, p.514.

21. Olmsted, *Journey in the Back Country*, pp.75–6.

22. Robert E. May, *John A. Quitman: Old South Crusader* (Baton Rouge, 1985), pp.131, 139.

23. Janet Sharp Hermann, *Joseph E. Davis: Pioneer Patriarch* (Jackson, 1990), pp.56–60.

24. Ingraham, *Southwest*, pp.54–7; D. Clayton James, *Antebellum Natchez* (Baton Rouge, 1968), pp.171–4; Christopher Morris, *Becoming Southern: The Evolution of a Way of Life. Warren County and Vicksburg, Mississippi, 1770–1860* (New York, 1995), pp.75–6; Daniel S. Dupre, *Transforming the Cotton Frontier: Madison County, Alabama, 1800–1840* (Baton Rouge, 1997), pp.204–5, 213–19.

25. *Code of Mississippi*, pp.513–19.

26. Woodville, *Republican*, 23 April 1836, 9 December 1839, 28 June 1845.

27. *Code of Mississippi*, pp.269, 534; Ingraham, *Southwest*, pp.58–61; Sydnor, *Slavery in Mississippi*, pp.98–9; John Hebron Moore, *The Emergence of the Cotton Kingdom in the Old Southwest: Mississippi, 1770–1860* (Baton Rouge, 1987), pp.279–81.

28. Wood, *Women's Work, Men's Work*; Robert Olwell, '"Loose, Idle, and Disorderly": Slave Women in the Eighteenth-Century Charleston Marketplace', in David Barry Gaspar and Darlene Clark Hines (eds.), *More Than Chattel: Black Women and Slavery in the Americas* (Bloomington, 1996), pp.97–110.

29. Woodville, *Republican*, 23 July 1836.

30. Lewis E. Atherton, 'Itinerant Merchandising in the Ante-Bellum South', *Bulletin of the Business History Society*, Vol.19 (1945), pp.54–5; Felix Flugel (ed.), 'Pages from a Journal of a Voyage Down the Mississippi to New Orleans in 1817', *Louisiana Historical Quarterly*, Vol.7 (1924), pp.414–40.

31. Ingraham, *Southwest*, p.61.

32. Olmsted, *Journey in the Back Country*, p.75; Charles C. Bolton, *Poor Whites of the Antebellum South: Tenants and Laborers in Central North Carolina and Northeast Mississippi* (Durham, 1994), pp.107–8; Moore, *Emergence of the Cotton Kingdom*, p.155.

33. *Vicksburg Advocate and Register*, 9, 13 April 1836; James, *Antebellum Natchez*, pp.168–9; Morris, *Becoming Southern*, pp.122–3.

34. James Lal Penick, Jr., *The Great Western Land Pirate: John A. Murrell in Legend and History* (Columbia, Mo., 1981), pp.106–57; Lawrence Shore, 'Making Mississippi Safe for Slavery: The Insurrectionary Panic of 1835', in Orville Vernon Burton and Robert C. McMath, Jr. (eds.), *Class, Conflict, and Consensus: Antebellum Southern Community Studies* (Westport, CT, 1982), pp.96–127; Christopher Morris, 'An Event in Community Organization: The Mississippi Slave Insurrection Scare of 1835', *Journal of Social History*, Vol.22 (1988), pp.93–111.

35. Sydnor, *Slavery in Mississippi*, pp.77–80.

The 11 O'clock Flog: Women, Work and Labour Law in the British Caribbean

MARY TURNER

The imperial government began to dismantle the slave labour system in the mid-1820s. Under pressure from the abolitionists and with the full support of the West India Committee, it set out a reform programme that defined significant changes in the slave labour laws and made special provisions to implement them. The proposed slave labour laws set out new terms for slave labour, regulated work place discipline, legalized and expanded certain customary civil rights the slaves had won and appointed a full time official, a Protector of Slaves, to implement the law. The declared aim of the reform package was to 'prepare the slaves for freedom'.

Planters in the representative colonies consistently opposed the amelioration policy. The Jamaica Assembly, which controlled the largest single unit of slaves in the British Caribbean, at first refused to even consider the proposed reforms, claiming the imperial government was trespassing on its constitutional privileges. Planters in the Crown colonies conquered from the Spanish and the Dutch during the Revolutionary wars (Trinidad, Demerara-Essequibo and Berbice) were scarcely more enthusiastic, but commanded less constitutional power. In Trinidad the imperial government implemented its model reform package by Order in Council in 1824. And in Demerara-Essequibo and Berbice on the South American mainland, new slave labour laws reflecting imperial guidelines were in place by 1826.

The co-operation of the Crown colonies was facilitated by the fact that in the colonial legal structures which the British took over from the Dutch and the Spanish there was an official whose duties included guardianship of the slaves. In the mainland colonies the *fiscals* and in Trinidad the *procurador fiscal* continued to function in this capacity, consistent with the terms of conquest, after the British take-over. The appointment of a Protector of Slaves therefore was not an innovation, but an adaptation of an established office. In Trinidad the existing *procurador fiscal* in fact took over as Protector.

The re-definition and implementation of the slave labour laws mark with some precision the moment of articulation between one system of labour extraction and another: chattel slavery into wage slavery. On the one hand, the existing laws reflect the slave labour system as established for perpetuity; on the other, the new laws devised by the first industrial imperial state, point the way to wage work.

This essay investigates the impact of the new laws on slave workers, particularly on women slave workers in Berbice. It reviews first the cases they brought against their owners and managers under the old slave laws before the Fiscal and then reviews the cases brought under the 1826 Code before the Protector. Berbice is the only mainland colony where the records allow this comparison to be made. No records of slave grievance cases, or of the Fiscal's summary judgements were kept in Demerara-Essequibo. Records exist for Berbice only because in 1819 Henry Beard, a qualified lawyer, was for the first time appointed President of the Courts of Civil and Criminal Justice; he persuaded the Fiscal, H.M. Bennett, that he should voluntarily (since no regulation compelled him to do so) record the cases he dealt with as guardian of the slaves. Bennett partially complied by making 'notes for his own satisfaction' of his investigations, but omitted to record his judgments except on the very rare occasion when cases were referred to a higher court. His deputy, J.M. Scott, was more conscientious and noted both investigation and judgment. These records, in conjunction with the detailed reports the Protector of Slaves was required by law to submit to the local and imperial governments, provide the basis for this investigation.[1]

Berbice was the last of the three colonies the Dutch established on the shoulder of South America and the slowest to develop. In economic terms its performance was quite outclassed by the sugar plantation dominated colonies of Demerara-Essequibo, which in the 1820s constituted the colonies' economic heartland. Berbice by comparison remained a frontier province. Its population in 1830 was almost 90 per cent slave and totalled only 23,000 people who were thinly spread along the coast and the upper reaches of the Berbice river and Canje creek. Many plantations there were isolated as many as forty miles from the nearest government outpost. As much as half the slave population was African born and was held, characteristically, in large scale holdings of 200 or more workers. The economy was comparatively diversified; sugar production occupied less than 50 per cent of slave workers (compared with 80 per cent in Demerara-Essequibo) coffee, cotton, provision and cattle production engaged most of the rest.[2]

Work conditions in Berbice, as in Demerara-Essequibo, were vitally influenced by the fact that the coastal plain was below sea level. Plantations there were polders, land claimed from the sea, and the maintenance of sea defences, drains and canals constantly demanded strenuous digging and building work from the slave gangs. At the same time, in contrast to the island territories, there was no sugar harvest period; the mills could be kept turning throughout the year, making the demand for night work in the factories continuous.[3]

Women slaves, who constituted slightly less than half the work force, were valued on the estates primarily as field and factory workers; supervisory roles and skilled work were male preserves. Women shared in the heaviest work and this conflicted with their role in reproduction. It is not surprising to find that the birth rate in Berbice, as elsewhere in the British Caribbean outside Barbados, was significantly below the death rate. Self-interest consequently encouraged owners, particularly after 1807 when abolition of the slave trade cut off their reserve army of African labour, to provide sick care. By the 1820s Berbice was comparatively well supplied with doctors with one for every 900 slaves employed by slave-owners at a fixed annual rate and some estates had hospitals.[4]

The statute laws regulating slave labour were embodied in a few local ordinances that dealt with slave discipline and subsistence rights. The maximum punishment for work-place offences was set in 1810 at 39 lashes, the Biblical standard, and pass laws of 1804 and 1806 confined slaves to the estates unless they had written permission from their owner. In 1806 their rations were defined as two full grown bunches of plantain weekly (nursing children excepted), or two common coffee baskets full of cassava or yam. To secure this supply coastal estates were to grow 75 plantain trees per slave, or 60 on the rivers, where the plantain grew better. Fines were fixed at 1,000 and 2,000 guilders for the first and second offence and criminal prosecution for the third, a punishment schedule that suggests a law more honoured in the breach than the observance. A few slaves also had the use of small plots, though these were not common on poldered land, to supply fruit and vegetables; in contrast to some of the island economies, however, market outlets for any surplus were limited.

The ordinances were supplemented by customs, a form of common law, which embodied slave rights established by tradition under pressure from the slaves, or rights which had been conceded by the Dutch and continued to be recognized by government officials. The slaves customary rights included the right to own most forms of personal property except firearms and small boats which were useful for escape along the rivers: a customary right to be either sold in families, or separated by consent: the right to give evidence in criminal cases, but not on oath: and a right, limited by works of necessity only, to Sunday free from forced labour as well as Christmas holidays. This right was widely established by law, or custom throughout the West Indies by the end of the eighteenth century and, when occasion arose, was defended in Berbice by the Fiscal. Customary rights, however, tended to be fragile and slave workers had to act on their own behalf to defend them.[5]

The Fiscal consequently administered a system with few legally defined pains and penalties. He had undefined discretionary power to punish the slaves for petty offences with flogging and imprisonment in a 'summary but moderate way'. And he took legal action against owners and managers found in breach of regulations. To facilitate this he enjoyed a general brief which entitled him to enter all properties where slaves were working to check the extent of grounds growing provisions, the scale of food and clothing supplied, the condition of estate sick houses and of the slave population in general.

The Fiscal's salary was 3,000 guilders a year plus fees and an under-sheriff and six 'dienaars', or justice officers assisted him. H.M. Bennett was a substantial slave-owner with a half interest in two sugar estates with a slave population of 288, together with ten domestics in his New Amsterdam household. He combined in his person every level of authority over slaves.[6] The lack of a systematic and comprehensive slave labour law, decision-making at the highest level in the hands of a slave-owner and the tradition of non-accountability, were problems the 1826 Ordinance was intended to resolve.

The pre-1826 records used here show that the Fiscal and his deputy dealt on average with three cases a month and noted one third with judgements.[7] These cases represented only a small proportion of the work-place disputes which occurred. As the case histories outlined below demonstrate, plaintiffs often made their grievances known to their manager, attorney or owner, even the local burger officer who combined the functions of magistrate and military officer, before requesting a pass from their manager to visit the Fiscal. Such disputes characterized the day to day working of the slave labour system throughout the Americas and helped to shape customary law and the informal contract terms on which slave labour was exacted. The slaves' ultimate weapon in these disputes was collective withdrawal of labour, or strike action; 'going to bush' pitted their ultimate ownership of their labour power against the owners' punishment capacity in efforts to shape their terms of work: hours worked, work loads, punishment norms, and food supplied.[8]

In Berbice appeal to the Fiscal offered an additional, constitutional-legal route to achieving these ends. The slaves' right to lay grievances before a high-ranking, salaried government official legitimized and, arguably, gave added value to their estate based struggles. This was more particularly the case since, under the Dutch system, owners and managers were penalized for failing to resolve conflicts on the estates; they paid 12 guilders for every slave worker who appeared before the Fiscal, which made collective complaints expensive, and more than double that (25 guilders) for each slave punished at the town jail for lodging a complaint judged unfounded.

The cases the slaves brought for redress to the Fiscal and, subsequently, to the Protector of Slaves, illuminate the working of the estate based labour bargaining system and raise the question, in what ways did the 1826 Slave Code impact on these processes?[9]

Women slave workers went to the Fiscal with charges against owners, managers and, on occasion, slave drivers. They acted individually and collectively; sometimes in a group with other women on behalf of themselves, or of the whole work force and sometimes with their male co-workers. In the latter case a man was usually spokesperson and women spoke in support. Groups of men appearing at the Office conveyed an element of threat, a hint of the physical force slave workers implicitly commanded – a factor which had added value after the August 1823 rebellion in neighbouring Demerara. All women collective protests to the Fiscal were comparatively rare and comprise only one in every eight of the total. They posited, arguably, a different sort of threat by showing that slave workers of the very lowest rank had been driven to combine and protest. Women, both individually and collectively, often opened up the process with managers and attorneys, or attempted to win redress when their men-folk had failed. In some cases, as at 'Reumzigt' for example, they filled both roles. 'Reumzigt' was a coffee property on the Berbice river with some 80 workers where punishment levels were first protested to one of the estate attorneys by an 11-man delegation. He sent them back to the estate to have their grievances flogged out of them, and to make sure the job was properly done and to preserve the authority of the gang's resident driver, floggers were hired to do the job. The delegation was then put in the stocks, making two punishments for one protest.

The workers then tried a different tack and sent one individual pregnant woman to see the second attorney who ordered her flogged as well. The manager was unwilling to do this and put her in the stocks to be 'fed sparingly' for a week. Methods of local redress had been exhausted, therefore, when the manager knocked down and kicked a woman because her box of coffee beans was not picked clean enough. At this point a four-woman delegation went to the Fiscal. They complained on behalf of the whole workforce that every trifling offence, such as a single unsound bean in a box of picked over coffee, earned flogging. They brought a box of coffee beans to show the standard they thought acceptable. The record does not, unfortunately, reveal what the outcome of this protest was. No judgment was recorded and, as was frequently the case, no law applied to it. The Fiscal's frequent practice in such circumstances was to tell the manager to moderate his conduct and give notice of a complaint to his employer. The case exemplifies, however, all the customary and legal methods available to slave workers in the absence of a resident owner to protest their work conditions and the roles played by women workers in this process.[10]

Women worker disputes with managers revolved around the issues taken up by the men: punishments, task size, over work, Sunday work, sickness and work, food and clothing, separation of families, and parent rights, sale or hire of their persons as individuals, or collectively. To these were added disputes concerning pregnancy, child rearing and sexual services. Most cases involved more than one issue since once before the Fiscal workers often took the opportunity to state all their grievances. Their fundamental purposes, however, were clear; they sought to limit the use of coercion and limit the demands on their labour power. The cases dealt with below illustrate both work-place conditions and the extent of legal redress available before the 1826 Ordinance was implemented.

The task-work system characteristic of Berbice and all the mainland colonies was a key focus of manager–worker conflict. Tasks were defined by managers and regulated, at best, by custom. Defined as a quantity of work, the task system notionally rewarded the industrious with free time and automatically penalized the lazy; in practice, it allowed managers to set tasks which filled the regular working day and then measure and punish shortfalls without necessarily taking into account weather and soil conditions which affected the quantity of labour needed. New managers also used the system to intensify labour exaction by setting higher production standards. The 11 o'clock flog was integral to task work; it took place when, after the morning's work was done and the slaves were due for their two-hour 11 a.m. to 1 p.m. break, it was found that less than half the task had been completed. The threat of the 11 o'clock flog sometimes drove slaves to work through their break in the hope of avoiding punishment.[11]

At 'Prospect' sugar estate worker discontent covered the entire spectrum of worker grievances, but was brought to a head by the task issue and the 11 o'clock flog. The manager's work and punishment regime had already prompted an all-male delegation to the attorney and cuts in rations had sent a woman to complain to him also; neither appeal was successful and the female petitioner was flogged. The women were sparked into action by an 11 o'clock flog. They were employed relieving and supplying canes and found behind hand with their task. The manager said the task was one row of 49 roods (a rood being 12 feet) and they had only done 15 by break time. They claimed the work went slowly because the ground was dried out and had first to be watered before they could chop it and plant the cane. As they explained to the driver, if the cane was not properly planted they would be flogged for that. At noon the manager, who clearly thought they were under-exerting themselves, sent the headman, the highest authority in the slave village, to go and flog each of the strong (not the weak, or pregnant) women 12 lashes each.

The women made it clear that the manager's regime at 'Prospect' maximized workloads and minimized subsistence. They were obliged to do night work at the mill for sugar manufacture, to bring firewood in from the canal mouth, to do occasional work, such as moving a corn store in the evening. On Sundays they had to collect firewood for the kitchen and steam engine as well as grass. At the same time individual workloads had been increased; for example, only four instead of five workers were employed to move megasse from the mill. The manager also deprived them of their rations; the attorney supplied their two bunches of plantain each week, but one was used to feed the stock together with all the molasses, and they were never issued tobacco, or rum. Even the sick were kept on short rations and received no fish.[12]

Once the slaves had stated their case the Fiscal or his deputy either visited the estate to collect evidence, or called witnesses, including owners, attorneys, managers, drivers, and slave workers not involved in the delegation, to his office. His power to redress grievances was strictly limited. He could rule that the size of the task was reasonable, but where he found it unreasonable he could do no more than suggest reduction. He could condemn a punishment regime as 'excessive' and declare the manager 'too frequently inflicted punishment without sufficient cause'. But if no evidence indicated that any one flogging exceeded the legal upper limit of 39 lashes he could only tell the manager to moderate his conduct and advise his employer to dismiss him if he failed to do so.[13]

Of the charges brought by the women at 'Prospect', Sunday work breached acknowledged custom and another related to the subsistence standards customarily afforded by the estate. Attorney and manager defended themselves as best they could. The manager professed not to know Sunday work was not customary in Berbice so he was simply continuing a practice he found operating when he took over the estate. In any case, he argued, the workers expending more labour could 'easily' move the twenty cords of wood in question over six nights. And he had 'paid' the slaves for overwork on the corn store with baskets of corn.

It is quite possible that Sunday work was customary at 'Prospect'; but slave workers subjected to new managers usually tried to resolve old grievances as well as win new concessions. And the exchange of additional rations, or of free time, or cash for additional work, was a well-established custom in Berbice as elsewhere. In this case, however, the exchange of corn for extra work simply aggravated the slaves' grievances about subsistence.

The ration issue was very sensitive both between workers and managers and between owners and managers because managers were commonly supposed to embezzle plantation supplies for their own profit. The managers in this case stoutly defended themselves. The overseer supplied a certificate of supplies issued to the slaves and the driver backed up the manager's denial that slave rations went to the stock. Nevertheless, it is clear that the manager was making economies. The slaves got two bunches of plantains one week and one bunch plus seven pounds of rice, or 25 ears of corn on alternate weeks. Plantains were, however, more nutritious than corn or rice, having twice the calorie content. The customary rum ration was cut and distributed only as a reward, a system that penalized average and elderly workers, and tobacco was no longer distributed. Customary standards of subsistence had been cut, but not below legal standards.[14]

The Fiscal used the occasion to condemn the 11 o'clock flog as 'premature'; he considered punishment for an unfinished task was appropriate, but only at the end of the working day. He affirmed the slaves' right to be free from work on Sundays. The plaintiffs, however, were reprimanded for complaining to him instead of to their master. By doing so they showed a lack of respect for a master who 'supplied their wants plentifully'. The women accepted defeat and made the necessary signals of regret and apology. The case had given them a political platform, obliged their bosses to defend themselves, cost the attorney Mr Ross 72 guilders, affirmed their right to a work-free Sunday and sent a warning signal to the manager about punishments and food supplies.

The case neatly exposes how the system worked. The Fiscal's chief role was to mediate conflict in the best interest of slave property owners, sparing the manager legal prosecution and reinforcing where possible the attorney's authority. Managers were warned in no less than 42 judgments recorded by the deputy Fiscal between May 1822 and July 1823 that any further complaint of equivalent ill treatment by their slaves would lead to prosecution. There is only one recorded instance, however, where a slave's complaint prompted a masters' immediate punishment and this involved a man who, at the behest of his wife, flogged, put in the stocks and threatened to put a chain round the neck of a slave woman who had supplied him with sexual services. This combination of harsh punishment and sexual exploitation prompted a 600 guilder fine. But when slaves complained that the manager at 'Plantation Scotland' had at various times taken over no less than 11 slave wives, he was only reprimanded and his employer advised to dismiss him.[15]

Excessive workload and punishment regimes were often combined with underfeeding and ill treatment of the sick. Two female and three male delegates from the aptly named sugar estate 'Plantation Profit', with its daily 11 o'clock flog of 25 lashes, its stocks full of people and a fish ration once a month, said when they complained of sickness they were flogged first then dosed with salts and camomile. One of the plaintiffs had asked for a blister (which would have kept her in hospital some days) and was flogged by the manager who said he would blister her backside: another was told 'the stocks is your physic'. Punishment and neglect of sick workers prompted numerous complaints from both men and women. As the judgements recorded by the Acting-Fiscal demonstrate, however, his powers were limited to recommending medical care, reprimanding managers for flogging the sick, or dismissing the complaint as frivolous.[16]

The workload, punishment, subsistence and health problems women slave workers shared with men were multiplied by their role as mothers. Once the slave trade was cut off, the reproduction of the slave workforce became, notionally, a priority for owners throughout the British Caribbean and more particularly in colonies such as Berbice with an internal frontier to exploit. But notional long-term benefits for owners inevitably tended to take second place to the immediate needs of plantation production and profit. Pregnant women labourers necessarily in the later months worked at reduced capacity while nursing women labourers threatened a longer term loss of hours in the field. The conflictive demands of work and reproduction which led in England, for example, to infants being born at the bottom of mineshafts, were intensified under slavery by the use of the whip.

Some estates in Berbice, as the cases outlined above indicate, made concessions to pregnant workers and modified workloads, deployed them in jobs suited to their capacity and punished them in the stocks rather than by flogging. But the evidence makes it abundantly clear these were not standard practices. Managers were more likely to take the attitude that 'they were not there to mind babies'. They forced women by threats of violence – one promised 'to break her belly with a foe – foe pounder', a stout wooden stick used to process plantain – to continue their regular work routine and subjected them with sadistic zeal to standard punishments.

Occasionally such managers were brought to justice. This happened at 'Plantation L'Esperance' coffee estate where Rosa, who was far advanced in pregnancy and protested she was too big to stoop, was sent to pick coffee. She had to do so on her knees. It was task work and at 11 a.m. when the driver checked, none of the women had picked their quota. The manager ordered him to lay all the women out on the coffee-drying platform and flog them one after the other. When the driver got to Rosa he stopped and said, 'This woman is rather big with child.' The manager said, 'Give it to her till the blood flies out.' The bush whip, the *carracarra*, had broken by then so he used a doubled cart whip. The next day Rosa was sent to the field again but had labour pains and was allowed to go to the hospital. The doctor examined her and declared sitting down would not be good for her. Many miscarriages, he considered, came from women taking no exercise and contracting lazy habits. So Rosa was sent back to the field. The next day she miscarried.

It was a hard labour and the midwife had to force it. Three women as well as Rosa and her husband saw the child; it was perfectly formed as she was near term, but born dead 'with one eye out, the arm broken, and a stripe visible over the head which must have been done with the double whip'. The parents told the manager the baby was dead, the father dug the grave and one of the helpers at the birth carried the body out. The next day the doctor saw Rosa and said, 'I suppose you have been eating green pines.'

The Fiscal heard evidence from all the actors involved and took particular care to get one witness to confirm the manager's order to 'flog her till the blood comes'. This case prompted instant action: the manager was immediately suspended and prosecuted. Despite a judicial system characteristically arbitrary in dealing with such cases he was eventually sentenced to three months in jail, fined 200 pounds and dismissed from his post.[17] Flogging women could induce a miscarriage at any stage of pregnancy and the question arises, did confinement in the stocks have the same effect? Two witnesses in one case, including the slave sick nurse attendant, testified this happened to a woman in the early stage of pregnancy who was put in the hospital stocks for a week for attacking a slave driver.[18]

When babies arrived safely and survived the initial hazards of death from disease, mothers faced the problem of securing time to nurse. Some managers allowed nursing women a shorter working day so they could feed the infant before work and at noon as well as in the evening; others insisted infants be weaned early and left in the care of women too old for field work. On 'No. 6 Canje Creek' sugar estate, the latter system applied and one worker named Laura, who claimed her child was weakly and left the field to feed it, was flogged. She complained to the Fiscal and requested assistance to carry out what the minutes term 'this natural favour'. The manager, called to the office to give his account, claimed that time at the beginning and end of the day (one and half hours) was allowed for nursing and four nurses were supplied. Further, 12 children had been raised in the last two years, which showed the method succeeded. None of this addressed Laura's problem of feeding her weak child at noon, but the Fiscal was evidently satisfied that nursery care at 'No.6 Canje Creek' met customary standards and the infant was left to take its chances.[19]

Slave workers as parents also turned to the Fiscal when they saw their children harshly punished and underfed. This happened at 'Plantation Leldenrust' where a couple brought charges against their owner on behalf of their four children and themselves. The children had insufficient allowances, inadequate clothing and regular flogging with a bush rope. The Fiscal found one of the boys with marks of severe beating on his posterior and the other, as his mother put it, 'lingers very much'. The parents were themselves forced to work until 4 p.m. on Sundays, got no holidays, half rations and short cloth allowances.

The Fiscal's investigation revealed that the parent's complaints represented the problems of the entire workforce. He called the slaves together with their owner and made it clear that they were entitled to Sundays free from work, entitled to their rations and the bush rope was not to be used. The clothing question, however, was not addressed and no penalty was imposed on the owner. To implement his instructions the Fiscal in this case relied on the slave workers themselves, who were instructed to complain to their nearest burgher officer if the owner did not comply. Although the children stood to benefit together with the rest of the workforce if these changes were implemented, they had no special right to protection by their parents or the law. The assumption was that children raised to the age of five were likely to survive one way or another and in any case property rights were paramount.[20]

Slave workers also looked to the Fiscal to punish managers who sexually exploited their wives and to prevent the break-up by sale of the nuclear family and of their kin and village units. Separation of families by sale contravened acknowledged custom in Berbice, but fear of sale and separation were pervasive, fed not only by local transfers, but by the export trade to Demerara. Slave sales disrupted not only nuclear families, but kin groups and village communities as a whole, as well as reviving memories barely a generation old of the traumas of forced migration. One group, sold from their homes, hired out and then threatened with separation, protested to the Fiscal that they were 'sent about like new negroes'. Such complaints, which challenged property rights, were considered offensive. Slaves were told to obey their owners on pain of exemplary punishment at the jail.[21]

The evidence here makes clear that the Fiscal presided over a conglomerate of estate based labour extraction systems barely regulated by law or custom over which he exerted very limited powers. Such powers as he had were, according to the recorded judgements, used more often to dismiss complaints and punish the plaintiffs than to redress grievances. Judgements in favour of slave plaintiffs, moreover, meant at best partial redress; managers were usually only reprimanded, or warned that prosecution was possible but actual prosecutions were rare.[22] Investigation by the Fiscal, however, requiring evidence from managers as well as workers, sometimes on the estate with the full knowledge of the workforce, may have had some effect. The fact that slave workers utilized the system suggests it may have done so.

The slaves' protests outlined here made clear what legal changes were needed to improve their work conditions: legally limited workloads, work time, and punishment schedules; adequate and secure subsistence: provisions for sickness, pregnancy, nursing and parenting: protection for family, kin and community groups from division by sale. Slaves also wanted the right to be sold to another employer and the right to secure the dismissal of managers who failed to apply the law. The slave workers' immediate needs required the labour laws to be more comprehensive and rigorously impose new limits on their owners' and managers' personal power.

From the imperial government's point of view, however, the aims and purposes of re-structuring the slave laws were more far-reaching and complex. To dismantle chattel slavery meant beginning the transition to wage work, preparing slave workers and slave-owners to become servants and masters, employees and employers. This process required first and foremost that owner – slave relationships be defined by law and systematically applied to both parties by enhancing the powers of the colonial state. The imperial government's 1824 blueprint consequently made implementation of the law its priority. Within the proposed new structural framework the labour laws modified customary methods of slave labour exaction and introduced elements of wage work. Imperial government proposals also took cognisance of the need, on the one hand, to award slave workers new statutory rights that adumbrated citizen status and, on the other, accustom owners to conceding such rights. And to reinforce and sanction ideological change in both classes the imperial government invoked the influence of the church and suggested regulations to facilitate the slaves' religious instruction.

The 1826 Berbice Slave Code reflected in essentials the imperial government's blue print. Drawn up under the energetic direction of the Lieutenant-Governor, Henry Beard, by his appointed Council between 21 July and 30 September 1826 and put into effect on 1 November, the 44-clause code incorporated substantial segments of the imperial government's 1824 Order in Council, as well as elaborating local innovations and caveats.

The Code, following the Order in Council, gave primacy to the implementation of the law. It endorsed the appointment of a full-time, salaried Protector of Slaves to hear charges brought by slave workers and slave-owners against each other and either deal with them summarily by applying the fines and punishments defined in the new regulations, or by referring cases to the courts. To assist the Protector in fulfilling his duties the administration of the colony was reorganized. The entire province was divided into districts based partly on divisions established by the Dutch; in each district the governor appointed one or more civil magistrates to take over all the civil duties of the burgher officers who retained solely military functions. The magistrates were designated assistant protectors of the slaves and bound to obey the Protector's instructions.[24]

The new administration clearly articulated with pre-existing structures. The Fiscal's part-time role as protector of slaves became a full time office and the burgher officers, who had from time to time been called on to act as his assistants, were superseded by civil magistrates officially charged to do so. To maximize local support for the new Protector and the new Code the Lieutenant-Governor chose of a new raft of civil magistrates. The magistrates, however, who were fined 2,000 guilders if they turned down their appointment, were unpaid. The new structures marked a clear expansion of local authority and were also directly responsive to the imperial government. An English official, David Power, was appointed Protector at a salary of £1,000 sterling a year to be paid by the colonial government. In due course the civil magistrates were superseded by full-time assistant protectors of slaves.[25]

The Governor ordered the new magistrates to promulgate the law by visiting all the estates in their district to read and explain it in person to the slaves so as 'to remove any erroneous expectations which they may have formed of anything being in contemplation regarding their state and condition beyond the provisions of this Code'. Where managers were delegated to perform this function they were obliged to report that they had done so to the magistrate. Comments on its reception were to go directly to the Governor.[26] Implementing the new law nevertheless presented serious problems. As the Protector David Power told the Colonial Secretary, it would go against the 'uniform experience of mankind' to expect that 'legislation so novel and so opposed to the ordinary prepossessions of those upon whose instrumentality its efficiency mainly depended' would be effective on 'mere promulgation'. Power feared he could count neither on the co-operation of planters and magistrates, nor the support of the Fiscal and the Courts of Civil and Criminal Justice when he tried to put the law into effect.[27] But the 1826 law and his own appointment expanded the colonial state's authority to mediate between owners and slaves. The number of cases dealt with almost doubled (an average of five rather than two–three a month), investigations were regularly carried out on the estates rather than in the Protector's office, and most significantly, despite substantial legal costs, cases against owners and managers were referred to the courts. The process of implementing the rule of law between owners and slaves had begun.

The new code, again in conformity with imperial guidelines, targeted the problem of labour discipline. It limited the use of the whip and defined alternative methods of punishment. The whip, a focus of slave complaints and of anti-slavery propaganda, symbolized the physical brutality, the barely restricted personal power owners exercised in the workplace, and the archaic nature of the labour extraction methods which characterized chattel slavery. The code eliminated the 11 o'clock flog for all slave workers by making it illegal for slave supervisor's even to carry a whip in the field on pain of a 600 guilder fine. It prohibited flogging of women on pain of a 1,400 guilder fine, or one to six months in jail, and imposed new regulations on the flogging of male slaves. Flogging was to be administered the day after the offence was committed and in the presence of witnesses, either one free person, or six slaves and the number of lashes was limited to 25 on pain of a 900 guilder fine, or six months in jail.

The Code then spelt out alternative punishments which could be used for both women and men: solitary confinement for no more than three days with, or without work, in a place licensed by a medical practitioner, confinement, solitary or otherwise, for one hour at noon: confinement in the public stocks for up to three hours for each offence by day: in the house stocks, with seats, for up to six hours, or in bedstocks for confinement at night. Food was to be supplied to women held longer than 12 hours. For women estate workers alternative punishments included wearing handcuffs, distinguishing dress, or lightweight collars. Corporal punishments continued to be legal, however, for slave children under the age of 12 to the degree customary for free children.

To implement these regulations managers and owners were corralled into a self-policing exercise, set out in the 1824 Order in Council, which was extended in Berbice to cover domestic, hired and jobbing slaves. All owners or managers of more than six slaves had to keep a 'Punishment Record Book' to record within 48 hours of inflicting punishment, the offence, the witnesses as well as time and place of punishment. This record was to be sworn on oath before the civil magistrate every quarter, submitted to the Protector and forwarded to the Colonial Office.

The new regulations appear to have benefited slave workers. The Protector dealt with fewer complaints about punishments than the Fiscal had done although, interestingly, such complaints continued to comprise about 25 per cent of the total. Women workers presented only three per cent of these cases, which all related to punishment in the stocks, not illegal flogging. The removal of the whip from the field impacted significantly on the proportion of complaints from male workers about punishments for protesting against workloads and tasks, which were reduced from one in every three or four to one in every nine or ten cases.

According to the records the new laws also reduced the intensity of workplace punishments. The maximum number of lashes inflicted on men for 'disobedience' and for 'insubordination' by from July to December 1827 was 75; in 1830, just before a revised code went into effect, it was 25 and by that date two-thirds of male as well as all female slave workers were punished by the stocks and imprisonment.[28] The maximum punishments for women for the same offences in the period 1829–30 was reduced from 71 hours in solitary to four hours in the public stocks for 'disobedience' and from three days in solitary confinement to six hours in the public stocks for 'insubordination'.[29] These modifications benefited owners and managers by minimizing work-time lost. But the scale of punishments in relation to the offence, whether in reduced number of lashes, or reduced hours of confinement still measured the grossly inflated powers in the hands of estate managers to punish and to punish for offences described only in the most general terms. It is easy to see why the overall rate of slave complaints about punishments remained the same.

Estate-based discipline was, nevertheless, backed up by a new method of summary punishment which was placed in the hands of the Protector and the civil magistrates, the treadmill. The treadmill, introduced in British prisons to discipline convicted criminals in 1818, was rapidly imported into the Crown colonies and installed in Trinidad by 1824. The severity of the punishment it inflicted depended in part on how the machine was regulated in terms of weight and speed and it easily became an instrument of brutal torture.[30] Time on the treadmill in New Amsterdam's jail provided an adjunct in Berbice to summary punishments administered on the estates and for women workers who obdurately opposed their owners and managers it substituted for flogging. The Protector sentenced women to it on only one occasion in the period 1826–30 but it was also used by the civil magistrates. Eight days on the treadmill, one woman complained, made her very weak and it readily promoted miscarriages.[31] So the modern instrument available to the fledgling colonial state authorities to inflict physical punishment on workers judged ill-disciplined was no less ferocious than the archaic instrument it partially replaced.

The regulation of labour time and the introduction of modern labour incentives paralleled the regulation and modernization of labour discipline. The customary 12-hour working day for field slaves with two hours for meals and the customary six-day working week, ending by sunset on Saturday and beginning sunrise on Monday, became the legal standard enforceable by fines. Some customary exceptions, however, in the length of the working week were legalized, the most important of which was work needed for 'the preservation of crops'. On sugar estates this meant boiling-off cane juice produced on Saturday and potting on Sunday: turning and drying cotton and coffee already picked, but not cured and picking cotton and coffee during harvest. Enforceable statutory limits on the slaves' working time were in themselves innovative. More significantly, however, following imperial guidelines, the 1826 code ruled that slave workers not engaged in sugar production were to be paid wages in cash, not kind for such 'additional exigible labour' at rates set by the Protector. The rates were set at 11.5 pence (sterling) for field workers for one to four hours' work while artisans, boiler-men and drivers earned 11.5 pence for one–two hours and one shilling 4.5 pence for two–four hours. Owners failing to pay a slave on these terms faced a 50 guilder fine.

The 'wages in cash for overwork' clause built on the well-established Americas-wide custom of paying slaves for over-work in cash, kind or free time; the women at 'Prospect', for example, who moved the corn store were paid in baskets of corn (see above) and the complaints about over-work frequently made to the Fiscal may have reflected lack of payment. It is interesting that the new regulation did not lead to a rash of wage claims: wages were claimed just once before the Protector, by ferrymen flogged for refusing a Sunday fare. This may reflect the fact that cash was in short supply and paper money widely relied on.[32] In practical terms the regulation may have served to secure the slaves more regular and possibly more adequate payments of wages in kind.

The significance of the clause, however, extends beyond its immediate practical effects; to require the exchange of cash for work struck at the heart of the slave labour system which in essence denied labour exchange value. Making wages for slaves a legal requirement in certain circumstances precisely paralleled the abolition of flogging for women and both innovations planted a marker pointing the way to replacing an archaic with a modern system of labour exaction. The attack on the central feature of chattel slavery was complemented by measures intended to make adjustments to the relative status of owners and slaves. The 1826 Code, again following imperial guidelines, awarded the slaves a range of civil rights, which their owners were necessarily obliged to acknowledge. Slaves acquired a statutory right to attend church and receive religious instruction; a right to marry; to qualify to give evidence in court; to become substantial property owners and, most significantly, to purchase manumission. In practical terms these rights were little exercised. Religious instruction was available from one London Missionary Society minister and, on Sunday afternoons only, from one Anglican clergyman. Sunday markets were, nevertheless, closed at 11 a.m. to allow slaves to exercise of this right without curtailing the working week. In these circumstances slaves rarely married, or qualified to give evidence in court. And of the substantial new rights opened up to slaves as potential property owners, to own land, cattle, agricultural implements, furniture and money which could be deposited on interest in a Savings Bank, the slaves commonly utilized only the right to claim payment from their debtors for goods sold to them. Women traders in particular regularly went to the Protector to claim small debts. In the same way the right to manumission proved useful only to a few privileged slaves. Nevertheless, these clauses shifted the legal parameters of slave–owner relations simultaneously awarding new rights and curbing old privileges in an effort to influence the ideological formation of both classes.[33]

The impact of the 1826 Code on the slaves terms of work, the main focus of this study, is complex; it generated new problems and left old ones unresolved. The 12-hour day was defined for 'field workers' and the question arose as to whether it applied to field workers engaged in sugar manufacture. Sugar estate owners were specifically exempted from the obligation to pay their slaves for over-work and the lack of clarity in this definition allowed them to continue night work. Women workers first protested against this practice; four women from 'Plantation Smithson's Place' charged they had cut cane by day and tied and carried megasse by night. At the inquiry the head boiler confirmed that they got no more than three hours sleep a night. They took refuge in being sick, but were punished as malingerers and put in the stocks in solitary over the three-day Christmas holiday. Within weeks workers from 'Plantation Canefield' corroborated their complaint where the manager instituted night work at his own discretion. Nightwork was better organized at 'Canefield'; the slaves worked alternate shifts changing over at 12 p.m. But the question remained, was night work legal?

The issue was taken up during Power's absence while on leave in England by his deputy, Charles Bird, who called for opinions from the Fiscal, H.M. Bennett, and the King's Advocate, M. Daly. The slaves, Bennett urged, were not engaged in night work on the manager's inclination, but from the necessity of maintaining production levels. It would be impolitic and detrimental to prevent it. Daly dissented. On appeal to London the Colonial Secretary briskly opined, a year after the women protested, 'This defect in the law cannot be too speedily remedied.' He ordered a supplementary ordinance to define the slaves' hours for repose each night and punishments for their owners.[34]

Confusion in the definition of the working day was compounded by the lack of any legal definition of the task scale. In contested cases the Protector, like his predecessor the Fiscal, determined judgment and on this issue the owners were prepared to use his services. At 'Plantation Overyssel' for example, where a new manager had taken over, the 18 workers in the 'strong women's gang' went on strike one Monday morning. They refused to begin weeding the 12-by-72 feet task the driver measured out for them on the grounds they would do 'no more than in Mr. Downer's (their previous owner) time'. They claimed they were defending their customary workload. When mediation by a neighbouring planter proved ineffective, the owner called in the Protector.

On the estate Power listened to all parties. The women maintained the task was 'too much' while the manager claimed their task was eight feet shorter than other estates required and produced certificates from neighbouring planters to prove it. He claimed further that a task 80 feet long could be completed in seven hours. The driver backed management and accused some women of intimidating the rest. But all the women stuck to their point. Power concluded that this was a collective effort to reduce the workload and was determined to crush such combinations. He sent the four women identified as ringleaders to jail for seven days for three sessions a day on the treadmill. The rest spent their weekend locked up in the sick house under threat of losing their Christmas holiday and Christmas presents.

The proprietor was well satisfied with this judgment, which from his point of view had the 'happiest effect'. The women completed the task 'with ease', their holidays and presents were restored and the four sentenced to the treadmill subsequently apologized to him at the Protector's office. Once resistance was quelled and production restored on his own terms, the owner tried to convince the women their behaviour had been irrational; who, he asked, had put them up to it? But the women, who evidently thought that attempting to reduce their workload was rational, kept their own counsel.[35]

Slave workers' rations, their regular wages in kind, were not improved by the 1826 legislation, but complaints about short ration supplies featured in 25 per cent of complaints to the Fiscal dropped sharply after 1826, possibly because the likelihood of prosecution increased and penalties were enhanced. The slaves' frequently contested customary right to run poultry and small stock on estate land was made dependent on the owners' express permission. Slave sick care was improved in the sense that the new code made licensed doctors, 'commodious' estate hospitals supplied with medicines and attendants mandatory on pain of a 600-guilder penalty and hospital procedures were tightened up. Patient's names, diagnoses and treatments were to be registered by the medical attendant on pain of a fine for each omission. As a result, when slave complaints revealed that managers had dosed them because no doctor was available, their owners were recommended for prosecution by the Protector for failing to supply 'a legally qualified medical practitioner'.[36] But delivery of medical care remained a problem. Slave complaints that they were denied treatment, worked and punished when sick continued; but the Protector, like the Fiscal, could only investigate, refer to the doctor and request the owner to act on his advice.

Substantively, benefits to women workers began and ended with the prohibition of flogging. Pregnant women continued to charge they were overworked and ought not to be put in the stocks; but, like the sick, they could only be sent to the estate doctor for examination and re-definition of their task.[37] Nursing and parental rights continued to be contested with managers and slave families continued to be exposed to separation by sale. While the code prohibited the separation of husbands and wives, but only families (husbands and wives with children under 16) sold for debt were to be sold in the same lot, to the same person and the responsibility for implementing the rule was placed on the Marshal and his clerk in charge of the sale. The onus of proof lay with the slave family in question until such time as planters submitted records of marriages and births to the Protector. Slave families sold in the ordinary way continued dependent on the 'acknowledged usage of the colony'.

Slaves continued to claim other rights on their own behalf before the Protector, just as they had before the Fiscal. They wanted some control over their occupation and disputed job changes imposed by managers and owners, particularly when they were sent from home as task workers to other estates. They wanted the right to change employer by being sold. This claim was made not only by individuals, but also by slave worker communities. Delegates from a workforce of more then a hundred slaves sold as a group by their owner in England to a neighbouring estate, told the Protector they knew perfectly well the life they would lead under the manager there and requested public sale. Better the chances of the sale room than the certainties of an 'indifferent' management.[38] More frequently slave workers claimed the right to be sold as a community. The law afforded them no assistance in this, so it is not surprising that some abandoned legal-constitutional methods of appeal in favour of strike action; the whole 226-strong workforce at 'Catherine's burg', for example, retired to the bush determined not to be sold separately.[39]

Slave workers making these claims challenged the owners' right to use their persons as property, the legal premise that sanctioned chattel slavery. In doing so they sharply illuminated the limitations of the 1826 code which did no more than slightly adjust the parameters in which their struggle continued. These limitations were also established in statistical terms by the massively detailed documentary evidence the Protector and his assistants garnered from the 'Punishment Record Books'. Systematizing and implementing the slave labour law revealed more fully than ever before the terms on which slave labour was exacted. The Colonial Office officials, who closely supervised the dismantling process and commented in detail on the Protector's reports, were forcibly struck by the sheer number of punishments inflicted on the workforce and by the fact that year after year the number showed no sign of diminution. Between 25–33 per cent of the total population were affected, almost one third, by flogging and all for minor infractions of work-place discipline. The figures abundantly confirmed the superiority of the labour system 'where man is left either to work, or want'.[40]

Viewed in historical perspective the code and its implementation outlined briefly here exposes the ways in which the law which aimed to dismantle the slave labour system, engaged with the regulations intended to perpetuate it. The new law modified and regulated work-place punishments, partly replacing archaic with modern disciplinary measures, set limits to the hours of labour, aimed to translate workers' customary payments in kind for over-work into mandatory, legally fixed cash payments. It nudged slave workers and slave-owners toward wage work. In society at large the law proclaimed the slaves' right to elements of citizen status, signalling the abolition of slave status.

The 1826 code is also significant in that its provisions and omissions indicate continuities between chattel slavery and the wage work system that replaced it. The particular needs of women workers at the workplace, the prohibition of flogging aside, were ignored. Subsistence was kept at the same low level, prefiguring minimal wage rates. And perhaps most significantly, implementing the labour laws both before and after abolition meant punishing, by different methods, workers who withdrew their labour and collectively protested their terms of work.

NOTES

I am indebted to Dr Donald Wood for permission to refer to the manuscript of his book *British Berbice.*

1. PP HC 1825 XXV 476 Further Papers relating to Slaves in the West Indies: Demerara and Berbice (hereafter SWI), Bennett to Beard, 19 Feb. 1825
2. B.W. Higman, *Slave Populations of the British Caribbean, 1807–1834* (Baltimore and London, The Johns Hopkins University Press, 1984), pp.63, 77, 104–5.
3. Ibid., p.183.
4. There were 31.4 births per thousand in Berbice compared with 52.3 per thousand in Barbados 1817–34. Ibid, pp.76, 262, 270.
5. CCJ, Appendix A, pp 144–5; Alvin Thompson, *Colonialism and Underdevelopment in Guyana 1580–1803* (Bridgetown, Barbados, Carib Research and Publications, Inc., 1965), pp.114–21; Higman, *Slave Populations*, pp.180, 205, 209.
6. PP HC 1828 X111, 577 Second Report of the Commissioners on Criminal and Civil Justice in the West Indies and South America, Appendix J, p.250, Appendix A, pp.91, 148 (hereafter CCJ); D.J. Murray, *The West Indies and the Development of Colonial Government, 1801–1834* (Oxford, Clarendon Press, 1965), p.86.
7. SWI 144 cases in all were dealt with February to June 1819: July 1820 to December 1823.
8. M. Turner (ed.), *From Chattel Slaves to Wage Slaves, the dynamics of Labour Bargaining in the Americas* (London, James Currey, Bloomington, and Indianapolis, Indiana University Press, 1995), Introduction, pp.1–32.
9. 1 pound sterling = 1.4 guilders. CCJ, Appendix A, p.90.
10. SWI, 18 July, 1823
11. Higman, p.180; SWI, 3 March, 10 November 1823.
12. SWI, 4 September 1823.
13. SWI, 3 March, 10 December 1823.
14. Thompson, p.123; Higman, pp.205, 209.
15. SWI, 2 July, 14 August, 23 August 1822.
16. SWI, 21 October 1823.
17. SWI, 10 June 1819; Extract from the Register of the Proceedings of the Commissioners of the Court of Criminal Justice, 1819, CO 116/139, cited in Emilia Viotti da Costa, *Crowns of*

Glory Tears of Blood, the Demerara Slave Rebellion of 1823 (New York and Oxford, Oxford University Press, 1994), p.328, note 129.

18. SWI, 14 June 1819.
19. SWI, 4 June 1819.
20. SWI, 15 March, 17 April 1819.
21. SWI, 15 October, 1821.
22. Of the judgments recorded by the deputy Fiscal 44 cases resulted in punishment for the plaintiffs or dismissal of their cases.
23. CO 111/102, Beard to Bathurst, 21 July 1826, no.13,14: 1826 Slave Code, *Berbice Royal Gazette*, 30 September 1826, f.166.
24. CO 111/102, Beard to Bathurst, 23 October 1826, no.30.
25. CO 111/102, Beard to Bathurst, 31 August, 1826, no.24; 22 September, 1826, no.27; PP HC 1830–1 XV 262, Protectors of Slaves Reports (hereafter PSR 262) Murray to Beard, 1 September, 1829. Experience in Trinidad demonstrated that this post could not be trusted to a colonial official. The appointment of civil magistrates also modified the precedent established in Trinidad where the existing officials, called commandants of quarters, were simply transformed into assistant protectors.
26. CO 111/102, Beard to Bathurst, 23 October, 1826, Encl.3, Circular to Magistrates.
27. PP HC 1829 XXV 335, Protector of Slaves Reports (hereafter PSR 335) Power to Beard, 1 September, 1828.
28. PSR 335, List of Offences committed by Male and Female Slaves in the Colony of Berbice, 1 July–31 December, 1827, pp.38–9; PSR 262, Abstract of Offences committed by Mate and Female Plantation Slaves in the Colony of Berbice I July–31 December 1829, pp.103–9.
29. PSR 262, Abstract of Offences... 1 July–31 December 1829, pp.103–9; Abstract of Offences, I January–14 May 1830, pp.119–20. The magistrates played a comparatively small role awarding slave punishments. In the six months 1 July–31 December 1829, for example, out of more than 5,000 punishments inflicted the magistrates determined only 37, and of these only 4 affected women. 'False complaints' and 'riotous behaviour' earned them up to two weeks' solitary, or 14 nights in the bedstocks. Male 'insubordination' earned 70 lashes from the magistrates and neglect of duty, one of the most common charges brought against all slave workers, 80 lashes.
30. W.L. Burn, *Emancipation and Apprenticeship in the British West Indies* (London, Jonathan Cape, 1937; reprint 1970), pp.282–3.
31. PSR 262, 16 September 1828.
32. Wood ms.
33. Higman, p.381; PSR 262, Bird to Beard 1 March 1830.
34. PSR 335, Bennett to Bird, 2 January 1828: Murray to Beard, 24 November 1828.
35. PSR 262, 12 December 1829.
36. PSR 262, 12 February 1829.
37. PSR 262, 29 March 1830.
38. PSR 262, 31 December 1829.
39. PSR 262, 7 November 1828.
40. PSR 262, Murray to Beard, 1 September 1829: Power to Beard, 1 September 1829.

'A Most Useful and Valuable People?' Cultural, Moral and Practical Dilemmas in the Use of Liberated African Labour in the Nineteenth-century Caribbean

ROSANNE MARION ADDERLEY

In 1807 the British parliament passed an act which outlawed the African slave trade after almost three centuries of legal British commerce in African lives. Over the next decade other European countries and the United States followed the British action with similar legislation of their own. However, the passage of legislation did not automatically terminate the activity of slave traders. On the contrary, the sale and transport of African men, women and children continued at least until the 1860s and possibly even later. More so than any other nation, Great Britain acknowledged the problem of this illegal traffic and sought to interdict it. British naval squadrons in Africa and the West Indies became slave trade policemen, stopping and searching suspected slave ships and seizing those vessels found guilty of illegal activity. This naval campaign – known as slave trade suppression – created one of the most unique social problems of British, African and African diaspora history: what to do with the African people found on confiscated ships? When government authorities confiscated a cargo of weapons, rum or other material goods these products could be used or sold for profit. Obviously, human cargo could not be so disposed. Ideally, the would-be slaves might have returned to their respective home communities. However, in the eyes of British authorities both logistical problems and African local politics precluded any such repatriation. The British government thus became responsible for thousands of African refugees. Those captured in or near the slave ports of Havana and Rio de Janeiro became wards or apprentices to selected planters, merchants and tradesmen in these territories. Those Africans seized in the Caribbean Sea also became indentured servants and publicly supervised settlers in various British islands. Those seized along the African coast became similarly subsidized settlers in the colony of Sierra Leone or in some cases on the island of Saint Helena.[1] Beginning in 1841, some of the rescued Africans also travelled to Caribbean territories as voluntary labourers. Thus, between 1810 and 1869 the English-speaking West Indies received a sizeable new African migration, albeit much smaller than the slave migration of previous centuries.

The Caribbean colonies, which received African immigrants, may be divided into two categories: large plantation colonies and smaller peripheral islands. In the former group, planters and administrators viewed the liberated Africans as a convenient source of labour that could replace the thousands of slaves who rejected plantation employment after emancipation. In the smaller peripheral islands, liberated Africans were seen more as unanticipated new additions to the existing labouring population. Both government officials and private citizens expected the new immigrants to accept apprenticeship or indenture in a variety of occupations, as the economy demanded.

Slave trade suppression and the rescue of Africans from slave ships began in 1809, roughly a year after the abolition law came into effect. However, this social, economic and diplomatic campaign did really take off until almost a decade later when Britain obtained its first co-operative legal agreements with the major slave trading powers of Spain and Portugal. The expansion of the legal apparatus related to slave trade suppression contributed significantly to the growth of liberated African settlement as a more calculated and organized phenomenon. Most importantly, after the first Anglo-Spanish and Anglo-Portuguese treaties in 1817, Britain would succeed in negotiating a series of increasingly powerful agreements with Spain, Portugal and Brazil for the mutual policing of illegal slave traffic. With these major slave trading nations (and also with the Netherlands) Britain would establish a group of bilateral mixed commission courts staffed by officials from each nation involved and charged with determining the legal fate of ships seized for allegedly participating in the illegal African slave trade. The commissions had no authority to either detain or prosecute suspected slave traders whose fate fell under the jurisdiction of their own respective nations. The commissioners would simply declare a seizure either proper or improper; in the case of vessels properly seized, they were empowered to condemn the ship as prize of war and liberate the Africans on board.

By the end of 1820 there existed a total of six mixed commissions: an Anglo-Portuguese commission at Rio de Janeiro, an Anglo-Spanish commission at Havana, an Anglo-Dutch commission in Suriname; and three commissions, Anglo-Spanish, Anglo-Portuguese and Anglo-Dutch at Freetown, Sierra Leone. When Brazil declared its independence from Portugal in 1822, Britain pursued comparable anti-slave trade treaties with the new nation, and by 1828 there also existed Anglo-Brazilian mixed commissions, one at Rio de Janeiro and one at Freetown.[2] The majority of

Britain's naval campaign against the slave trade continued to take place off the coast of West Africa. Thus, the mixed commissions at Sierra Leone saw the greatest volume of activity. According to Leslie Bethell's calculations, between 1819 and 1845 the mixed commissions at Sierra Leone addressed a total of 528 cases, in comparison to 50 cases at Havana and only 44 cases at Rio de Janeiro.[3] However, in the settlement of liberated Africans in the British West Indies, the mixed commission at Havana in particular would prove to have great importance.

Under the provisions of the treaties and related agreements, which established the mixed commissions, the governments involved initially agreed that Africans liberated from slave ships at these sites should become free people in the territory – Cuba, Brazil or Sierra Leone – where the adjudication took place. This provision would prove unproblematic in the British colony of Sierra Leone, but in the slave societies of Cuba and Brazil numerous observers reported that the so-called *emancipados* received treatment little better than slaves. In addition, Cuban and Brazilian authorities hardly welcomed the responsibility of monitoring the distribution and subsequent well-being of hundreds or even thousands of free Africans. Such authorities also worried that the introduction of these uniquely emancipated Africans might foment rebellion among their own enslaved populations. After years of diplomatic exchanges on this matter, in 1833 Britain and Spain finally came to an agreement under which British, not Spanish, authorities would take responsibility for Africans liberated at the Havana mixed commission, and furthermore Britain would transfer such Africans to its own Caribbean possessions.[4] The two nations would formalize this agreement in the 1835 revision of the Anglo-Spanish treaty for the abolition of the slave trade. British officials engaged in similar discussions with their counterparts in Brazil, but unlike the Anglo-Spanish case, it appears that they never did arrive at a formal treaty agreement on such transfers.[5] Nevertheless, during the 1830s and early 1840s Britain and Brazil did transport some liberated Africans from Rio de Janeiro to British West Indian colonies in a process similar to that applied at Havana.

The early 1830s also marked the dawn of British emancipation with the law ending British slavery passed by Parliament in 1833. Historian David Murray thus correctly points out the opportunistic concerns which heavily shaped British behaviour in developing this new policy of liberated African settlement. With respect to the removal of liberated Africans from Havana, Murray writes: 'As usual British motives were mixed. The abolition of slavery had led to labor shortages in the British West Indies and the liberated slaves, or *emancipados* ... might help to fill the gap.'[6] Murray further points out that British West Indian governors even competed with one another in seeking to obtain African immigrants under these new arrangements. The Colonial Office, however, did not give automatic priority to the most labour-hungry or plantation-dominated territories in this process. Quite the contrary, the body of civil servants charged with the everyday implementation of slave trade suppression policies debated at some length the course of action they should follow in the distribution of rescued Africans from Cuba among different British colonies. These Havana debates provide the starting point for the present study. Colonial Office authorities specifically considered the benefits of sending liberated Africans to the nearest available colony regardless of its labour needs or demands – in this case the Bahamas – versus sending them to more distant colonies with larger economies and very vocal labour requests – in particular the island of Trinidad, along with the colonies of British Guiana and British Honduras which also expressed interest. While nineteenth-century British bureaucrats seem unlikely guides for a social and cultural evaluation of the liberated African experience in the Caribbean, their comparative discussion in this case provides several preliminary insights into the different material and conceptual concerns which shaped the liberated African labour experience both in large plantation colonies and in smaller more peripheral ones. The present essay focuses on the cases of Trinidad and the Bahamas respectively.

In October of 1835 the Colonial Office prepared a detailed 'Minute on the Condition and Disposal of Captured Africans at the Havana'.[7] This document, apparently written by several Under Secretaries of State, sought to elucidate four specific questions. Firstly, should the process of transferring liberated Africans from Havana continue? As indicated above, the system had already begun operation in 1833. Secondly, if the policy should continue, should officials persist in attempting to organize emigration groups according to criteria of age, gender and health? In the groups already sent to Trinidad between 1833 and 1835, the governor of that colony had requested equal proportions of males and females, no-one over 30 years of age, and everyone in good health. (The question of gender balance in particular would linger for many years as a key social concern in the speculations of British authorities about the possible impact of liberated African immigrants on West Indian societies.) Meanwhile in their third question, the Colonial Office bureaucrats asked one another explicitly:

> If [the liberated Africans at Havana] are all to be removed how shall they be disposed of? Shall they be sent to Trinidad & those Islands only in which their labor may be profitable for commerce? Or shall some be sent to the Bahamas to be located there: providing their own subsistence & receiving the benefit of British Laws & Manners?[8]

Finally, as a concluding question, the 'Minute' invited respondents to suggest alternative solutions to distributing the refugee Africans – although given the fact that transfers of liberated Africans to Britain's West Indian colonies had already begun, this last enquiry seems something of an afterthought.

The 1835 'Minute' in fact arose in part as a response to the competing claims of different West Indian governors. In addition to the arrangements with Governor George Hill of Trinidad, the British Commissioners at Havana had also received requests from Governor Carmichael-Smyth of British Guiana and Governor Francis Cockburn of British Honduras, this latter request seeking liberated Africans not as plantation labourers but as woodcutters for the colony's intended development as a timber exporter. But perhaps even more than responding to these arguably predictable requests, the Colonial Office 'Minute' sought to respond to a 'fourth application of a somewhat different nature' presented by Lieutenant-Colonel William Colebrooke, the governor of the Bahamas. Passing through Havana on his way to Nassau, Colebrooke had had the opportunity to observe the stranded situation of the Africans from captured slave ships and to learn of the plans then afoot to send them to those British colonies which had requested them for use as labourers. Colebrooke did not directly criticize the proposals of other colonies, however, instead according to the Colonial Office, the Bahamian governor 'made up his mind that a considerable number of [the Africans] *might be favorably* [for themselves at least] settled in the Bahamas' (my emphasis).[9] This suggestion from Governor Colebrooke prompted the Colonial Office to consider precisely the criticism posited by twentieth-century historians such as David Murray, as well as by some nineteenth-century anti-slavery activists concerning the self-serving quality inherent in Britain's use of liberated Africans to fill her own West Indian labour needs; and in that self-interest a possible departure from the best interests of the Africans themselves.

The early part of the 1835 'Minute' engaged this debate largely as a moral abstraction, considering whether or not Britain would compromise the 'spirit of [her] national policy' on slave trade suppression if the Colonial Office chose a course of action which would benefit both the liberated Africans and British commercial interests 'in preference to' a course of action which would benefit the Africans alone. The authors seemed particularly worried that the less economically attractive option – sending the Africans to the Bahamas – would in fact prove more beneficial to the Africans themselves; and if this were found to be the case, to send such emigrants to labour-hungry, plantation colonies would seem almost certainly immoral. Consistent with much British public discourse in the wake of the 1833 Emancipation Act, these Colonial Office functionaries conceived of their government as the unquestionable benefactor of Africans whom other less honourable nations continued to enslave. The several authors of the 'Minute' therefore concluded, at least in principal, that the 'moral & physical improve[ment] of the Africans liberated at Havana' should form the 'single object' of any policy decision.[10] Their document, nonetheless, went on to explore in more detail the specifics of the different settlement options. And these colonial officials would ultimately rationalize a viewpoint, which held that both choices for settlement had sufficient positive qualities to justify their use. In other words, for the settlement of liberated Africans from Havana, any British colony could suffice.

Regardless of this eventually inconclusive policy position, the 1835 explorations of the hypothetical advantages and disadvantages of different settlement options highlighted several of the distinctions which would in reality differentiate the experience of liberated Africans not only between the very different colonies of Trinidad and the Bahamas but also within each individual colony under different settlement circumstances. To begin with, the authors of the 'Minute' presented a clear case favouring the idea of 'forming [the Africans] into independent settlements' on 'lands granted for the purpose', and having them cultivate that land for their own subsistence. These Colonial Office functionaries argued that, while arrangements such as this would prove more costly, they would have the advantage of placing the immigrants under the direct 'care of the Government, and under the influence of moral civilization'.[11] On the issue of 'care', the language here implies a Colonial Office scepticism toward the prospect of planters or even other employers treating liberated Africans fairly or well. The officials further seem to have envisaged that, for such settlements, government authorities could arrange a missionary presence and perhaps also other education. In the case of the Bahamas, such missionary arrangements had already begun for previously established liberated African communities and would continue at least through the 1840s. Most ironically, in reviewing the advantages of 'independent liberated African settlements', the Colonial Office authorities even suggested that new African immigrants might simply be 'unaccustomed' or 'unfitted by their previous habits' to any kind of 'regular labour' such as that which employers would require either on sugar plantations or in other contexts.[12] One might expect twentieth-century anthropologists or perhaps pro-peasant advocates to make an argument in favour of land grants and subsistence agriculture over wage labour for Africans newly arrived in the Caribbean. But such a suggestion seems strange indeed in the writings of British government bureaucrats. After all, during the nineteenth century even the most ardent emancipationists and professed African advocates generally viewed people of African descent as little more than potential labour for European-dominated economies. And, in fact, the same authors who made the case for 'independent [African] settlements' proved equally adept at arguing in favour of having liberated Africans hired by planters and other private citizens. The very nature of the 'Minute' as a decision-making tool required the juxtaposed presentation of both possible policies.

In support of the proposals to use liberated Africans as plantation labour, the Colonial Office authors suggested that such 'a system of dependence and subjection' along with the inevitable interaction with other 'more civilized' segments of the population could possibly prove even more effective in guiding liberated Africans into becoming productive and socially adjusted members of West Indian societies. In presenting this argument, the officials particularly expressed a concern that separate communities of liberated Africans alone, would encourage these immigrants to maintain patterns of culture, custom or behaviour from their African past rather than adopting the norms of British colonial society. Attorney General Stephen Rothery had in fact already expressed such a concern in response to regulations prepared by the Board of Council in Trinidad for the distribution of liberated African labourers in that colony. Rothery had argued that allowing the immigrants to congregate in 'large numbers' would encourage them to 'form a society of themselves and ... retain the savage habits of their nation'.[13] He recommended instead that Trinidadian authorities should distribute such Africans widely 'amongst small proprietors ... resident on their own property & superintending the work of their own laborers'.[14] Rothery's preference for small proprietors did not become practice in the Trinidad experience, but the principle of dividing the Africans from Havana into small groups for consignment to individual employers became a defining feature of this phase of liberated African immigration to that colony. The Colonial Office 'Minute' further pointed out that the idea of creating subsistence communities of liberated Africans might also prove difficult given the gender imbalance of slave ship cargoes which had far more males than females: 'A body of men without women ... cannot form a community by themselves'.[15] With respect to the Africans brought from Cuba, the Trinidadian government did seek to maintain a practice of accepting only gender-balanced lots. However, in the broader experience of liberated African immigration to both the Bahamas and Trinidad such balance did not occur. Contrary to the compartmentalized musings of these Colonial Office authors, the pursuit of marital liaisons would become only one of many levels of social interaction between the new immigrants and the existing non-white populations.

Paradoxically, in the effort to determine a preference between the Bahamas and the so-called sugar colonies as settlement locations for the Africans from Havana, the Colonial Office 'Minute' would move away from these attempts to measure comparative material and social environments and return once more to the realm of moral abstraction. In a somewhat tortuous argument, the authors pointed out that the placement of liberated Africans as sugar workers in Trinidad or British Guiana might actually prove beneficial to the greater cause of international slave emancipation. They contended that if the use of liberated African labourers successfully improved the efficiency of sugar production in these territories and thereby lowered the price of non-slave sugar, Britain could strike an economic blow at the slave-sugar economies of Cuba and Brazil. The authors thus implied that even if liberated Africans themselves might fare better if settled in the Bahamas, by going to the sugar colonies they could in theory assist in improving the lives of thousands of other Africans by reducing the economic incentives which continued to fuel both slavery and the illegal slave trade.[16] British authorities would in fact return to this argument in later years when they implemented the planned emigration of thousands of liberated Africans from Sierra Leone and the island of Saint Helena to work as indentured labour in Trinidad and other sugar colonies. Before this premeditated immigration scheme began, however, Trinidad would receive 'over eleven hundred' liberated Africans from Cuba as the island's first major influx of this unique immigrant group.[17] Labour-hungry colonies, however, did not monopolize this transfer process. Although the Colonial Office 'Minute' provided more than sufficient justification for prioritizing such colonies, the Bahamas nonetheless received over 900 Africans from the Havana Mixed Commission between 1836 and 1841.[18]

One key explanation for this pattern probably lay in the identity of the two men appointed successively to assist the Mixed Commission in the supervision of the African refugees. During the mid-1830s and early 1840s the post of Superintendent of Liberated Africans at Havana fell successively to two committed long-time emancipationists and advocates for African well-being: Dr Richard Robert Madden and his successor David Turnbull.[19] Both men belonged to the British and Foreign Anti-Slavery Society and both sought to discharge their duties holding the interests of the liberated Africans as their primary concern. In fact Madden came into open personal conflict with one of his British colleagues in Havana, Commissioner Edward Schenley, who himself owned slaves. Madden argued that, although slave ownership remained legal in Cuba, Schenley compromised the integrity of Britain's mission against the illegal slave trade by participating in the Cuban slave economy which supported that trade; not to mention the fact that under British law, all slaveholding had become illegal in 1834.[20] Meanwhile, during his tenure as Superintendent, David Turnbull several times faced threats of incarceration or worse at the hands of Spanish authorities who accused him of interfering with legal slave ownership within Cuba. On more than one occasion such threats forced him to flee the island in fear for his freedom and safety. During the course of one such escape, Turnbull passed through the Bahamas on his way to London; while in the town of Nassau he visited and worshipped with a group of liberated Africans then under the tutelage of a British Methodist missionary.[21] Yet, in the end, even these two activists had only a short-lived effect on the shape of liberated settlement patterns in British Caribbean. David Murray explains that the whole debate over where to send liberated Africans from Havana would prove to have limited consequence in that four groups of liberated Africans emigrated from Cuba to Trinidad before the formalization of the transfer policy in the 1835 Anglo-Spanish treaty; and after that formalization, between 1835 and 1841, the Havana Mixed Commission would process only six cargoes of Africans which they distributed between the Bahamas, Grenada and British Honduras as indicated above.[22] Furthermore, despite the depth and apparent sincerity of this 1835 debate, throughout the years of liberated African settlement even sympathetic officials viewed these slave trade refugees first and foremost as agricultural and otherwise manual labourers – the long ordained lot of all people of African descent in the Caribbean world.

In letter to his superiors at the Colonial Office in 1832, the Governor of the Bahamas, Sir James Carmichael-Smyth,[23] made the following prosaic observation concerning the behaviour of liberated African immigrants in the colony under his governance: 'The real truth is, as far as I have been enabled to see, that the African, like every other Man [sic], will exert himself or not exert himself in the exact proportion as he finds his own interests affected'.[24] In much of the British West Indies during the years after emancipation this description would have applied equally well to the behaviour of former slaves. After 1834 planters and other employers complained quickly and at great length that once freed, their black working population would no longer co-operate with the long-established labour demands of the Caribbean agricultural economies. Of course, unlike the sympathetic Governor Carmichael-Smyth, these white West Indians usually did not address the 'interests' of the emancipated people and the ways in which those 'interests' affected worker behaviour. As historians such as William Green in *British Slave Emancipation* and more recently Thomas Holt in *The Problem of Freedom* have demonstrated, these post-emancipation labour complaints focused on the vain hope of planters that freedpeople would perform the same volume of labour which they had done during slavery, under roughly the same working conditions, for whatever meagre wages or other compensation that employers deemed appropriate.[25] Nevertheless, even the most intransigent former slaveholder recognized an inherent quality of disarray of the post-emancipation world. In other words, while they expressed displeasure at the lack of co-operation of their former chattel, they did not claim surprise at the problems they encountered. Quite the contrary, most planters portrayed their labour difficulties as evidence of the folly of emancipation, a fulfilment of their own predictions that economic and social collapse would follow the end of slavery.

Indeed, even most ardent abolitionists did not anticipate an uncomplicated transition to free labour. Many British anti-slavery activists did hope (unrealistically) that the majority of newly freed slaves would continue as plantation labourers; and that, with encouragement and oversight from the British government, former slave-owners would pay their new employees fairly and treat them well. However, along with these most sanguine hopes, abolitionists also expressed concern about the ability of the newly emancipated to handle their novel status. Some leaders expressed this concern in terms of straightforward matters such as the need for education or the desirability of continued Christian conversion and increased Christian religious instruction. Meanwhile, other voices worried more abstractly about the capacity of former slaves to function independently without the dependency and supervision of slavery. Some couched these worries in terms of perceived African or 'negro' inferiority, while others criticized the institution of slavery for hindering the development of Britain's black Caribbean subjects as potential free workers and citizens. Thus, people from both sides of the emancipation issue viewed the universal establishment of West Indian free labour as an experimental process fraught with practical and cultural difficulties.

In contrast, such justifiable concern and even pessimism usually did not characterize discussion of the various labour experiments embarked on with liberated Africans both before emancipation in the Bahamas and after emancipation in both the Bahamas and Trinidad. Carmichael-Smyth, a committed although not strident opponent of slavery, made the comment quoted above in the context of a statement comparing the so-called 'industry' of liberated Africans settled in the Bahamas with the alleged lack of industry on the part of Bahamian slaves. The governor argued that while slaves had no incentive to work diligently, free African men, having responsibility for supporting their families, exerted themselves 'as readily and cheerfully as labourers in any part of the world'.[26] This kind of argument followed standard anti-slavery rhetoric of the period, and in the same statement Carmichael-Smyth also made unfavourable comparisons between the labour of slaves and that of European peasants. But where this latter comparison served only as a metaphoric tool, the liberated African experience constituted a social and economic policy already in the process of implementation. With his positive review of liberated African behaviour, whether exaggerated or not, Carmichael-Smyth reflected a widespread optimism about the role that these newly arrived Africans would play in

British West Indian economies. Even in the Bahamas, where white inhabitants had initially expressed hostility to the arrival of these unusual immigrants, both agricultural and other employers came to view the slave trade refugees as a promising supplement to their local labouring population. Governor William Colebrooke, who succeeded Carmichael-Smyth in the mid-1830s, described the liberated Africans as a 'most useful and valuable people'.[27] One finds no hint of caution in this accolade or fear about the capacity of the newly arrived Africans to function effectively as free labourers. Even more strikingly, in the case of Trinidad the whole process of liberated African labour recruitment rested on the belief that these immigrants would serve local labour needs, where recently emancipated slaves had proven either insufficient in number or unaccepting of the wages and working conditions desired by sugar planters.

Unwittingly, in his 1832 statement, Governor Carmichael-Smyth in fact foreshadowed the failure – or perhaps more accurately the under-fulfilment – of liberated African labour schemes both in his own colony and elsewhere. On the whole, liberated Africans did indeed 'exert themselves' according to 'their own interests'. And of course those interests often did not coincide with those of their employers. Much like former slaves, after the conclusion of their indentures, liberated Africans balanced wage labour with more independent economic activities. Furthermore, even during their indentured servitude the presence of liberated Africans did little to change the patterns of labour usage in either colony. The mixed economy of the Bahamas involved a combination of some plantation agriculture along with maritime pursuits such as fishing and wrecking; salt raking in southern parts of the archipelago; and as one would expect diverse trades and shopkeeping activity within the town of the Nassau. Throughout the 30-odd years of liberated African immigration to the colony, new arrivals found themselves serving indentures in all of these various activities. In contrast, in the sugar-dominated economy of Trinidad, most economic activity revolved around the plantation production of this staple crop. Accordingly, the majority of liberated African immigrants began their Trinidadian lives serving terms of indenture on sugar plantations. The only notable exception to this rule involved the practice of assigning children under the age of 12 to fulfil their terms of indenture as household or personal servants, often with individuals living in the town of Port of Spain. That liberated Africans became integrated into the working population of each colony, and indeed served required periods of indenture ranging from three to 14 years, seems to demonstrate a significant degree of success for the hopes of those people who viewed the rescued Africans as an ideal potential labour source. But these immigrants neither solved the labour shortage complaints of Trinidadian planters nor provided Bahamian employers – particularly in agriculture and salt raking – with a workforce any more productive, stable or guaranteed than their own former slaves.

One reason for this lack of radical success for employers lay in the peculiarly protected status which liberated Africans possessed. Both the Bahamas and Trinidad had labour management mores rooted in the institution of slavery. Therefore, when local whites and even the colonial governors looked hopefully upon the labour potential of liberated Africans, they envisaged arrangements which would grant large measures of control to employers and minimal autonomy to workers. The Colonial Office, however, exercised especially vigilant oversight of the treatment of these unique refugees, regularly intervening to protect the Africans from treatment as quasi slaves or captive free workers. For the most part, this policy did not reflect London hostility to the exploitation of the Africans as menial labourers. Rather, it demonstrated a mixture of genuine concern and political sensitivity on the part of various civil servants. Many abolitionists within the civil service justifiably feared the possibility of African mistreatment at the hands of planters who had developed abusive habits under slavery. Meanwhile, most Colonial Office functionaries, whatever their political views, felt vulnerable to criticism which alleged that the practice of slave trade suppression in fact served as a scheme through which Great Britain seized Africans bound for slavery in Cuba or Brazil only to misuse the very same Africans as labourers in her own colonies.

Significant contrasts of course existed between the experience of Africans who worked as tradesmen or personal servants in Nassau or Port of Spain and those who worked on plantations in Bahamian Out Islands or in rural Trinidad. However, there did not exist a simple demarcation between labour exploitation in the sugar-dominated and profit-hungry economy of Trinidad and less exploitation in the more diverse and less profitable economy of the Bahamas. In both places employers made various attempts to restrict the scope of liberated African freedom only to have colonial authorities intervene on behalf of this uniquely protected class – never to remove the expectation that the Africans, like the rest of the black population, should function primarily as labourers; but rather to attempt to protect them from violence and other treatment too closely akin to slavery. Such interventions had two effects. Firstly, as noted above, liberated African labourers never became the tightly controlled labour force for which many employers had hoped. Secondly, through their observation of the actions taken on their behalf, the Africans themselves came to recognize their own unique status and the way in which official liberated African policy could often turn to their advantage. This recognition not only affected their behaviour in some dealings with employers, but also later influenced the development of their understanding of their social and cultural place within the British Caribbean world. All the same, in both colonies, in the disposition of their labour these African immigrants blended quickly with prevailing local modes.

One important difference between the Bahamian and Trinidadian cases lay in the fact that over one third of all liberated Africans who entered the Bahamas arrived before emancipation. And most evidence indicates that these people often worked and sometimes lived directly alongside slaves. Indeed much of the early concern by Bahamian whites over the consequences of accepting liberated African immigrants revolved around fears that these free strangers would disrupt the discipline of the slave community. Ultimately, of course, white Bahamians did receive liberated Africans into their slave society, and those early fears proved largely unfounded. However, the situation of free African immigrants working among slaves raises automatic questions about the treatment of the free group. During the 1820s the British Parliament established a commission to investigate the condition of liberated Africans settled in the West Indies. Two commissioners involved with this effort visited the Bahamas in 1827 and 1828 and compiled lengthy reports, which provide some sense of the work experience of the earliest liberated African arrivals.[28] The commissioners traced the whereabouts and circumstances of hundreds of rescued Africans, even though by 1827 many of such immigrants had lived in the Bahamas for over a decade and had already completed any terms of indenture or apprenticeship established when they first arrived.

In the commissioners' records some people appear listed as 'domestics' or 'washerwomen', which occupations they may have begun during their indentureships. Other entries indicate clear changes from one occupation to another. Thus, for example, a man apprenticed as a 'herdsman' ended up working as a 'porter'. However, for significant numbers of people – especially those described as self-employed in subsistence cultivation – no direct evidence exists about the nature of their initial apprenticeships. Given the fact that slavery dominated the labouring sector of the economy, liberated Africans and slaves inevitably shared the world of work. Anecdotal examples illustrate not only the intermingling which occurred between these two groups, but more importantly the way in which the African immigrants seemed to become an integral yet free component of the slave society. One group of 93 liberated Africans had arrived in the Bahamas in May of 1827 and had therefore spent less than a year in the colony at the time of the parliamentary investigations. These newcomers were still serving six-year indentures when the commissioners arrived. An 'Ebo' [sic] woman from this group provided the following report concerning her own employment: 'That she is employed by her Holder in Agriculture. Has no fixed allowance but gets quite enough to eat. Receives also proper clothing and is very well treated. Cohabits with a slave of her Holder by whom she has one child.'[29] The phrase 'cohabits with a slave' in fact appeared with particular frequency throughout the 1828 report. Yet most strikingly, the majority of the above description suggests a working experience indistinguishable from slavery, except for the fact that this woman knew that she would serve only a limited term, and perhaps also the claim of 'very good' treatment. At the same time, however, the mere fact that emissaries from London actually interviewed hundreds of these immigrants about their condition sent a powerful message to both Bahamian society at large and to the Africans themselves about the special position which they held. In fact, during most of this pre-emancipation era, a report on the condition of liberated Africans did not occur only as a one-time event. The 1828 effort had a unique quality both in its thoroughness and in the fact that it originated from a specific parliamentary mandate; moreover, during the first two decades of slave trade suppression, the employers of liberated Africans also faced an annual check from the Collector of Customs with the same monitoring purpose.

This pattern of special attention continued in the post-emancipation years, although the Collector of Customs did not continue to make annual reports for the large numbers of Africans who arrived in the 1830s. What also continued was the pattern of African immigrants being intermixed with the wider labouring population – now all free – rather than occupying any separate niche. For example, in 1838 Lieutenant Governor Cockburn ordered the preparation of written agreements for the apprenticeship of over one thousand Africans who had arrived in the colony that May taken from two Portuguese slave ships – the 'Diligente' and 'Camoens'. Local officials drafted three formats: one for 'Minors or domestics &c under 16 years', one 'for Prodial [sic] laborers above the Age of Sixteen' and one for 'Mariners & others above the age of 16 years'.[30] This latter category in particular reflected the peculiar economic diversity of the Bahamian archipelago. In less than two weeks after the arrival of this extraordinary number of people, the Lieutenant Governor had executed over 800 of such apprenticeships, leaving no room for doubt as to the demand for these labourers.

These particular indentures, however, did not survive Colonial Office scrutiny. Africans rescued from Portuguese vessels (such as the 'Diligente' and 'Camoens') in the Caribbean were sent to the Bahamas as a measure of expediency while the Royal Navy escorted the illegal slave ships to the British-Portuguese court at Sierra Leone. The Colonial Office informed Lieutenant Governor Cockburn that he should not have executed such agreements until the conclusion of the legal matters at Freetown. Cockburn at first protested, saying that it would prove impractical to cancel the indentures as so many employers had taken their new labourers to islands away from the capital. He also questioned whether or not he could legally nullify the agreements at all.[31] However, after several months of arguing via trans-Atlantic communications, in November of 1838 the Lieutenant Governor capitulated and published a notice cancelling the adult apprenticeships and indicating that the apprenticeships of minors should end when they reached the age of 16.[32] In addition, Cockburn advised Stipendiary Magistrates[33] in the various islands that 'should this arrangement be such as to throw any Africans out of employment, without affording them the means of elsewhere obtaining wherewithal to duly support themselves, you will take the necessary measures for sending them to the charge of the African Board in Nassau'.[34] (The African Board consisted of a group of local authorities responsible for the management of liberated African immigration.) Cockburn expressed concern that large numbers of Africans would end up returned to government custody. He also worried that the employment of future African arrivals would prove difficult without the control of indentures.

During this period most liberated Africans who entered the Bahamas came from Portuguese ships like the *Diligente* and *Camoens* for which legal work had to be completed in Sierra Leone. In 1831, facing a parallel situation, Governor Carmichael-Smyth had settled a group of roughly 150 people from the Portuguese slaver *Rosa* in their own independent village called Adelaide, on the south-west coast of the island of New Providence.[35] Cockburn, however, seems never to have considered such free village settlement as practical or even desirable for the large numbers of African immigrants whom he faced in 1838. Indeed, even as he stated his concern that liberated Africans would prove more difficult to hire out without the power of apprenticeships, he simultaneously expressed a degree of confidence that the immigrants would find employment. In December Cockburn reported that 300 Africans had returned to government supervision as a result of the cancelled indentures, but he anticipated that 'many of these would be disposed of very shortly'.[36] With this conclusion, the experience of the one thousand Africans from the ships *Diligente* and *Camoens* presented a fair reflection of the broad experience of liberated African labour in the case of the Bahamas. That experience involved the dispersion of the Africans throughout the economy performing the same diverse range of occupations (although mostly agricultural) performed by the rest of the black labouring population, both in and around Nassau and in the Out Islands. That experience, however, also entailed various regulatory efforts, dictated by the social management imperatives inherent in British liberated African policy.

In Trinidad, liberated Africans likewise followed a pattern of labour similar to that long established for the island's working classes as a whole.

That is to say, the majority of liberated African immigrants became menial agricultural labourers in the sugar plantation economy. Reverend Thomas Gilbert, an Anglican priest who supervised a parish in south-central Trinidad characterized the life of the recently arrived Africans as follows: 'the Planters ... are almost to the exclusion of others, the persons under whose superintendence and care the African are placed'.[37] Gilbert wrote this comment during the summer of 1850 in the context of a lengthy letter enumerating his concerns about the treatment of these immigrants. The year of 1849 had seen well over a thousand liberated Africans arrive in the colony via the programmes of labour recruitment from Sierra Leone and the island of Saint Helena. Indeed, the entire decade of the 1840s marked the height of such immigration. Addressing his remarks to Lord Harris, the governor of the island, and also to the colonial government in London, Gilbert offered a detailed critique of what he perceived as the British failure at both local and imperial levels to properly attend to the physical and spiritual needs of the Africans. Not surprisingly, the priest directed his most serious concern toward the related issues of Christian conversion, church attendance and both religious and secular education. However, Reverend Gilbert's letter and the months of controversy which it generated, also provide a review of the overall integration of liberated Africans into the world of Trinidadian agricultural labour – a world which they shared in most, although not all, respects with the colony's former slaves.

In promoting the cause of Christian conversion and instruction, Reverend Gilbert more than once in his letter advocated the implementation of measures to either induce or require the employers of liberated Africans to set aside the Sunday Sabbath for their attendance at church and at religious classes. Gilbert lamented of the 'the habit, which is not uncommon of occupying the Africans on Sundays'.[38] On this subject, he further implied a significant contrast between the experience of the newly arrived Africans and that of other segments of the labouring population. The Anglican priest explained: 'I have seen [the Africans] when others from different directions have been assembling in the house of prayer, gathering Cane tops in the field, in the same dirty, ill-clad condition in which they appear through the week.'[39] This statement suggests that some employers may have taken advantage of the immigrant labourers by setting them to work on Sundays at times when the emancipated slaves would not. Of course, this interpretation requires some caution in that, as people not yet converted to Christianity, the Africans may very well have viewed their Sunday labour as no more or less intolerable than their work on other days of the week. Also, in a letter written to support Gilbert's appeal, the Bishop of Barbados pointed out that the roots of the particular Sabbath problem with respect to liberated Africans lay in part in the patterns of Caribbean agricultural life carried over from slavery. Slaves or free labourers who spent most of the week working at the arduous business of cane cultivation for masters or employers often made use of whatever time off they had on Saturdays or Sundays 'engaged in marketing [sic], or in cultivating their own provision grounds, or even in sleep or amusement'.[40] Bishop Parry therefore recommended the most specific provisions possible to mandate Sunday religious activities for the African immigrants. Like many planters (and even some abolitionists) who hoped that liberated Africans might function as model free labourers, Bishop Parry seems to have believed that, given the opportunity, Reverend Gilbert and others could similarly shape these people into idealized Christian converts, independent of the habits or mores of the wider labouring population with whom they worked.

Liberated Africans would eventually express some of their greatest distinctiveness in their religious lives, although not at all in ways of which the Anglican bishop would have approved! Their incorporation into the society as labourers, however, would proceed in ways that followed the experience of former slaves, and the rest of the black agricultural workforce. Reverend Gilbert and Bishop Parry certainly did not achieve any of the aggressive socio-religious programming attached to plantation employment as they had hoped. Moreover, in the early 1850s the Colonial Office had fallen into a pattern of allowing only limited one-year indentures for all free African immigrants sent to the Caribbean under the labour recruitment schemes. Thus, approximately a year after their arrival liberated Africans faced roughly the same set of choices about how to dispose of their time and labour in rural plantation Trinidad as had emancipated slaves. Reverend Gilbert gives indirect testimony that, like newly emancipated slaves in previous decades, liberated Africans immediately took advantage of the option of labour mobility.

In the context of his concern for the good treatment and educational improvement of the Africans, Gilbert made a strong plea for the use of periods of indenture longer than a year. With language that often seems incongruous in a letter written by a priest, he argued that, with the short indentures, individual planters had no incentive to provide the best possible clothing or accommodation for their African immigrant workers. If such workers elected to leave after twelve months, the planter had no way to recoup his investment. Gilbert explained, for example: 'If [a planter] erects consonant [sic] houses for [liberated African] reception, they may leave his Estate for any where [sic] or reason or for none at all ... and his capital which might other be otherwise usefully employed is thus locked up in an unoccupied dwelling'.[41] In this statement, the Reverend clearly seems to argue not from hypothesis but rather from his own observation of such behaviour by immigrant Africans. And indeed, complaints about precisely this problem appeared with regularity in the voices of planters and other prominent citizens who wrote editorials and letters contemplating the economic future of the colony in Trinidad's several nineteenth-century newspapers. Of course, by 'leaving estates for anywhere, any reason or no reason at all' liberated Africans did nothing more than follow in the emergent patterns established by former slaves and other segments of the black labouring population. In Trinidad's post-slavery sugar economy, the combination of labour-hungry planters and plentiful vacant land for squatting gave all of these workers a measure of mobility and bargaining power in the disposition of their labour – mobility and bargaining power which the liberated Africans apparently came to make use of as had other groups.

When Governor Harris himself responded to Gilbert's various criticisms and requests, he in fact argued that, as labourers, liberated Africans constituted nothing more than one component of the black working population as a whole. And as such, he had neither resources nor inclination to make extra or legally binding provisions for their religious and secular education, beyond the efforts already in progress for the 'Creole [or black Trinidadian] race'. Lord Harris asked:

> Are these [liberated Africans] to be placed in a more advantageous position than the rest of the population? [I]f so, can it be effected? Doubtless it would be very desirable to achieve a superior degree of civilization for them and for the others also, but I have great doubts whether it be possible to do more for them than for the rest of the laborers.[42]

Ultimately therefore, in neither the Bahamas nor Trinidad did liberated African immigration result in a set-apart class of workers. The immigrants stood out because of their special status and the attention which they received, and also because of their cultural difference, as African-born people, from the rest of the black population. They did not, however, carve out separate economic niches or alter the existing labour markets in any dramatic fashion. Trinidad eventually turned to East Indian indentured labour in order to create a new set apart labouring class, along with a new body of restrictive rules to bind these new workers more effectively to sugar plantations. The Bahamas meanwhile had no such large-scale labour demand to fulfil after liberated African immigration had ceased.

British policies in the case of liberated African labour should not necessarily be interpreted as either lax or cynical in their professed attempts to fulfil moral imperatives. There is now significant consensus among historians of the nineteenth-century Caribbean that agents of the British Colonial Office sincerely and aggressively sought to convince West Indian employers to comply with the long series of regulations and revised regulations which London put forth to safeguard the interests of various categories of indentured workers during the post-slavery era. Indeed, their repeated efforts to revise such regulations imply that they genuinely believed that they could eventually produce just the right package of guidelines to satisfy both the wishes of employers and the well-being of the workers. Thomas Holt sympathetically points out that these officials faced a daunting task in trying to morally and creatively manage labour relations not only in the unprecedented era of emancipation but also in the midst of 'the ongoing capitalist revolution and its problematic implications for human relations'.[43] Holt explains: 'How was one to conceptualize freedom in a society where social relations of labor were rapidly changing? Freedom was an abstract concept, difficult to define in substance ... Slavery on the other hand [had been] clear-cut and concrete.'[44] A sceptic might argue that Colonial Office authorities ought to have known that ultimately any arrangements that truly protected liberated Africans (or later East Indian labourers) could not simultaneously satisfy West Indian employer's demands. However, these British colonial functionaries would hardly be either the first or the last public officials to pursue a course of action, which was more wishful than it was realistic. Yet one might also more radically charge that the Colonial Office agenda – however sympathetic to Africans – was never wishful enough, in it never seriously envisioned any other fate for liberated Africans than that of a labouring class working for British employers.

Of course, in neither colony did the integration of liberated African immigrants into existing economic frameworks at all imply their disappearance into the wider population. Quite the contrary, while these 'new Negroes from Africa' did not inhabit separate economic spaces, they did very much create distinctive cultural ones. That however is another story – a story which has left a lasting mark on African diaspora culture in the Bahamas, Trinidad and elsewhere in the Caribbean, but one which did not significantly alter the economic and social world of the mid-nineteenth century. Ironically, despite all the expectations and often noble ideas which British policy-makers invested in the liberated African experiment, the experience of these unique free immigrants demonstrated above all how little fundamental change had in fact occurred in British expectations for Africans and people of African descent in the post-emancipation Caribbean.

NOTES

1. For the most part Saint Helena served as a temporary stopping place for liberated Africans ultimately transferred elsewhere. For discussion of the processes of liberated African settlement and relocation at Sierra Leone and Saint Helena see: Johnson U.J. Asiegbu, *Slavery and the Politics of Liberation 1787–1861: A Study of Liberated African Emigration and British Anti-Slavery Policy* (New York, Africana Publishing Corporation, 1969).

2. Leslie Bethell, 'The Mixed Commissions for the Suppression of the Transatlantic Slave Trade in the Nineteenth Century', *Journal of African History*, Vol.7, No.1 (1966), pp.79–82.

3. Ibid., p.84.

4. David R. Murray, *Odious Commerce: Britain, Spain and the Abolition of the Cuban Slave Trade* (New York, Cambridge University Press, 1980), pp.271–81.

5. Leslie Bethell, *The Abolition of the Brazilian Slave Trade: Britain, Brazil and the Slave Trade Question, 1807–1869* (New York, Cambridge University Press, 1970), pp.114 and 380–3.

6. Murray, *Odious Commerce*, pp.120–1.

7. CO 318/123. 1835 Volume 4. Removal of Liberated Africans from Cuba. 'Minute on the Condition and Disposal of the Captured Africans at the Havana. 24th October 1835'.

8. Ibid.

9. Ibid.

10. Ibid.

11. Ibid.

12. Ibid.

13. Cited in: CO 318/123. 'Minute on the Condition and Disposal of the Captured Africans at the Havana. 24th October 1835'.

14. Ibid.

15. CO 318/123. 1835 Volume 4. Removal of Liberated Africans from Cuba. 'Minute on the Condition and Disposal of the Captured Africans at the Havana. 24th October 1835'.

16. Ibid.

17. Murray, *Odious Commerce*, p.280.

18. These nine hundred refugees came from three separate Spanish vessels condemned at Havana: 393 Africans from the 'Empresa' in 1836; and in 1841, 233 from the 'Jesus Maria' and 282 from the 'Segunda Rosario'. See: Murray, *Odious Commerce*, p.281. CO 23/97. William Colebrooke, Bahamas Governor to Lord Glenelg, Principal Secretary of State, Colonial Department, 19 November 1836. CO 23/109. Enclosure in Sir Francis Cockburn, Bahamas Governor to Lord John Russell, Principal Secretary of State, Colonial Department, 8 February 1841. David Turnbull, Superintendent of Liberated Africans at Havana to Cockburn 21 January 1841.CO 23/109. Enclosure in Cockburn to Lord John Russell 6 March 1841. Turnbull to Cockburn, 23 February 1841.

19. For discussion of the role of British officials working in Havana during this era see: Luis Martinez Fernandez, *Fighting Slavery in the Caribbean: the Life and Times of a British Family in Nineteenth-Century Havana* (Armonk, New York, M.E. Sharpe, 1998). The work of Martinez-Fernandez explores the life of John Backhouse who, like Madden and Turnbull, worked with the British-Spanish Court of Mixed Commission.

20. CO 318/127. 1836 Volume 4. Removal of Liberated Africans from Cuba. Dr. Richard Robert Madden, Superintendent of Liberated Africans at Havana to Lord Glenelg, Principal Secretary of State, Colonial Department, 6 November 1836.

21. Correspondence, John Corlett, Nassau, Bahamas, 22 November 1842. Wesleyan Methodist Missionary Society Collection, School of Oriental and African Studies (hereafter cited as WMMS Papers). MMS. 4C. West Indies (Various) 1833–1906. Box 218 (?), File 1842.

22. Murray, *Odious Commerce*, p.281.

23. Carmichael-Smyth, already identified above as the Governor of British Guiana, served as Governor of the Bahamas in the late 1820s and early 1830s before transfer to the British Guiana post.

24. CO 23/86. Sir James Carmichael-Smyth to Goderich, Colonial Department, 5 February 1832.

25. See William Green, *British Slave Emancipation: the Sugar Colonies and the Great*

Experiment 1830– 1865 (Oxford, Clarendon Press, 1976) and Thomas C. Holt, *The Problem of Freedom: Race, Labor and Politics in Jamaica and Britain, 1832–1938* (Baltimore, Johns Hopkins University Press, 1992). In a work of British colonial history prepared without particular attention to the lives former slaves, Green demonstrates that, as they had feared, planters did indeed face declining economic fortunes in the years after slavery. He does not blame these problems entirely on the behavior of the freedpeople but demonstrates how the reluctance of the newly emancipated to continue regular plantation work combined with the end of preferential sugar tariffs to undermine most West Indian sugar economies. Thomas Holt, in contrast, devotes much less attention to the economic details of the post-emancipation decline, and instead focuses his study on the different expectations which white West Indians, colonial officials and former slaves held for the birth of a free Jamaica. According to Holt, although some colonial officials often spoke in progressive terms about the rights of freedpeople, the Colonial Office ultimately joined forces with planters in a lengthy and often fruitless struggle to balance their desire for cheap wage labour with the peasant aspirations of Jamaica's black majority.

26. CO 23/86. Carmichael-Smyth to Goderich, 5 February 1832.
27. CO23/94. Colebrooke to James Stephen, Under Secretary of State, Colonial Department, 19 August 1835.
28. CO 23/79–80. Duplicate of Report on the State and Conditions of Liberated Africans in the Bahamas, 1828 (hereafter cited as 1828 Liberated African Report).
29. CO 23/80. 1828 Liberated African Report.
30. CO 23/102. Enclosures in Cockburn to Glenelg, 19 May 1838.
31. CO 23/102. Glenelg to Cockburn, 10 August 1838 with enclosures. CO 23/103. Cockburn to Glenelg, 4 October 1838 with enclosures and responses.
32. CO 23/103. Cockburn to Glenelg, 8 November 1838 with enclosures.
33. Special magistrates appointed after the Emancipation Act of 1834 to supervise the treatment of former slaves who were to serve terms of 'apprenticeship' before full emancipation. Such men were sometimes called upon to perform similar monitoring services with respect to liberated Africans.
34. CO 23/103. Enclosure in Cockburn to Glenelg, 8 November 1838.
35. CO 23/84. Carmichael-Smyth to Goderich, 23 July 1831. Patrice Williams, *A Guide to African Villages in New Providence* (Nassau, Bahamas, Bahamas Department of Archives, 1979), p.3. This village of Adelaide and another (southwest of Nassau) named Carmichael in honour of the Governor, have received considerable attention in Bahamian local history studies addressing the liberated African experience. A group of Africans themselves apparently founded Carmichael in the early 1820s, presumably after the conclusion of apprenticeships served during the first decade of liberated African settlement. In later years, Governor Carmichael-Smyth and others would draw upon public funds to provide both religious and secular education for this community. Furthermore, in 1836 Governor William Colebrooke sent numbers of Africans from two Portuguese slave ships to join the Carmichael settlement. Indeed, in December of 1838, Lieutenant Governor Cockburn also sent 'twenty to thirty Children' from a Portuguese vessel to this village. Nevertheless, the majority of liberated Africans did not have this independent settlement experience. Also, as noted above, some of the Africans at Carmichael initially served terms apprenticeship in the wider economy. And, in later years, other village residents would take employment elsewhere on the island to supplement their subsistence community. See: CO 23/86. Carmichael-Smyth to Goderich, 5 February 1832. CO 23/94. Colebrooke to Glenelg, 15 December 1835 with enclosures. CO 23/96. Colebrooke to Glenelg, 25 April 1836 with enclosures. Williams, *Guide to African Villages*, pp.5–7.
36. CO 23/103. Cockburn to Glenelg, 21 December 1838.
37. CO 295/170. Enclosure in Harris to Grey, 3 July 1850. Letter of the Reverend Thomas Gilbert, Rector of Saint Paul's parish, Trinidad, 3 June 1850.
38. Ibid.
39. Ibid.
40. CO 295/171. Enclosure in Harris to Grey, 26 August 1850. Letter of Right Reverend Thomas Parry, Bishop of Barbados to Earl Grey, Secretary of State for the Colonies, 19 August 1850.

41. CO 295/170. Enclosure in Harris to Grey 3 July 1850.Letter of Reverend Gilbert, 3 June
    1850.
42. CO 295/171. Harris to Grey, 11 September 1850.
43. Holt, *The Meaning of Freedom*, pp.25–6.
44. Ibid.

Rites and Power: Reflections on Slavery, Freedom and Political Ritual

JULIE SAVILLE

Only as abstract symbols, wrenched from social contexts, can slavery and freedom be construed to denote unrelated or opposite conditions. Whether analysed as a global phenomenon, as a social process, or as a model of power relations, the history of slavery and freedom is a matter of interrelationships rather than fixed antagonisms. Since the turn of the century a substantial body of scholarship has viewed 'Atlantic studies' as a particularly well-suited vantage from which to explore the changing interrelationships between slavery and freedom. The work of many historians, anthropologists, and more recently, specialists in cultural studies – notwithstanding interpretative differences whose consideration lies outside the scope of this discussion – has approached 'Atlantic studies' as something other than an organizational rubric for studying the land masses and archipelagoes that rim an ocean.[1] In political philosophy no less than in labour systems, an 'Atlantic world' – a shifting realm of production, exchange, and consumption whose networks began in the seventeenth century to link the experiences and imaginations of peoples in various parts of Europe, Africa, the Americas, and eventually parts of Asia as well – has been an arena of necessary connections between slavery and freedom, colony and metropole, the so-called 'primitive' and the so-called 'modern'.[2]

Trans-Atlantic slave emancipations themselves, whether viewed from the tumult of slaves' experiences or from the seeming finality of proclamations of abolition, were not uni-directional. Reversible, contingent changes in labour and property relations, in rule and resistance, and in the political standing of individuals no less than of states mark the trail of slaves' emancipations from the eighteenth through the mid-twentieth centuries. The renewed enslavement in the British West Indies of the 'vast majority' of slaves whom Anglo-American loyalists transported from the southern states after the American Revolution and the re-introduction of slavery in the French colony of Guadeloupe eight years after a revolutionary government had decreed abolition are perhaps only among the earliest, dramatic illustrations of an instability that remained fundamental.[3]

Finally, because such upheavals in public institutions as abolition entailed are interconnected with personal perception and daily practice, emancipation, like enslavement, was a moral no less than a material project. The power that linked slavery and freedom in inseparable and continuing tension was both substantive and symbolic. Hannah Johnson, the daughter of a slave fugitive who had successfully escaped from Louisiana to New York State some 40 years before the American Civil War, memorably underscored the religious, military, economic, political, and personal domains that slavery and its abolition simultaneously traversed.[4] In July 1863 rumours had reached her that President Abraham Lincoln might withdraw his proclamation of emancipation, perhaps in response to the Confederacy's refusal to extend prisoner-of-war status to African-American soldiers. At the prompting of a 'good friend', she urged Lincoln to ponder the possibilities for historic transformation and for his personal redemption that lurked in his state paper: 'They tell me some do you will take back the Proclamation, don't do it. When you are dead and in Heaven, in a thousand years that action of yours will make the Angels sing your praises I know it.' Just as Johnson's regard for eternal salvation did not lead her to slight politics, her religious conviction also embraced physical struggle. She was proud that her son was a member of the 54th Massachusetts Colored Volunteer Infantry and frankly accepted physical force as a means of bringing God's will to earth. She extended this obligation to soldiers when she reflected, 'I know it is right that a colored man should go and fight for his country, and so ought to a white man'. She urged a similar view upon the President, when she proposed that Confederate prisoners be subjected to forced labour in retaliation for any violations of the rules of war. 'It would seem cruel, but their no other way', she advised, 'and a just man must do hard things sometimes, that shew him to be a great man'. With enviable economy, she further explained to Lincoln how slavery ravaged the spirit for living no less than the means of living. 'Robbing the colored people of their labor is but a small part of the robbery', she explained. 'Their souls are almost taken, they are made bruits of often'.

Notwithstanding her great expressive power, the force of Johnson's judgments does not derive from metaphor. What seems noteworthy is the consistency with which she portrays power – whether wielded to support or to destroy – as having both physical and emotional aspects. Such clarity nevertheless leaves us with a puzzle. Legislatures and armies possessed means to drive slavery from states and territories; by what powers is spirit brought to life?[5]

This essay explores in admittedly preliminary fashion how attention to ritualized communication can open a window onto the ways in which the mobilization of ex-slaves in the immediate aftermath of slavery construed power as having both a material and a spiritual locus.[6] Ritual, employed here somewhat loosely, refers to repeated patterns of collective behaviour and not to ceremonies of state formation or public memorialization. These public rites have been reconstructed from accounts of the public behaviour of ex-slaves that are admittedly more fragmentary and episodic than the dense personal narratives that have provided the basis for investigations of the dynamic human interactions that underlay masters' and mistresses' authority under slavery. Additionally, it has been necessary to interpret the rites acted out on particular plantations in relation to somewhat generalized models of antebellum plantation authority. Only rarely has it been possible to take account of idiosyncrasies of personal interactions on a given plantation. Nevertheless, even this somewhat limited contextualization allows us to see how slaves, like other non-literate social groups, came to write social judgements in the language of collective rites.

There is now perhaps diminished need to establish that slaves possessed a complex social consciousness. The view that only brutes could come to flower in degraded circumstances – that it was unreasonable to expect that 'the typical slave on the ante-bellum plantation in the United States' could have 'a fantasy-life not limited to catfish and watermelons' – seems no longer to inform scholarly examinations of enslaved humanity in any part of the world.[7] The premises of slaves themselves, as the following example illustrates, have rendered no small assistance to this interpretative shift. Hence, using somewhat different language in the fall of 1865, a group of former slaves also alluded to the burden of enslavement. 'We have, for the last four yars', they advised President Andrew Johnson, 'been studing with justis and the best of our ability what step wee should take to become a people'.[8] On the one hand, their language acknowledged an alienation from self and society that has been characterized as 'social death'.[9] At the same time, they revealed that it was such passivity and atomization as slavery enforced that had led them to envision freedom as a process of becoming a 'people'. Their interactive formulation thereby explains freedom in terms that acknowledged the toll of slavery. The prospects of an acknowledged community life promised a means by which they could act together and thereby begin to undo the links of paternalist obligation which, under slavery, had sought to tie them individually to their masters and mistresses. In the wake of emancipation, then, former slaves saw political mobilization as inseparable from community organization, anticipating that continuing process of reception, initiation, education and incorporation of newcomers into myriad community groups which formed the backbone of grassroots community organizing in the freedom movements of the 1960s.[10]

Slaves' emancipations, therefore, have perhaps also freed historians to see slavery with new eyes. While slaves were indeed dead as recognized political subjects, studies of the social processes of emancipation have revealed them to have been live students of political affairs. They manipulated whatever military, civil, or religious institutions that warfare, ameliorative legislation, or metropolitan plans of gradual abolition brought their way.[11] The distances and speed with which an amalgam of written report, rumour, hope, and alarm could radiate along webs of communication set in motion by the journeyings of more mobile slaves – such as sailors, peddlers, and carriage drivers – have been explored.[12] Finally, conditions under which significant numbers of urban and rural ex-slaves greeted emancipation with enthusiasm and sense of rightful involvement in political affairs have received close examination.[13] Documentation, analysis, and interpretation of the nature and consequences of such efforts can help to bring discussions of slaves' political lives onto terrain where issues more closely resemble the debates that have enmeshed studies of the political lives of other servile and disenfranchised groups. Discussions can begin to interrogate the processes and consequences of politicization rather than their existence.

Throughout the Americas former slaves seem to have announced their political awakenings with the formation in public of enthusiastic crowds whose vibrant assemblies typically antedated – sometimes by decades – legislative expansion of rights of suffrage. These post-emancipation assemblies seem to share several features. First, the groups that presented themselves announced their opinions as collective rather than individual views, formed through processes of decision-making that deserve closer comparative study. Second, they communicated many of their views in highly expressive, gendered patterns of group behaviour in which symbolic expressions and instrumental goals commingled. In general, the rites themselves, particularly in the countryside, were materially impoverished. They employed objects close at hand in hardscrabble environments: sticks, articles of clothing, farming tools, and most importantly, the participants' bodies and voices. Third, the collective demonstrations mounted by former slaves in an era in which non-servile wage earners had only begun to gain recognition of corporate rights, provoked fear of 'riot', almost independent of the crowd's actual behaviour. Comparative study of the ideologies, organization, and consequences of post-emancipation civil disturbances can illuminate the political, economic, and cultural contexts of the social reasonings and popular views of justice expressed in the crowd's activities.

In post-emancipation Jamaica, to consider one of the more richly studied examples, crowds engaged a striking range of issues.[14] Former slave men and women paraded on behalf of candidates for whom they were ineligible to vote, variously protested or celebrated the outcomes of electoral contests in which they could not cast ballots, attacked property in denunciation of the island's tax structure, protested against the island's rumoured annexation to the United States, and, driven by a crisis in access to land, seasonal wage rates, and the administration of justice, made public, ritualized preparations for what climaxed as Morant Bay's brutally suppressed 'peasant war'. Such behaviour is an important reminder that in the history of political institutions casting ballots is a fairly recent means of expressing opinion. Examining forms of political expression other than voting by ballot can shed light on the means by which and the purposes for which socially subordinate groups, in this instance former slaves, acted to effect social change.

Overt, public demonstrations represented a new departure in the collective behaviour of slaves in the American South. The crowd behaviour and forms of mass action of nineteenth-century southern slaves seem notably weak when viewed in comparison with Caribbean saturnalia, the festive mock elections of New England's Pinkster Day, or the market days that variously figured in Caribbean and Brazilian slave societies.[15] Of course, slaves' prior participation in ritualized public expressions of conflict did not guarantee tolerance after abolition.[16] Nevertheless, like their counterparts elsewhere in the hemisphere, ex-slaves in plantation districts of the southern United States seized emancipation as occasion to act collectively. Their new public presence visibly altered the terms of public conduct permissible under slavery and drew on gendered expressions of solidarity to lay the infrastructure of a political life. The remainder of the essay sketches the contours of ex-slaves' mobilization in plantation districts of the lower South – principally South Carolina and Louisiana – identifying the organizational forms and ideologies that underlay the ritual practices of five somewhat different expressions of political ritual – the communal riot, the folk court or local 'justice committee', the folk militia or 'marching company', the plantation-centred demonstration, and a plantation harvest rite.

The coming of the Civil War was a direct stimulus to slaves' communal uprisings. Much like contemporary peasants in continental Europe, southern slaves did not attempt insurrectionary mobilization without signs of an impending disruption in local power relations.[17] Although the secession crisis of 1860 seems to have inspired plantation slaves in west central Mississippi to attempt surreptitious organization, their elaborate conspiracy was uncovered.[18] Plantation-centred rebellions – communal uprisings – erupted chiefly during the Civil War, when Federal occupation of Confederate territory created the social chaos that slaves of the densely concentrated plantation majorities of South Carolina's and Georgia's rice coast and the sugar parishes of southern Louisiana judged favourable to their protests.[19] Some of slaves' earliest rioting protested against worsening conditions of material life triggered by wartime coastal blockades and spiralling prices. The combined influences of war-born shortages of items basic to slaves' allowances of clothing, blankets, and dietary staples, an unprecedented reliance on the use, not simply the threat, of deadly force, and the arrival of armies rumoured to be liberators, subjected the network of reciprocal obligations between master and slave to unprecedented, and, in some instances, irreparable strain. Where slaves threatened violent assault against plantation residents (chiefly overseers, though some masters were also targets), such uprisings were responses to specific wartime events. In areas of the South Carolina low country, for example, armed escorts who fired at recalcitrant slaves to drive them beyond the reach of invading Federal armies starkly violated antebellum ideals of standardized, measured force. Slaves' terror yielded to explosive outbursts of violent assault when Union forces subsequently reached the region. On occasion, slaves' wartime unrest seems to have responded, at least in part, to brutalities directed against Union soldiers. Hence, a Federal commander attributed the 'symptoms of servile insurrection', which a subordinate officer reported widespread outside New Orleans in November 1862, to slaves' outrage at the execution of seven Federal soldiers 'who had surrendered themselves prisoners of war [and] were in cold blood murdered'.   Even behind Confederate lines, slaves experienced adverse changes in daily life when Federal invasion threatened. Plantation regimen underwent unprecedented militarization when Confederate soldiers were posted to overseers' duties and to recapture fugitives attempting escape. As Confederate hopes of military victory receded, work became a form of warfare; overseers responded to fairly common infractions of plantation work rules, such as tardiness in reporting to the fields, or unexcused departures from the plantation, by hanging or shooting the offenders. War pressed slavery to defences not routine in times of peace.

Such wartime violations of paternalist obligation precipitated on South Carolina's and Georgia's rice coast the largest, most riotous demonstrations that slaves had attempted since scattered eighteenth-century uprisings of the colonial era and the upheavals of war during the American Revolution.[20] Civil War festivals of insurrection targeted symbols of the old order, as suggested by an outburst precipitated by Federal invasion of Port Royal Island, off the South Carolina coast, in November 1861. As masters and mistresses fled Port Royal during Union invasion, slaves made their way from outlying plantations toward the slave-owning families' residences in the village of Beaufort.[21] Their forays turned the symbols of the old order upside down. What had been an object of taste or an emblem of power, the slaves now marked for contempt. They smashed furniture, shredded clothing, and smeared luxury furnishings with excrement. Such humiliations sought to efface an old order and summon a new, as the slaves' festival of frenzy fused natural symbols of corruption or decay with symbols of life and rebirth. Instrumental purposes also drove some forays. Like their counterparts during the American Revolution, slaves' Civil War-era seizures of plantation articles also attempted to remedy shortages of necessary goods. On Port Royal, they redistributed basic articles of daily use – soap, candles, salt, stored grains – among plantation communities. The penetrations of groups presumably composed of men and women field workers into the unfamiliar, probably forbidden spaces of plantation residences brought master's and mistresses' personal luxuries within unaccustomed reach. Silk dresses, canes, feather mattresses, and in one instance a piano – fell prey to more individualized seizures when slaves carried such finery back to huts in the slaves' quarters or put the booty to personal use. In general, however, slaves had apparently vented their collective rage in assaults against property, not people.

Or had they? Masters' and mistresses' personal possessions seem to have fallen victim to particularly expressive attacks. Although differences in the sources make comparisons hazardous, it is worth wondering whether the social relations and symbols of antebellum slavery had fostered more intimate assaults against property than the seemingly more systematic plunder, murder, and re-distributions of property that southern slaves had undertaken during military conflicts of the American Revolution.[22] Civil war-era slaves' violence is somewhat more reminiscent of the unrest of peasants in south-western France during the Revolution, who removed and burned pews from churches, seized weather vanes, destroyed grain measures used to collect seigneurial dues – all symbols of noble privilege – and at times insisted on banishing social distance by demanding a fraternal embrace or a feast within the walls of the château.[23]

Slaves emboldened by Federal invasion seem to have convened plantation courts to sit in judgment of masters and mistresses with notable infrequency. Rarely summoning former owners to direct judgment, they were more likely to organize something like police forces and folk juries on the plantations to keep order among themselves. Although details require closer study, it is unclear whether slaves' greater interests in self-regulation rather than in settling scores with their former owners, reflected the relative absence of owners from the plantations, internal divisions produced by conflicts under slavery, the uneven successes with which slaves had been able to bring areas of familial life and independent production within a framework of customary expectations, or some yet unexplained combination of these and other influences. What little summary judgment slaves administered was encouraged by Federal soldiers. Hence, to the dismay of his superior officer, when a commander of black soldiers occupying coastal Virginia, encountered 'half a dozen *women*' whose owner had 'whipped [them] unmercifully, even baring their whole persons for the purpose in presence of *Whites and Blacks*', the soldier decided that the slaves should exact retribution in kind. 'I laid him bare', he reported, 'and putting the whip into the hands of the Women, three of Whom took turns in settling some old scores on their masters back'.[24] Slaves themselves, in behaviour anticipating more typical expressions of popular justice during Reconstruction, solicited assistance from black soldiers and forced masters to appear before military or civilian authorities in order to air grievances about workloads, compensation, and corporal punishment. Few slaves seem to have regarded the combination of physical force and brittle negotiations by which work was driven forward under slavery as institutionally guaranteed rights of negotiation. Hence slave carpenters in Plaquemines Parish, Louisiana, thought to bolster the 'woman strike' with which field workers had launched wage negotiations with their recalcitrant owner by erecting a gallows outside the overseer's cabin.[25]

Most days of reckoning, nevertheless, found plantation slaves subjecting representations of their owners, rather than their owners themselves, to ritualized forms of degradation. On the heels of Confederate surrender in the Carolina rice region, for example, a former driver did not interfere when slaves dismantled the planter's family portraits and went on to re-mount them in their cabins, sell them at bargain prices in the neighbourhood, or leave them outdoors to be vulnerable to effects of rain, dew, and undoubtedly, some man-made moisture.[26] Some of the rituals as acted out by former slave men were consistent with transformative rituals to possess an enemy's spirit. For example, a driver formerly owned by rice planter Charles Manigault made a present of Thomas Sully's portrait of Manigault to a woman friend, telling her, Manigault furiously reported, that '*she* must take this Portrait home with her, TO REMEMBER HIM !! ... My Portrait, to remember this Nigger!' As Manigault's rage suggests, the indirect, symbolic absorption of master by slave, more than the theft itself, touched a raw nerve. Civil War-era slaves perhaps aimed at reclaiming something of their own souls, something of their owner's spirit, and their past labour services as well in the more expressive assaults on material possessions that were part legitimization of property by public display, part absorption of an enemy's spirit, and part remedy of a daily necessity. Something other than blind pillage was at work in the slaves' frenzy. Retaliations for particular abuses, combined with revenge for justice long denied and movements to restructure the terms of work guided the wartime courses of slaves' communal violence.

Post-emancipation political rituals drew not only on pre-industrial forms of crowd action such as had erupted during the war. They also came to reflect the influences of gendered patterns of group behaviour common to nineteenth-century military and civilian institutions. In their popular adaptations of the quasi-military marching company, which had become a staple of nineteenth-century popular politics in the United States, former slave men found a means to give organized expression to the political role envisaged for them under the terms of the March 1867 Reconstruction Acts.[27] By contrast, ex-slave women, encountering no national institution to shape their collective expressions of evolving social goals, structured a collective presence from local practices of work and household.

An episode in coastal South Carolina offers a glimpse of the passion for electoral politics widely expressed by ex-slave plantation workers in the southern United States, after the United States Congress extended voting rights to former slave men two years after the abolition of slavery. On the first day in which newly eligible ex-slave voters in South Carolina were to be registered under the federal act, a party of some 1,000 black men marched to a registration site in a rice-growing parish north of Charleston, arriving well before the board of registrars had assembled to begin its duties. Two hundred of the marchers, armed with guns or muskets, served as a kind of guard for the plantation labourers who formed the largest portion of the party. Judging from the group's reported size, virtually every man among the three or four hundred eligible black voters in St. Thomas Parish must have participated in this registration foray. Marching along with them in apparently equal numbers were several hundred men younger than 21 years of age, who seem to have joined the march even though they were not yet old enough to vote. By what paths and toward what ends did this band of marching men, huge by any parish standard, exuberantly make its way toward the registration site?[28]

When they formed themselves into a visible, public procession on that Wednesday morning in August 1867, the assembly of these ex-slave marchers began to adapt a military structure of male relations widespread throughout the Atlantic world. Over the course of Reconstruction, quasi-military marching societies played a range of symbolic and social roles. They provided slightly enhanced physical security to ex-slave Republican voters marching to the polls, became a ceremonial presence in freedpeople's post-emancipation sociability, and co-ordinated the administration of justice in rural neighbourhoods by taking alleged offenders before military or civil officers. Unlike antebellum duelling among the gentry, where transactions in affairs of male honour were driven by written exchanges, the main action of the marching company was in drilling.[29] The marchers' co-ordinated movements symbolically linked the power of a victorious national army to the individual bodies of workers for whom, like other manual labourers, physical well being and freedom from corporal punishment were central symbolic and ideological concerns.[30] Drilling and marching therefore became a form of political practice, as ex-slave men took the lead in fashioning an organization that would express their burgeoning claims to social authority. Ex-slave soldiers, like the Union veteran James Bowen, who in December 1866 drilled 30 male labourers on a rice plantation north of Charleston, South Carolina, as they negotiated with their employer about wages during the next agricultural year, formed part of a persistent if shadowy stratum of local leadership. Under their tutelage, the concerns of an emerging labourers' movement would drill and march its concerns onto the terrain of Reconstruction politics.[31]

Internal relations in these marching bands have so far proved to be unrecoverable in the absence of written proceedings. But their public impact was visible and audible. Against the backdrop of political terror that came to be politics in the Reconstruction South, some marching clubs manifested a remarkable political discipline in the face of overwhelming odds. Even from a distance, it is easy to understand why faith doctor and grassroots activist Henry Adams heard about Peter Williams and Joe Calvin when he travelled through the cotton country of Claiborne Parish, Louisiana, organizing voters in 1876. Two years earlier, Williams had been at the head of a group of men marching to the polls in Homer, Louisiana. When shots rang out, he fell dead, his fellow marchers reported, and 'Joe Calvin took charge of us, and we went on to Homer'.[32] Courage seems to have circulated as widely as leadership in this neighbourhood club of Louisiana's cotton country. Men's political societies nevertheless fostered different models of leadership. A more hierarchical model of leadership and perhaps more permanent officeholding were touted by ex-slave Wade Hampton, the president of a local political club, or Union League, formed among cotton workers in the South Carolina low country. 'I, as the commanding officer of the league', Hampton boasted, 'order the League to do anything'.[33] A little learning could be stretched a long way in these associations, and complaints about members' overbearing behaviour or exaggerated professional claims of some literate members probably reflect more than the hostility of ex-masters or the disgusted complaints of the Federal military officers. At the same time, however, relationships within these largely labourers' clubs, where outsiders joked that there were as many officers as members, did not reproduce established social hierarchies in the way that antebellum militia organizations had mirrored social divisions between slave-owning gentry and yeoman farmers.[34]

Former slave women do not seem to have participated in most of the practices that neighbourhood Republican clubs or Union Leagues associated with active membership. They quickly disappeared from post-bellum drills and marches, even though theirs had been a routine presence in the dances that slaves had sometimes devised in emulation of antebellum militia.[35] They were more likely to keep watch than to have been drawn within a circle of regular attendance when circumstances permitted clubs to hold scheduled meetings. At the same time, cultural practices of reckoning kinship along extended family ties may have provided a means for at least some women to exercise an influence in ostensibly all-male marching clubs and political leagues. Hence, labouring men in a South Carolina Union League expressed their political ties to each other in terms of their shared kinship to particular women. For example, Adam Bookart, a farm labourer who in 1868 was arrested along with eight other men on spurious charges of theft while they were on League duty, explained, 'These colored men are all second cousins to my wife ... I know all of these men and they are all related to me'.[36] Tantalizing silence surrounds Mrs Bookart's influence in this 'men's' League.

Somewhat distinctive patterns of political ritual shaped the paths by which ex-slave men and women plantation labourers initiated a remarkable political mobilization. Circumstances of birth, place of work and residence, and interpretations of personal 'destiny' remained essential to ex-slave women's mobilization. Slaves had determined that one of their number was destined for leadership by collective interpretation of certain traditional signs – including unusual occurrences during birth or uncommon physical marks, such as grey hair in children, infants born with teeth, or substantial size in adults.[37] Their interpretations of such traditional signs do not seem to have noticeably favoured either men or women. Hence the elderly freedwoman Margaret Crinerall, who strongly impressed a northern school teacher when they met in Charleston, South Carolina, after the war, could readily explain how, since her marriage at the age of 12, she had purchased the freedom of four men, including her first husband (for whose freedom she paid his owner $1,775), had hidden Union prisoners in her house for six months, and had come to own three lots in Charleston. Crinerall, who insisted that at one time in her eventful life she had weighed 375 pounds, looked to her birth to explain her feats: 'I was born with four jaw teeth and grey hairs', she revealed, 'to show that I am foremost in the call and I know all things beforehand!'[38]

Plantation-centred demonstrations and post-war meetings relied on variant forms of household representation in which freed women played somewhat different roles. A work stoppage on a coastal South Carolina cotton plantation illustrates how some women's circumstances might have excluded their direct participation when plantation residents directly confronted a plantation manager in St. Peter's Parish in September 1865. Of the 11 or 12 households whose members still lived and worked on planter W. M. Robertson's cotton plantation, six households were directly represented when seven men turned out in late August 'armed with sticks & clubs and marched to the overseer's house and used abusive language because the hogs had broken the fence and got into the corn field'. Only the household of driver Harry Gantt had more than two men present at the protest. Absent from the demonstration were women whose household residents were all described as 'children' in the planter's list of his workforce. Hence Clarinda had probably been personally assertive about spending less time in the cotton fields, since the planter regarded her as 'idle & insolent', but she had not turned out. Nor had Eve, 'an old woman' whom the landowner found 'very imputinent [sic]'. Their circumstances as lone women heading households of young children perhaps inclined them to stay away because they shared a vulnerability akin to that of Matilda, mother of 'three children', the only person on the plantation whom the planter rated 'very well behaved' during the six months since Charleston had surrendered. Although gendered dimensions of protest deserve closer study, it seems clear that among these cotton workers, at any rate, planned post-emancipation demonstrations on the plantation were the work of adult men who did not live alone.[39] Some things a man had to do for himself and his household. The account is silent as to whether he was also obligated to act on behalf of women's households.

Where work groups rather than households led the confrontation, women assumed a more visible role in plantation-centred demonstrations. Their fellow male workers called on women labourers for assistance when unexpected circumstances seemed to require female fury. In the spring of 1866, for example, men and women on 'Keithfield' rice plantation on Georgetown's Black River summoned the work gang, which was composed primarily of women, to mount forceful resistance to the labour regimen supervised by freeborn black plantation overseer Dennis Hazel. When Hazel reduced the driver Abram's supervisory role by insisting that he 'must take his hoe and work under the contract with the rest', the driver summoned the men's and women's field gangs. Wielding a classic peasant tactic which assumed that lethal force would not be exerted against women, the men's gang rallied the women with cries of 'Kill him, now is your time, dont let him get away'. Wielding hoes and sticks, the women's group answered the call and played a notably prominent role in driving off the overseer, the estate's managers, and a small detail of federal soldiers. The overseer later recalled that Sukey, Becky, Charlotte, Susan, Clarissa, Sally, Quasheba, and Magdalen had pummelled him with sticks and bricks. An estate manager who tried to protect the overseer later recalled that Becky had struck him over the eye with a club, while Sukey, Quasheba, Charlotte, and Susan continued an assault that drove the manager to appeal in desperation to several male labourers 'to stop and force back the maddened women'.[40] Such feminized styles of collective assertion were wielded by women who shared pre-existing ties created by virtue of common residence on the same plantation or by labour in the same plantation work group.

It is not a coincidence that ex-slaves' attempts to hold on to plantation lands drew on both women's pre-industrial forms of collective political expression and also men's adaptations of more general conventions of nineteenth-century popular political practices. On the South Carolina sea islands adjacent to Charleston, a movement to resist restoration of plantation lands in the winter of 1865–66 combined the parliamentary tactics of the folk court or 'justice committee', the gender-specific, pre-industrial rituals of dissent of the plantation demonstration, and the militaristic manner of the all-male folk militia. Freedpeople's most deeply held convictions inspired their most complex language of political ritual. Whether former slaves regarded land as an organic element of a plantation-centred identity, or as political reward for their loyalty and military service to the Federal government during secession and civil war, or as recompense for unrequited toil, or as the indispensable material foundation of self-government and freedom from physical coercion, ex-slaves understood freedom as inseparable from the possession of land.[41] Therefore, on the sea islands of South Carolina, their attempts to prevent the post-war restoration of plantation lands on which they had been settled under the terms of Union general William Tecumseh Sherman's Field Order 15 of January 1865, drew on the widest idiom of protest that they could command.

On Edisto, John's, and Wadmalaw islands, a group of literate ex-slave artisans and religious leaders, at least one of whom had reportedly fled North in the late antebellum era, took the lead in sponsoring the formation of parliamentary styled clubs. Sometimes called 'justice committees' by their members, the clubs seem to have been based on notions of representation that linked male members in a loosely structured, decentralized authority of direct household representation and rotating leadership. Perhaps in consultation with a sympathetic northern teacher, the islands' men were feverishly organizing quasi-parliamentary 'justice committees' in the early winter of 1865–66, in response to official announcements that the abandoned plantation lands on which they had been settled under wartime auspices of Sherman's order would be restored to pardoned landowners. Membership and attendance in these justice committees cannot be determined. It is interesting to note, however, that one year later men's names figured exclusively among the 63 petitioners from Edisto Island who addressed a written appeal to Bureau commissioner Oliver Otis Howard regarding obstacles to their committee's weekly meetings.[42] Through the weekly meetings of the 'justice committees', they explained, the reading of newspapers was a chief item of business. In that way, the committees kept island residents apprised of the progressively narrow terms by which the federal government would permit them to claim sea-island lands.

Linked to the parliamentary activities of the sea-island justice committees were tactics of direct action and popular demonstration. These mobilizations reflected gendered patterns of crowd behaviour that characterized many of the freedpeople's public protests. Male marching companies composed the sea-island land movement's orderly, visible, public face. In January and February 1866 squads of men drilled and marched as they guarded island landings and halted parties of former landowners and prospective buyers who visited the islands. Women and children, on the other hand, monopolized ritualized expressions of disorder. The women's patterned, rhythmic vocalizations ('shrieking' or 'yelling' to their victims), verbal denunciations, and physical assault with small projectiles (sticks and stones) created the illusion of seemingly 'spontaneous' outcries of anger or alarm. A party of prospective northern buyers and the former slave-owners who escorted them to John's Island in February 1866 found themselves literally standing between these distinctive forms of political ritual. An armed guard of ex-slave men stopped the group at an island landing, marched them to a plantation residence, and required them to wait for a federal officer 'with a heavy guard of men in front of them, and a crowd of women behind; the former ready at any moment to fire upon them, and the latter abusing the prisoners not only with horrible language, but by poking them with sticks, &c'.[43]

Thus, popular agitation that was more or less 'spontaneous' in appearance, that was centred in the near vicinity of the plantation quarters, that was expected to stop short of deadly force, and that was expressed in an indirect, protopolitical idiom of chants, song, or dance claimed the special efforts of ex-slave women. In the early summer of 1865, for example, women rice workers of Guendalos plantation north of Charleston, South Carolina, ceremonialized in dance the tension with which plantation workers awaited the arrival of a squad of Union soldiers who were to determine whether a recently returned landowner was authorized to take possession of keys to a storage building that were in the custody of the plantation's ex-slave foreman. Women 'revolved around us', so the planter's sister later recalled, 'holding out their skirts and dancing – now with slow, swinging movements, now with rapid jig-motions, but always with weird chant and wild gestures'.[44] More deeply than ex-slave men, emancipated women labourers drew on pre-industrial forms of collective behaviour that, on coastal rice plantations of South Carolina and Georgia, incorporated creolized forms of African dance and Gullah chants. While non-lethal demonstrations centred in the quarters were characterized by women's forms of militancy, men had taken the lead in the quasi-parliamentary activities of neighbourhood clubs and in creating the more militaristic, public face of actions and demonstrations that crossed plantation boundaries. Suffrage rights forged in Congress in 1867 therefore encountered gendered forms of a rural activism that had germinated earlier, without authorization, in the shade of political life.

FIGURE 1
'RETURNING FROM THE COTTON FIELDS IN SOUTH CAROLINA', c.1874

Source: Collection of the New York Historical Society.

At the same time, the continuing mobilizations of an emerging post-emancipation labourers' movement projected intriguing contrasts in the nature of the public images of men and women rural workers. Male authority, whether in the militaristic manner of a marching company or the disciplined control of a quasi-parliamentary 'justice committee', gained in symbolic representation as some forms of women's authority faded from view. The symbolism of a post-emancipation harvest celebration photographed on a cotton plantation outside Mount Pleasant, South Carolina, suggests something of the changing representations of the various men and women who mounted these rural movements. Photographed in the fall of 1874 or 1875 by a photographer who had travelled with Ulysses Grant's Army of the Mississippi, the composition of the single-file procession of 27 people, at least four of whom are adults, probably reflects the input of both the subjects and the photographer.[45] On the one hand, the procession symbolically called attention to workers' roles in the production of the harvested cotton crop and thereby departed from the intended lessons of plantation rituals that had developed during slavery. Plantation rituals under slavery ceremonialized antebellum plantation power relations by idealizing 'Master's' role as provider in the dispensing of plantation allowances or as patriarchal leader of household prayers presiding over a newly Christianized plantation body. By contrast, this post-emancipation harvest observance celebrated the creative power of labouring households, not 'Master's' largesse. A lengthy procession of adults, children, and infants winds its way through picked fields, with both women and men bearing large bags of harvested cotton on their heads. An elderly man heading the procession, dressed in what appears to be a battered but serviceable top hat and swallowtail coat, holds aloft a decorative wooden stick, emblematic of a special authority. Another man in the procession also carries some article – either a large book reminiscent of a Bible or a folded banner reminiscent of a federal flag – that also signals his special capacities. By contrast, the most visible women only occupy positions directly behind men who presumably headed their households. Even the oldest woman in the procession, the only woman who carries some kind of non-utilitarian object, perhaps a bell, to suggest her special powers, marches behind the elderly man who leads the procession. The configuration thereby represented hard-won household authority idealized in fairly well-defined patriarchal forms. Significantly, there is scarcely a place for the women workers whose households march in the procession without a male head; their white aprons and bags of cotton are shadowy traces scarcely visible at the rear of the procession. Feminine forms of aggressive militancy essential to some rituals of dissent have scarcely a place in the elements from which harmony and workers' freedom were represented in this image. The harvest ritual of this plantation community perhaps betrays the impact of a masculinization of workers' social ideals even while their social struggles remained dependent on women's efforts.

This search for patterns in ex-slaves' collective behaviour during and immediately after emancipation has suggested how cultural practices shaped by experiences of slavery mediated former plantation slaves' public expressions of political claims. Men and women shared some basic elements of practical philosophy about how the world worked. Their ritualized behaviour therefore showed a common concern with temporal and spiritual dimensions of power relations. Similarly widespread practices of extended kinship and mechanisms of interpreting traditional emblems of leadership helped prevent masculinist versions of citizenship from proving incompatible with women's political activism. At the same time, however, women played a less prominent role in political rituals grounded in networks of household representation than in rituals that drew on ties formed in fieldwork groups. Former slave men and women assumed somewhat different burdens as they faced the tasks of becoming a free people.

NOTES

Earlier versions of this essay were presented at the 1994 annual meeting of the Organization of American Historians, Atlanta, Georgia; the colloquium 'Les Dépendances Serviles: Une Approche Comparative', Paris, France, June 1996, sponsored by the Centre de Recherches Historiques, Ecole des Hautes Etudes en Sciences Sociales, C.N.R.S.; and the Tulane–Cambridge Atlantic World Studies Group, Inaugural Conference, New Orleans, LA, November 1996. In addition to the helpful comments offered by participants and panelists at these meetings, I would also like to express appreciation to Thavolia Glymph and Kenneth L. Jackson for their criticisms and suggestions.

1. Classic assessments of the evolution and interpretive significance of Atlantic studies models are offered in the corpus of writings of W.E.B. DuBois, C.L.R. James and Eric Williams. For some more recent formulations, see Elizabeth Fox-Genovese and Eugene D. Genovese, 'Slavery: The World's Burden', in idem, *Fruits of Merchant Capital: Slavery and Bourgeois Property in the Rise and Expansion of Capitalism* (New York, Oxford University Press, 1983), pp.391–414; Sidney Mintz, *Sweetness and Power: The Place of Sugar in Modern History* (Penguin Books, 1985), especially xiii–xxx; Barbara L. Solow, 'Slavery and Colonization', in Barbara L. Solow (ed.), *Slavery and the Rise of the Atlantic System* (Cambridge, Cambridge University Press, 1991), pp.21–42; Bernard Bailyn, 'The Idea of Atlantic History', *Itinerario*, Vol.20, No.1 (1996), pp.19–44; Stuart B. Schwartz, 'Expansion, Diaspora, and Encounter in the Early Modern South Atlantic', *Itinerario*, Vol.19, No.2 (1995), pp.48–59. I am indebted to conversations and joint teaching with Thomas C. Holt for provocative discussion of many of these questions.

2. In addition to sources cited in note 1 above, the following works explicitly address global dimensions of slavery and the slave trade, slaves' emancipations, and colonialism: Eugene D. Genovese, *The World the Slaveholders Made: Two Essays in Interpretation* (New York, 1969); Walter Rodney, 'African Slavery and Other Forms of Social Oppression on the Upper Guinea Coast in the Context of the Atlantic Slave Trade', *Journal of African History*, Vol.7, No.3 (1966), pp.431–43; idem, *A History of the Guyanese Working People, 1881–1905* (Baltimore, Johns Hopkins University Press, 1981); David Brion Davis, *The Problem of Slavery in the Age of Revolution, 1770–1823* (Ithaca, Cornell University Press, 1975); Barbara Jeanne Fields, *Slavery and Freedom on the Middle Ground: Maryland during the Nineteenth Century* (New Haven, Yale University Press, 1985); Rebecca J. Scott, *Slave Emancipation in Cuba: The Transition to Free Labor, 1860–1899* (Princeton, Princeton University Press, 1985); Robin Blackburn, *The Overthrow of Colonial Slavery, 1776–1848*

(London, Verso, 1988); idem, *The Making of New World Slavery: From the Baroque to the Modern, 1492–1800* (London, Verso, 1997); Peter Linebaugh and Marcus Rediker, 'The Many Headed Hydra: Sailors, Slaves, and the Atlantic Working Class in the Eighteenth Century', *Journal of Historical Sociology*, Vol.3, No.3 (Sept. 1990), pp.225–53; Sylvia R. Frey, *Water From the Rock: Black Resistance in a Revolutionary Age* (Princeton, Princeton University Press, 1991); Thomas C. Holt, *The Problem of Freedom: Race, Labor, and Politics in Jamaica and Britain, 1832–1938* (Baltimore, Johns Hopkins University Press, 1992); Paul Gilroy, *The Black Atlantic: Modernity and Double Consciousness* (Cambridge, MA, Harvard University Press, 1993); Frederick Cooper, *Decolonization and African Society: The labor question in French and British Africa* (Cambridge, Cambridge University Press, 1996); Ira Berlin, 'From Creole to African: Atlantic Creoles and the Origins of African-American Society in Mainland North America', *William and Mary Quarterly*, 3d ser., Vol.53, No.2 (April 1996), pp.251–88.

3. Frey, *Water From the Rock*, pp.172–90; quotation at p.190; Blackburn, *Overthrow*, pp.248–9.

4. The full text of Johnson's letter appears in Ira Berlin, Joseph P. Reidy, and Leslie S. Rowland (eds.), *Freedom: A Documentary History of Emancipation, 1861–1867*, Series II: *The Black Military Experience* (Cambridge and New York, Cambridge University Press, 1982), pp.582–3.

5. Toni Morrison's *Beloved* can be read as a compelling meditation on this question. Nell Irvin Painter, *Sojourner Truth: A Life, A Symbol* (New York, W.W. Norton, 1996), p.22 similarly considers emancipation in the context of structural and affective aspects of power. She observes, 'There is no denying that legal and economic status counted enormously in circumscribing slaves' chances in life; but the injuries of slavery went much deeper, into the bodies and into the psyches of the people who were its victims. In their experience, slavery meant a good deal more than lack of standing before the law and endless, unpaid labor, just as there would be a good deal more to freedom than being able to make a contract or earn a shilling.'

6. This discussion is informed by Rhys Isaac, *The Transformation of Virginia, 1740–1790* (Chapel Hill, University of North Carolina Press, 1982), especially 'A Discourse on the Method: Action, Structure, and Meaning', pp. 323–58; Sean Wilentz (ed.), *Rites of Power: Symbolism, Ritual, and Politics Since the Middle Ages* (Philadelphia, University of Pennsylvania Press, 1985); Eric Hobsbawm and Terence Ranger (eds.), *The Invention of Tradition* (Cambridge, Cambridge University Press, 1983); Susan G. Davis, *Parades and Power: Street Theater in Nineteenth-Century Philadelphia* (Philadelphia,Temple University Press, 1986).

7. Stanley M. Elkins, *Slavery: A Problem in American Institutional and Intellectual Life*, 3d ed. (Chicago, University of Chicago Press, [1959], 1976 ed.), pp.137, 136; the interpretation is criticized in Lawrence W. Levine, *Black Culture and Black Consciousness: Afro-American Folk Thought from Slavery to Freedom* (Oxford and New York, Oxford University Press, 1977), p.35.

8. The petition appears in Mary Ames, *From a New England Woman's Diary in Dixie in 1865* (Springfield, MA, Plimpton 1906), pp.99–100 and in Herbert Aptheker (ed.), *A Documentary History of the Negro People in the United States* (Citadel Press, 1951), pp.543–44.

9. Orlando Patterson, *Slavery and Social Death: A Comparative Study* (Cambridge, Harvard University Press, 1982).

10. Holt, *Problem of Freedom*, p.5, locates the freedpeople's collective aspirations in broader context: 'For most of humankind throughout most of human history the highest value or good has been to achieve a sense, not of autonomy, but of belonging, that psychic and physical security of incorporation into the group'. The 'organizing tradition' is described in Charles M. Payne, *I've Got the Light of Freedom: The Organizing Tradition and the Mississippi Freedom Struggle* (University of California Press, 1995), especially pp.67–102.

11. The literature is vast. Particularly useful for me have been Benjamin Quarles, *The Negro in the American Revolution* (Chapel Hill, University of North Carolina Press, 1961), pp.38–40, 42–5; Blackburn, *Overthrow*, pp.333–79; Frey, *Water From the Rock*; Emilia Viotti da Costa, *Crowns of Glory, Tears of Blood: The Demerara Slave Rebellion of 1823* (Oxford and New York, Oxford University Press, 1994), pp.45–6; Scott, *Slave Emancipation*, especially

pp.174–81; David Barry Gaspar, 'Working the System: Antigua Slaves and their Struggle to Live', *Slavery and Abolition*, Vol.13, No.3 (Dec. 1992), pp.131–55; Ira Berlin *et al.*, *Slaves No More: Three Essays on Emancipation* (Cambridge and New York, Cambridge University Press, 1992).

12. Carolyn Fick, *The Making of Haiti: The Saint Domingue Revolution from Below* (Knoxville, University of Tennessee Press, 1990); Julius S. Scott, III, 'The Common Wind: Currents of Afro-American Communication in the era of the Haitian Revolution' (PhD diss., Duke University, 1986); W. Jeffrey Bolster, *Black Jacks: African American Seamen in the Age of Sail* (Cambridge, MA, Harvard University Press, 1997); Peter P. Hinks, *To Awaken My Afflicted Brethren: David Walker and the Problem of Antebellum Slave Resistance* (Philadelphia, Pennsylvania State University Press, 1997); Winthrop D. Jordan, *Tumult and Silence at Second Creek: An Inquiry Into A Civil War Slave Conspiracy* (Baton Rouge, Louisiana State University Press, 1993), especially p.204; Steven Hahn, '"Extravagant Expectations" of Freedom: Rumour, Political Struggle, and the Christmas Insurrection Scare of 1865 in the American South', *Past and Present*, Vol.157 (Nov. 1997), pp.122–58.

13. Thomas C. Holt, *Black Over White: Negro Political Leadership in South Carolina during Reconstruction* (Urbana, University of Illinois Press, 1977); Peter J. Rachleff, *Black Labor in the South: Richmond, Virginia, 1865–1890* (Philadelphia, Temple University Press, 1984); Joseph P. Reidy, *From Slavery to Agrarian Capitalism in the Cotton Plantation South: Central Georgia, 1800–1880* (Chapel Hill, University of North Carolina Press, 1992); Eric Foner, *Reconstruction: America's Unfinished Revolution, 1863–1877* (New York, Harper and Row, 1988); Elsa Barkley Brown, 'Negotiating and Transforming the Public Sphere: African American Political Life in the Transition from Slavery to Freedom', *Public Culture*, Vol.7, No.1 (Fall 1994), pp.107–46; Julie Saville, *The Work of Reconstruction: From Slave to Wage Laborer in South Carolina, 1860–1870* (Cambridge and New York, Cambridge University Press, 1994).

14. Holt, *Problem of Freedom*; Gad J. Heuman, 'Post-Emancipation Protest in Jamaica: The Morant Bay Rebellion 1865', in Mary Turner (ed.), *From Chattel Slaves to Wage Slaves: The Dynamics of Labour Bargaining in the Americas* (London, James Currey; Indianapolis and Bloomington, Indiana University Press, 1995), pp.258–74; idem, *'The Killing Time': The Morant Bay Rebellion in Jamaica* (Knoxville, University of Tennessee Press, 1994); Lorna Elaine Simmonds, '"The Spirit of Disaffection": Civil Disturbances in Jamaica, 1838–1865' (MA thesis, University of Waterloo, 1982).

15. Robert Dirks, *The Black Saturnalia: Conflict and Its Ritual Expression on British West Indian Slave Plantations* (University of Florida, Monographs in Social Sciences, No. 72, University of Florida Press, 1987); Joseph P. Reidy, '"Negro Election Day" and Black Community Life in New England, 1750–1860', *Marxist Perspectives*, Vol.1 (1978), pp.102–17; David Barry Gaspar, 'Slavery, Amelioration, and Sunday Markets in Antigua, 1823–1831', *Slavery and Abolition*, Vol.9 (May 1988), pp.1–28; Sidney W. Mintz, 'The Origins of the Jamaica Market System', in Mintz, *Caribbean Transformations* (New York, Columbia University Press, 1989 ed.) João José Reis, *Slave Rebellion in Brazil: The Muslim Uprisings of 1835 in Bahia* (Baltimore, John Hopkins University Press, 1993 trans.), pp.41–9; Shane White, '"It Was a Proud Day": African Americans, Festivals, and Parades in the North, 1741–1834', *Journal of American History*, Vol.81 (June 1994), pp.13–50.

16. Ana Maria Alonso, 'Men in "Rags" and the Devil on the Throne: A study of protest and inversion in the carnival of post-emancipation Trinidad', *Plantation Society in the Americas* (1990), pp.73–120.

17. E.J. Hobsbawm, 'Peasants and Politics, *Journal of Peasant Studies*, Vol.1 (Oct. 1973), pp.3–22; Peter Kolchin, *Unfree Labor: American Slavery and Russian Serfdom* (Cambridge, Harvard University Press, 1987), pp.241–357; Daniel Field, *Rebels in the Name of the Tsar* (Unwin Hyman, 1989).

18. Jordan, *Tumult and Silence*.

19. Discussions of slaves' wartime rebellions is based on Willie Lee Rose, *Rehearsal for Reconstruction: The Port Royal Experiment* (Oxford and New York, Oxford University Press, 1964), pp.106–7; Berlin *et al.* (eds.), *Destruction of Slavery*, pp.219–35, quotations at 228; Ira Berlin *et al.* (eds.), *Freedom: A Documentary History of Emancipation, 1861–1867*

Ser. 1, Vol. 3: *The Wartime Genesis of Free Labor: The Lower South* (Cambridge and New York, Cambridge University Press, 1990), pp.401–4, 405–6, 489–91, 535–6, 548–50; Clarence L. Mohr, *On the Threshold of Freedom: Masters and Slaves in Civil War Georgia* (Athens, University of Georgia Press, 1986); Eric Foner, *Nothing But Freedom: Emancipation and Its Legacy* (Baton Rouge, Louisiana State University Press, 1989), pp.79–82; Saville, *Work of Reconstruction*, pp.11–16, 32–4; Dusinberre, *Them Dark Days*, pp.209–10, 376–84; Leslie A. Schwalm, *A Hard Fight For We: Women's Transition from Slavery to Freedom in South Carolina* (Urbana, University of Illinois Press, 1997), pp.126–35; Thavolia Glymph, '"This Species of Property": Female Slave Contrabands in the Civil War', in Edward D.C. Campbell, Jr. and Kym S. Rice (eds.), *A Woman's War: Southern Women, Civil War, and the Confederate Legacy* (Charlottesville, University Press of Virginia, 1997), pp.55–72.

20. Regarding eighteenth-century slave revolts in these regions, see Peter H. Wood, *Black Majority: Negroes in Colonial South Carolina from 1670 through the Stono Rebellion* (New York, Knopf, 1974); Frey, *Water from the Rock*; Robert Paquette, 'The Great Louisiana Slave Revolt of 1811', Paper delivered to the Southern Historical Association, 1990.

21. Accounts of the slaves' foray into Beaufort appear in Rose, *Rehearsal for Reconstruction*, pp.106–7; Saville, *Work of Reconstruction*, p.34; Schwalm, *Hard Fight*, pp.126–31.

22. For plantation slaves' insurrections during the American Revolution, see Frey, *Water from the Rock*, pp.53–5, 59–63, 86–7, 101–2, 114–16, 169, 225–30.

23. P.M. Jones, *The Peasantry in the French Revolution* (Cambridge, Cambridge University Press, 1988); Steven G. Reinhardt, 'The Revolution in the Countryside: Peasant Unrest in the Périgord, 1789–90', in Steven G. Reinhardt and Elisabeth A. Cawthon (eds.), *Essays on the French Revolution: Paris and the Provinces* (Texas A&M University Press, 1992), pp.12–37. John T. O'Connor kindly brought the latter essay to my attention.

24. Berlin *et al.* (eds.), *Destruction of Slavery*, pp.96–7.

25. Ibid., p.234; Armstead L. Robinson, '"Worser dan Jeff Davis": The Coming of Free Labor during the Civil War, 1861–1865', in Thavolia Glymph and John J. Kushma (eds.), *Essays on the Postbellum Southern Economy* (Texas A&M University Press, 1985), pp.25–6.

26. Dusinberre, *Them Dark Days*, pp.209–10, quotation at p.209. The characterization of postbellum rituals of social transformation has been influenced by analysis of a Dahomean legend of ritual absorption in Michel-Rolph Trouillot, *Silencing the Past: Power and the Production of History* (Beacon Press, 1995), pp.64–9 and interpretation of Dessaline's ritualized dismemberment in Joan Dayan, *Haiti, History, and the Gods* (University of California Press, 1998), pp.29–39. For a stimulating discussion of social and ideological constructions of property relations among slaves, see Dylan Penningroth, 'Slavery, Freedom, and Social Claims to Property among African Americans in Liberty County, Georgia, 1850–1880', *Journal of American History*, Vol.84, No.2 (Sept. 1997), pp.405–35.

27. The Reconstruction Acts adopted between March and July 1867 placed all former Confederate States except Tennessee under military government and ordered the commanders of the military districts to draw up new lists of voters for mandated elections regarding the calling of state constitutional conventions in which black men over the age of twenty-one would be eligible to vote.

28. Charleston *Daily Courier*, 29 Aug. 1867, p.2, col.2, 30 Aug. 1867, p.2, col.4. The federal census of 1870 reported the black population of St. Thomas parish to be 1952 people. Ninth Census, 1870, *Population*, p.258.

29. For analysis of dueling in the antebellum South, see Steven M. Stowe, *Intimacy and Power in the Old South: Ritual in the Lives of the Planters* (Baltimore, Johns Hopkins University Press, 1987), pp.5–49; Kenneth S. Greenberg, *Honor and Slavery*, pp.62–4, 73–4.

30. This discussion has been informed by Alf Lüdtke, 'Organizational Order or *Eigensinn*? Workers' Privacy and Workers' Politics in Imperial Germany', in Wilentz (ed.), *Rites of Power*, pp.303–33; Wolfgang Kaschuba, 'Popular culture and workers' culture as symbolic orders: Comments on the debate about the history of culture and everyday life', in Alf Lüdtke (ed.), *The History of Everyday Life: Reconstructing historical experiences and ways of life* (Princeton, Princeton University Press, 1991 trans.), pp.169–97.

31. Michael William Fitzgerald, *The Union League Movement in the Deep South: Politics and*

Agricultural Change during Reconstruction (Baton Rouge, Louisiana State University Press, 1989); Saville, *Work of Reconstruction,* pp.143–51; Nell Irvin Painter, *Exodusters: Black Migration to Kansas after Reconstruction* (New York, W.W. Norton, 1976), pp.76, 82–5.

32. For pioneering analysis of the 'executor/constituency' relationship on which such circulating leadership is based, see Painter, *Exodusters,* pp.22–6, 85, 132–4; quotation from 46th Congress, 2d Session, Senate Report 693 Pt 2, *Select Committee ... to investigate the causes of the Removal of the Negroes from the Southern States to the Northern States* (Washington, 1880), p.187.

33. Affidavit of Wade Hampton in the Case of Patrick Feilds vs Theodore Cordes, [Dec. 1867?], 2d Military District, Letters Received, ser. 4111, RG 393 Pt 1 [SS-84]. Copies of documents from the National Archives that were consulted at the Freedmen and Southern Society Project at the University of Maryland, College Park, appear with the project's accession number in brackets. For a similar claim expressed by another Union League organizer, see Charleston *Daily Courier,* 31 July 1868, p.4, col.2, 29 Aug. 1868, p.1, col.1, 9 Sept. 1868, p.1, cols. 3–4, 14 Sept. 1868, p.2, col.3; Jno B. Hubbard, Report of an investigation at Santuc Depot, 3 Sept. 1868, Robert K. Scott Papers, South Carolina Department of Archives and History.

34. For analysis of social divisions within fraternal relations in antebellum militia organizations, see Stephanie McCurry, *Masters of Small Worlds: Yeoman Households, Gender Relations, & the Political Culture of the Antebellum South Carolina Low Country* (Oxford and New York, Oxford University Press, 1995), pp.265–71.

35. For an 1843 'mock military parade' on a South Carolina plantation, see Levine, *Black Culture,* p.17; see also Brown, 'Negotiating and Transforming the Public Sphere', pp.109, 118–26; Fitzgerald, *Union League Movement,* pp.37–66.

36. Proceedings of a Commission of Inquiry, convened at Orangeburg [June 1868], enclosed in Bvt. Capt. James Chester, Recorder to Lieut. Louis V. Caziarc, 26 June 1868, 2d Military District, Letters Received, ser. 4111, RG 393 Pt 1 [SS-126].

37. In addition to the biographical details of Crinerall's life in the text, see, for example, Kenneth S. Greenberg (ed.), *The Confessions of Nat Turner* (St. Martin's Press, 1996), pp.44–5; Margaret Washington Creel, *'A Peculiar People': Slave Religion and Community-Culture among the Gullahs* (New York, New York University Press, 1988), pp.290–2; Testimony of Henry Adams, in 46th Congress, 2d Session, Senate Report 693 Pt 2, *Select Committee ... to investigate the causes of the Removal of the Negroes from the Southern States to the Northern States* (Washington, 1880), p.138.

38. 'Margaret [Crinerall?]', from Miss J.A. Van Allen, Charleston, n.d., American Missionary Association, Letters Received. The ex-slave woman's surname is scarcely legible in the manuscript.

39. W. [M]. Robertson, 'Statement of the conduct of the colored people ...' [Sept. 1865], enclosed in Lt. W. Wood to S. Baker, 16 September 1865, Department of the South, Letters Received, ser 2384, Subdistrict of Coosawatchie, RG 393 Pt 2 No 141[C-1593]; W. M. Robertson to Capt. J.J. Upham, 8 Sept. 1865, ibid. The exact number of households is uncertain because of idiosyncrasies in the planter's list. My account differs from Schwalm, *Hard Fight,* p.174, who regards as women's individual resistance the patterns of behaviour that I have tried to relate to workers' household circumstances.

40. B.F. Smith to H.W. Smith, 6 April 1866, National Archives, Washington, DC, Microfilm M 869, r 34, 0486–88; [Statement], F.S. Parker [Sr.], 3 April 1866; Affidavit of Francis S. Parker, Jr., 4 April 1866; Affidavit of Dennis Hazel, 4 April 1866; all in Letters Received, ser. 2393, Department of the South, RG 393 Pt 2 No.142 [C-1606], Lt. Col. B.F. Smith to Capt. M.N. Rice, 7 April 1866, Vol.154 DS, pp.62–3, Letters Sent, ser. 2389, Department of the South, RG 393 Pt 2 No.142, Freedmen and Southern Society Project, University of MD, [C-1606]. For other cultural variants in working-class women's public behaviour, see Christine Stansell, *City of Women: Sex and Class in New York, 1789–1860* (Urbana, University of Illinois Press, 1987); Mary H. Blewett, *Men, Women, and Work: Class, Gender, and Protest in the New England Shoe Industry, 1780–1910* (Urbana, University of Illinois Press, 1988).

41. More detailed examination of ex-slaves' views of land appears in Saville, *Work of*

Reconstruction, pp.18–20, 41–3, 188–92; Edward Magdol, *A Right to the Land: Essays on the Freedmen's Community* (Westport, Greenwood Press, 1977); William S. McFeely, *Yankee Stepfather: General O.O. Howard and the Freedmen* (New Haven, Yale University Press, 1968); Douglas Hall, 'The Flight from the Estates Reconsidered: The British West Indies, 1838–1842', *Journal of Caribbean History*, Vols.10–11 (1978), pp.7–24.

42. Colored Planters of Edisto Island to O.O. Howard, 3 Nov. 1866, National Archives, Washington, DC, Microfilm M 752, r 37, 0460–69.

43. Charleston *Daily Courier*, 1 Feb. 1866, p.2, col.2; see also Charleston *Daily Courier*, 3 Feb. 1866, p.2, col.5; 6 Feb. 1866, p.2, col.1; 15 Feb. 1866, p.1, col.2; 16 Feb. 1866, p.2, col.4; 17 Feb. 1866, p.2, col.5; James C. Beecher to Lieut M. N. Rice, 31 Jan. 1866, Beecher Papers, Perkins Library, Duke University; Lawrence N. Powell, *New Masters: Northern Planters during the Civil War and Reconstruction* (New Haven, Yale University Press, 1980), pp.99–101.

44. Elizabeth W. Allston Pringle, *Chronicles of Chicora Wood* (Boston, Christopher Publishing House, 1940), p.273.

45. The photograph 'Returning from the cotton fields' was taken by George N. Barnard and can be found in the collections of the New York Historical Society; a reproduction is found in Saville, *Work of Reconstruction*, p.142. See also Keith F. Davis, *George N. Barnard: Photographer of Sherman's Campaign* (Kansas City, MO: Hallmark Cards, Inc. [1990]).

'Stubborn and Disposed to Stand their Ground': Black Militia, Sugar Workers and the Dynamics of Collective Action in the Louisiana Sugar Bowl, 1863–87

REBECCA J. SCOTT

A few hours' ride on the railroad south-west from New Orleans, or on horseback along the Mississippi River to Donaldsonville and then down Bayou Lafourche, there occurred in 1887 a most remarkable set of events. The formal end of Reconstruction was already a decade in the past, and the electoral disfranchisement of African Americans in Louisiana would be completed over the next 11 years. A white-supremacist Democratic governor was entrenched in the statehouse and the state militia had become almost a branch of the White Leagues. But somehow into this unpromising environment there erupted a tenacious expression of militancy by thousands of plantation workers, the great majority of whom were either former slaves themselves or the direct descendants of former slaves.

In late October and early November 1887, on the eve of the harvest, black, mulatto, and white sugar workers on estates in St. Mary, Terrebonne, and Lafourche Parishes took the remarkable step of declaring allegiance to the Knights of Labor and insisting on the right to bargain with their employers. After being rebuffed by the planters' association they downed tools and refused to cut cane until employers would negotiate with them. They sought regular payment of better wages, in cash not scrip, and extra compensation for night work.

Planters brought in strike-breakers from out of state, but the replacement workers were met with hostile crowds at the railway depot, and, on occasion, with birdshot as they tried to get the equipment going. Local authorities asked the governor to send in the militia. Those deployed to the estates met defiant strikers: 'the negroes hooted and used violent language, the women waving their skirts on poles, and jeering'.[1]

The region remained in tumult through the month of November, as the militia evicted strikers to enable planters to house the strike-breakers and resume production. For reasons that are still not entirely clear, by 20 November most of the militia withdrew, leaving planters to enforce security on their own. Shortly after the formal withdrawal of the militia, a Peace and Order committee of white citizens tried to hem in strikers evicted from the estates who had taken refuge in the town of Thibodaux. An unexplained shooting triggered an attack by the white vigilante forces on strikers. Going from house to house and street to street, vigilantes killed dozens of strikers and injured perhaps a hundred more. The viciousness of the repression broke what remained of the strike, sowing fear through the region.[2]

There are several ways to fit these events into narratives of southern history in this period. The presence of black and white Knights of Labor organizers encourages one to view the strike as an unusually bold instance of the cautious policy of cross-racial alliance followed by the Knights in this period. The failure of the strike, and the inability of the Knights to protect their members from repression, might be seen to illuminate the limits of that policy.[3] Alternatively, one can situate this conflict in the story of modernization and consolidation of industry, a Sugar Bowl variant on the Gilded Age pattern of large-scale capital investment and large-scale labour repression. On this view, the breaking of the strike eliminated an obstacle to the hegemony of a particular elite vision of the organization of production and of labour relations.[4] Finally, one can understand the Thibodaux massacre alongside the 1873 Colfax massacre and the 1874 Battle of Canal Street in New Orleans, Louisiana's macabre and outsized contributions to the violent imposition of white supremacy through a combination of local white mobilization and what Lawrence Powell calls 'silk-stocking vigilantism'.[5]

This essay is somewhat less ambitious. Rather than situate the events of November of 1887 in one or another story about where Louisiana was headed, it will ask a different pair of questions: how could a strike of this magnitude ever get off the ground in a setting as hostile to African-American mobilization as the Louisiana sugar parishes in the 1880s; and what might we learn about the politics of freedom by looking at the decades that separated the end of slavery from the events of 1887? These questions are addressed on three levels: the structure of production on sugar estates; patterns of mobilization by African Americans in these parishes in the 1870s; and the social geography of the bayou country, with its implications for networks of support and points of vulnerability.

The Structure of Production

Union occupation of the sugar parishes of Louisiana during the Civil War had triggered the breakdown of slavery, but did not immediately replace it with a thoroughgoing system of wage labour. On plantations abandoned by Confederate owners, former slaves sought in some cases to cultivate the land in collective 'labour companies', with an emphasis on locally consumable crops.[6] Some planters remained in place and continued cultivation under Union auspices, but they were reluctant to plant new cane, and sugar output fell abruptly due to the disruption occasioned by war and conscription of labourers, as well as the reliance on lower-yield rattoon cane, regrown from the previous year's roots. Workers and administrators continued to tug and haul over the choice of overseers, the right to garden plots, and the pace of work in the fields.[7]

With the end of the war came the end of formal experiments like the labour companies, though on one plantation in Terrebonne Parish something similar seems to have persisted into 1866. In April 1866 the Freedmen's Bureau agent reported that Orange Grove Plantation was leased by 'William James (colored)', and worked by a force of 39 men, 36 women, and 11 children, accompanied by 57 dependent children. The agent clarified: 'the balance of the negroes on this place partners with him in the hiring and working of it. This place is rented for three years to the Freedmen. Wm. James is the head man ...' But by July of 1866 a new agent reported routinely that the Orange Grove estate was under the authority of one A. Verrette, and that 41 hands were working under contract for rations, clothing, quarters, fuel, and wages. William James had vanished from the record.[8]

Gradually the lines of a new free labour system were emerging in the sugar sector, to become dominant over the next years. Planters were generally 'averse to leasing land to the freedmen', as one Freedmen's Bureau agent in Lafourche Parish put it, and their insistence on controlling labour often made for unhappy relationships. Both planters and agents of the Freedmen's Bureau encouraged annual wage labour contracts, but former slaves were quick to see the disadvantages of arrangements that deferred their compensation to a year-end settlement in which they could easily be short-changed.[9]

When blocked from establishing themselves as tenants or smallholders, freedpeople used the occasion of the signing of a New Year's contract as a moment of bargaining. One agent near New Orleans reported in January of 1866, 'the freedmen are delaying to make a permanent contract in expectation of orders from the Bureau compelling the planters to hire labour and pay for it at the rate of fifty cents per hour, this idea originated probably among freedmen working on the levee in the city who have recently been "striking" for the aforesaid wages'.[10] In Terrebonne Parish during the same month the local agent apologized that he could file no monthly report on the number of freedmen on each plantation: having recently received their final pay from the previous year's contract, workers showed a disposition 'to look around and see where they can get the best wages before entering into new ones'.[11] This kind of negotiation put an upward pressure on wages, which climbed slowly.

By the time of the Bureau agent's report for Terrebonne Parish in April of 1868, the new system of free labour was largely in place. Labourers worked for rations, quarters, fuel, and wages, without a government-supervised contract. The average monthly wage on the seven major plantations that the agent inspected was said to be $13, one half paid at the end of each month, and one half reserved until the end of the year. A portion of land on each estate was given rent-free to the freedpeople, presumably for the cultivation of gardens. Male field hands outnumbered female. Many freed women and children had diminished their regular labour in the cane fields, turning to household tasks and to attendance at the newly established school.[12]

Some variant on this system was probably in force on most of the parish's other estates, though there were occasional reports of leasing of land to the freedmen. During the sugar harvest itself demand for labour was high, and workers travelled to the bayou sugar parishes from the poorer northern parishes or from out of state. Increasing numbers of white smallholders, many of them of Acadian origin, seem to have worked seasonally in the fields as well. Nevertheless, the overwhelming majority of permanent workers were still African Americans born in Louisiana.[13]

The overall recovery of production in the sugar sector was painfully slow. Louisiana's 1861 crop had weighed in at 264,000 tons. In 1866 and 1867 the crop barely broke 20,000 tons, less than one tenth of the earlier total. A decade later it had still not reached one half of the 1861 record. Labour was in flux; working capital was not easy to find; Louisiana's longstanding disadvantages of frost and flood were hard to overcome.[14]

The portrait of the first years after emancipation, then, is one of halting gains for freedmen and continuing frustration for planters, in the realm of production as in the realm of Reconstruction politics. But soon the financial crisis of 1873 brought sharp downward pressure on wages, as prices fell and planters sought to reduce their expenses. The monthly wages offered on sugar plantations fell abruptly from $18 to $13. These wage cuts were met by strikes in Terrebonne Parish, where workers combined demands for higher pay with an appeal for the right to form 'sub-associations' and lease land. The hostile *Daily Picayune* reported on January 16 that 'the negroes have been marching around the parish, preventing the field hands from working'.[15]

The results of the 1873–74 struggles were inconclusive. Labourers could block some concerted efforts to drive down wages, but few planters would countenance renting their land to former slaves. On those occasions when planters, faced with mounting losses, did choose to subdivide the land, white immigrants seem to have had priority. The newly installed tenants on the Rienzi Plantation outside of Thibodaux, in Lafourche Parish, were said to be 'Portuguese, English, Spaniards and colored', in that order.[16] Though planters were unable to hold themselves together in stable combinations to reduce wages over more than a narrow area, they could generally keep harvest wages well below 20 dollars a month, with rations.[17]

By 1880 certain basic patterns had been set. The majority of labour in the cane would be performed by groups of wage workers of African descent, under direct supervision, largely continuing patterns of gang labour that harked back to slavery. But these patterns also meant that landless workers had potential numerical strength, mechanisms of communication, and concentration of effort in moments of dispute. John Rodrigue has gone so far as to argue that sugar planters' dependence on collective labour at harvest helped to discourage the more blatant forms of 'bulldozing' and violent intimidation of African-American voters, for fear of disrupting the harvest.[18] At the very least, an awareness of the potential power of black sugar workers seems for a time to have encouraged a degree of discretion in the exercise of force.

Patterns of Mobilization

Louisiana had contributed more black soldiers to the Union Army, some 24,000, than any other state. Many came from the city of New Orleans, which had been occupied by Union forces in 1862. By 1863 Union recruiters were active in rural areas, as Federal control extended up the river and down the bayous into the sugar parishes. In testimony before the Freedmen's Inquiry Commission, one former cooper from St. James parish recalled the path he had travelled from plantation artisan, to runaway, to 'contraband' at Camp Parapet above New Orleans, to enlistment. By the end of the war he was a corporal in the Union Army.[19]

In the case of Louisiana, black soldiers not only shared in the Union triumph over the Confederacy, but also represented a significant fraction of the occupying troops in the aftermath of the surrender. Though the number of Federal soldiers fell sharply after 1865, some black soldiers from within and outside the state returned to or remained in Louisiana after being discharged.[20] The presence of demobilized soldiers among the workers on sugar estates was frequently commented on by officials of the Freedmen's Bureau, who made varying estimates of their impact. Some emphasized their orderly and disciplined habits as a good example to other workers, though a Bureau agent in Jefferson and Orleans Parish thought they had 'erroneous and incongruous notions of liberty' and were thus a bad influence.[21]

Union veterans, along with other supporters of Republican rule in the state, joined various associations designed to mobilize Republican voters and consolidate newly won rights. In rural areas in particular considerable caution was required, as African-American mobilization and Republican politics were equally anathema to many whites. But radical or Republican clubs were said to be thick on the ground in St. Mary parish, organized on every third or fourth plantation by John J. Moore, a former slave.[22]

Initiatives in electoral politics accompanied other forms of popular mobilization. Voters in Terrebonne, Lafourche, and St. Mary parishes elected numerous African-American officials during Reconstruction, including more than a half-dozen representatives to the state legislature. Although some came from a pre-war group of property-owning free men of colour, others were former slaves who lived and worked for wages in the countryside. Among them were John J. Moore and Isaac Sutton, both rural labourers who represented St. Mary Parish. Oscar Crozier, a mulatto sugar planter, served as a member of the police jury (town council) and as president of the school board in Thibodaux. Thomas A. Cage, born a slave in Terrebonne Parish, became sheriff and chair of the Republican state central committee. William Murrell, Sr., a minister and editor, served in the legislature from Lafourche Parish.[23]

The possibility of open political organization among African Americans depended, of course, on Republican rule backed up by the presence of Federal troops in the state. As white resistance to radical Reconstruction gained in strength, white supremacist leagues, clubs, and 'rifle companies' proliferated, portraying themselves as the legitimate representatives of the people. The Republican leadership scrambled to assemble a countervailing force by building on the Federal authorization to form a state militia.[24] In New Orleans, former Confederate General James A. Longstreet, now a Republican and a proponent of peaceful reconciliation with the North, was named adjutant-general of the state in 1870, and commissioned brigadier-general in the state militia in January of 1872. The militia was a fragile organization, combining some largely black municipal police units with assorted white recruits, including some former Confederate soldiers willing to work with Longstreet.[25]

As the 1872 election approached, the contradictions of Republican rule in Louisiana became more glaring. Fewer than 500 Federal troops were present in the entire state, under the command of William H. Emory, who had his doubts about the whole enterprise. This force was altogether insufficient to prevent intimidation of Republican voters. Rivalry between the parties and among factions at the top was mirrored in struggles among different groups at the parish level. The outcome of the election for governor was itself contested, complete with two inaugurations of rival contenders.[26]

During the year that followed, the legitimacy of governor William Pitt Kellogg rested on the most fragile of underpinnings, and the results of local elections were by no means definitive. In Grant Parish, on the Red River, electoral conflict ended in a bloody massacre of Republican supporters by local vigilantes. In the heart of the bayou sugar country, Lafourche Parish, the main Democratic paper piously regretted the bloodshed, but issued its own warning to local African-American officials, specifically addressing William Murrell, Sr., legislator and Methodist Episcopal pastor in Thibodaux: 'We sincerely hope that Murrell who flourishes in the Bayonet Legislature under the familiar cognomen of the 'Wild Man of Lafourche' will take note of the way things are done when it comes to a question of races, and that he and his like will know one for all that when color is arrayed against color the whites must and shall rule in Louisiana'.[27]

In Lafourche Parish, a dispute flared over the results of the elections for Sheriff, Recorder, Clerk, and Parish Judge Rev. Murrell feared violence, particularly from a group of 'bulldozers' (vigilantes) who were rumoured to be on their way from Texas. A contingent of Metropolitan Police came out from New Orleans to keep the peace, and perhaps at the same time install the defeated Republican contenders, but they were greeted with scorn and more or less passive resistance by the town's white notables. Further sarcasm was heaped on Reverend Murrell by the *Thibodaux Sentinel*, which ridiculed his stovepipe hat and gold-headed cane, mocked the way he parted his hair, and accused him of cowardice. The vulnerability of African-American activists in such circumstances was obvious. In response to a request to guarantee Murrell's safety, the sheriff simply replied 'No. I can guarantee no man's lives; I can not stand watch over any man.' The Metropolitan Police nonetheless returned to New Orleans.[28]

The town of Thibodaux itself had become bitterly contested ground, with competing parties, public officials, and associations. The *Thibodaux Sentinel* reported scornfully in May of 1873 that there was a 'secret society' in town, to which only 'pure blooded radicals' and people of colour were admitted, and which was characterized by initiation rites of a 'pronounced indecency'.[29] Republicans, in turn, feared violence from groups like the White League or from 'bulldozers' who might invade the parish.

In March 1874 a schoolteacher from Thibodaux named Benjamin Lewis came forward to offer his services and those of more than 50 companions to the state militia, in order to defend Republican rule and black citizens in the Lafourche Parish area. He was named captain of Company C of the Sixth Regiment Infantry, to be assisted by First Lieutenant Anatole Panale and Second Lieutenant William Robinson. His unit was mustered in by Major General Longstreet, and issued Enfield rifles. Owing to the 'revolutionary condition of the country', they 'suspended their drill in the manual arms' for a time. But in July a second unit, led by Benjamin Peney of Terrebonne, was mustered in. The militia soon made their presence felt.[30] The hostile former chairman of the Democratic Party in Lafourche Parish, H.N. Michelet, characterized the militia as 'warriors' able to rally the support of their wives and sisters, whom he described as 'colored Amazons'. He reported that this company of 'negro Militia armed with state arms' had been drilling every Saturday evening on the commons in the town of Thibodaux.[31]

The militia led by Benjamin Lewis seems to have served as a kind of countervailing force to the civil authorities in matters of day-to-day administration of justice. One white local official, Major I. D. Moore, fumed that 'The mere arrest by a civil officer of a drunken negro in the town of Thibodaux is the tocsin that sounds to arms and summons these Valiant warriors to bold heroic deeds to wit the rescue from the officer of his prisoner and of the provoking of the turbulent mob to the very verge of riot, bloodshed and arson'.[32]

Until enlistment registers or payrolls for the Terrebonne and Lafourche militia are located, it will remain difficult to determine the social and racial composition of the group. A historian of Reconstruction-era militia writing 40 years ago observed dryly that 'there was a noticeable mixture of Negro and white troops in the Tennessee, Louisiana, and North Carolina companies. The militia was nevertheless considered a "Negro militia", in keeping with the longstanding Southern indifference to logic when considering questions involving race'.[33] In describing Benjamin Lewis as 'of mixed negro and Indian blood, the Indian in him clearly predominating', and then characterizing his force as a 'Negro militia', Michelet was following the same reasoning. For him, this was a 'Negro militia' in part because most of its members were believed to be of African descent, but also because the rhetoric of white supremacy required that racial categories be clear and dichotomous.

The manuscript census of 1870 provides a glimpse of Benjamin Lewis, and hints at the networks he may have mobilized in order to form and sustain the armed unit Major Moore mocked as 'Valiant warriors'. July 1870 found Benjamin Lewis in Lafourche parish's Third Ward, near the railroad and sugar town of Raceland, a short distance along the bayou from Thibodaux. His was a remarkably diverse and complex household. The first inhabitant of the dwelling was William E. Kerr, age 37, white, born in Connecticut, who listed his occupation as retired United States soldier. Next was listed Tench Goodly, age 22, a black boatman born in Louisiana. Then came Taylor and Mary Nelson, he a black farm labourer born in Mississippi, she a black woman born in Louisiana, now occupied in 'keeping house'. Last was Benjamin Lewis himself, age 31, mulatto, a schoolteacher born in the state of Maine.[34]

With a little imagination, one can envision the links to different segments of the community that each member of this household may have provided. Tench Goodly would have travelled by boat up and down the bayou in the course of his work. Taylor Nelson may have laboured on several nearby plantations, and seems later to have become a member of the Republican Party executive committee in Thibodaux. Mary Nelson probably kept in touch with neighbours in the Third Ward, and travelled to Thibodaux for events of various kinds. William Kerr, meanwhile, remains a mysterious figure. 'Retired U.S. soldier' was not a conventional occupational description; perhaps he was injured in the war and no longer worked. Perhaps, but the evidence is silent on this question, he and Benjamin Lewis had both served in the invading Union forces.

Benjamin Lewis himself taught school a little further along the bayou, in the Second Ward of Terrebonne Parish. In 1872 he shared responsibility for 116 schoolchildren with Mary Ann Clay, and earned about $55 a month. His supervisor in 1875 judged him a 'faithful, hard working teacher' and termed his school (the Nichols School) 'among the best in the parish'.[35] It is not certain whether Captain Benjamin Lewis actively collaborated with the white-haired Reverend William Murrell, the young carrier of the Enfield rifle with the older carrier of the gold-headed cane, but they very likely knew each other, for Murrell served on the school board of Thibodaux, and had probably noticed the conscientious teacher in neighbouring Terrebonne even before Lewis came forward to form a militia.[36] During the 1870s their interests converged, as both sought to sustain the Republican rule that underlay their freedom of action.

Benjamin Lewis seems to have moved easily from the sphere of education to that of armed defence to that of electoral activism. In October of 1874 he stepped in as a substitute police juror in the Terrebonne Parish seat of Houma, just in time to help designate the polling places for the November election. (He himself would serve as commissioner of election at Poll #2, at the Lejeune Store on the old Beattie Place in upper Terrebonne.) Lewis thus joined that year as Terrebonne Parish police juror and election commissioner with W.H. Keys and Alfred Kennedy, African-American officials who had been denounced a few months earlier as inciters and supporters of the January 1874 strike of Terrebonne sugar workers. Keys was accused by the *Daily Picayune* of having called upon workers to seize the land and prevent strike-breakers from working; Kennedy was said to have headed an armed group of 50 who came down the bayou to stop work at Southdown Plantation.[37]

Benjamin Lewis's militia was a visible public presence in Lafourche Parish over the next two years. During the local elections of 1876, they intervened at one polling place as rival groups struggled for physical possession of the ballot boxes. A great deal was at stake in that election, and destroying the 'Negro militia' would be a high priority of local Democrats if they won. Indeed, the Democratic leader H. N. Michelet recalled that a group of Democratic supporters, most of them Confederate veterans, had been armed and eager to sweep away this group of 'vandals'. The 'gray heads' among the Democrats, he recalled, had with difficulty restrained the young, in the interests of adding the parish's vote for the Democrat Francis T. Nicholls to the state-wide total rather than risking the annulment of the vote.[38]

Out of that election, of course, came the famed Hayes–Tilden dispute at the national level, and eventually the installation of the Democratic Government of Nicholls at the state level.[39] Once in power, the Democrats moved quickly against Lewis's militia, declaring their terms expired. But Oscar Crozier, the African-American sugar planter who still held the office of tax collector, intervened with Governor Nicholls, and temporarily stalled the disbanding. Those connected with the militia held on to a certain public presence: Anatole Panale, who had served with Benjamin Lewis, remained on the school board in April of 1877, and in May the militia were said to be vocally involved in a court case bearing on the election for police jurors. Angry Democrats recalled that the militia's weapons were never turned in, and they believed that the militia members, with their guns, eventually 'scattered over the state'.[40]

Benjamin Lewis, at least, had not scattered anywhere. In 1880 the census recorded him as living in the First Ward of Terrebonne Parish. Married and the father of two children, he still listed his occupation as schoolteacher. The neighbourhood was similar to the one near Raceland where he had lived as a single man a decade earlier: large numbers of black and mulatto labourers lived alongside a smaller number of white farmers and labourers, and near a boarding house filled with black railway workers from Virginia, Mississippi, Tennessee, Alabama, and Maryland.[41]

Although 1876–77 marked the dramatic formal end to Reconstruction, streams of activism nonetheless continued over the next decade through narrowed channels. Black militia members could no longer parade with fife and drum in the streets of Thibodaux. A new, and presumptively white, militia had been organized under the command of Brigadier General John S. Billiu of Thibodaux.[42] The exercise of open political voice by black Republicans had become significantly more difficult, though a white Republican planter, Taylor Beattie, still held the office of district judge.

On occasion, however, black residents of the sugar parishes openly asserted their right to occupy the formal public spaces of town. In July of 1887, for example, the Vigilance Fire Company and Pride of Iberia Hook and Ladder Company arrived in Thibodaux from New Iberia with 'over five hundred excursionists'. The firemen formed in line at the depot, marched through the principal streets and then 'repaired to Eureka hall, where dancing was indulged in to a late hour'. It was reported that before leaving the firemen 'proceeded in a body to serenade the mayor, but the gentleman was either absent or did not want to receive *negro serenaders*'.[43]

The white elite did not soon forget what they sometimes termed 'Benjamin's militia'. An article in the Thibodaux papers in 1887 recalled the way in which the men and women who followed Benjamin Lewis had come to town from out in the country to dispute possession of the ballot box in 1876.[44] Although in the intervening years African Americans marched in town as members of fire companies rather than militia, activists continued to move back and forth between the plantations and the parish seat. Though they had to contend with an increasingly conservative leadership in the Republican party and with the renewed power of the Democrats, it seems likely that they too carried a memory – albeit a different one – of the sight of the 'Negro militia' drilling in front of the courthouse. Junius Bailey, for example, was a teenager at the time that the Lewis and Peney militias were active in Lafourche and Terrebonne parishes. Born a slave in Assumption Parish in 1857, he was part of a post-war generation of African-American children able to attend public schools. He trained as a schoolteacher, attended Leyland University, and then entered Republican politics in the unpropitious year of 1878, running for sheriff in Lafourche Parish in 1884. He became a member of the black Masonic lodge in Thibodaux and served as a teacher, probably on the Laurel Valley Plantation several miles outside of town. He seems to have moved around very widely, acquiring training in New Orleans, and taking up teaching positions in a variety of places. In 1887 he would emerge as a leader of the Knights of Labor in Lafourche Parish and a participant in the November sugar strike.[45]

The Geography of the Sugar Bowl

For Benjamin Lewis, as he moved back and forth from Raceland to Thibodaux to Houma to rural Terrebonne Parish, and for Alfred Kennedy, the police juror who accompanied 50 men down the bayou to the Minor plantation in support of the 1874 strike, physical mobility and political mobilization were intimately linked.[46] In seeking the roots of the bold actions of 1887 it may therefore be helpful to look briefly at the physical and social geography of the bayou sugar country.

The characteristic shape of a Louisiana sugar plantation is significantly different from the sugar estates of Cuba or Brazil. Louisiana's sugar plantations extended like ribbons along the rivers and bayous of the southern part of the state, each stretching back from a specified number of arpents of land along the waterfront. The depth of a sugar property, from the levee to the farthest reach of the plantation, was usually limited by ecological constraints: as the land slopes back from the levee, it eventually becomes too low to be drained and planted in sugar. The layout of the Laurel Valley plantation in Lafourche Parish provides a good example. Still a working plantation, it has narrow frontage along Bayou Lafourche, and then a deep rectangle of land extending back along a sandy ridge as far as the swamps.[47]

This layout helped to shape social life. The levees along the river and the bayous constituted thoroughfares that joined estates to each other and all of them to the nearby towns, permitting workers to travel by boat or on foot to and from the plantations. Already in the early months after the fall of New Orleans during the Civil War, word of the possibility of freedom had spread quickly along the Mississippi river, and triggered the flight of slaves by boat to Union lines downriver. Bayou Lafourche played a similar role as an axis of communication, though on a smaller scale: It is not surprising that a classic view of nineteenth-century Thibodaux shows a boatman in the foreground on the Laurel Valley and Rienzi Plantation side of Bayou Lafourche, with the town arrayed across the bayou.[48]

At the back of most plantations lay the swamplands. The swamps were a buffer and a resource, a point of intersection between the labouring world of the plantation and the world of moss-gatherers and woodcutters, often Acadian, who had long inhabited the land unsuitable for cane. Within these swamps lay the *brulées*, burned-over ridges that were the characteristic refuge of poorer Acadians and Canary Islanders.[49] Octave Johnson, the cooper from St. James Parish, recalled that during the war he and a group of 30 runaways had survived for months in the swamps four miles to the rear of the plantation house, relying on a fragile set of exchanges with those still enslaved.[50]

The built environment of the plantation itself had a characteristic form. The 'quarters' were generally facing rows of cabins, sometimes double cabins with central chimneys, each with a gallery in front. Life on those front porches has been memorably portrayed in the fiction of Ernest Gaines, and is revealed as well in the court records of the Parish of Lafourche. On the galleries took place everything from a dispute between neighbours over the loan of a frying pan, to tense discussions about debts and wages paid. However impoverished, sugar workers' dwellings had little of the isolation of a single sharecropper's or tenant's cabin in the cotton parishes, and the already lively world of the quarters became even busier with the arrival of migrant workers for the harvest.[51]

Beyond the quarters were the canefields themselves, reached on foot or on horseback, at times through a sea of mud. In the 1870s and 1880s one could still on some estates find provision grounds and kitchen gardens where the workers grew potatoes, corn, and vegetables. On others, barracks-like dwellings for migrant workers and a company store, combined with an immense mill, gave the plantation something of the feel of a 'factory in the field'.[52]

A dominant feature throughout was collective life and group activity. This was the ironic concomitant of planters' efforts to retain gang labour and exert full control. Moreover, continuity of residence in the quarters had not brought the docility and isolation from the world beyond the plantation that planters hoped to instil in their workers. Schoolteachers, migrant workers, mechanics, and blacksmiths came onto the plantation; women on their way to market, folks looking for a new job, and members of assorted organizations still went to town.

One of the many contested moments of the November 1876 election highlights the links between electoral politics and the interior world of the sugar plantation. The Republican supervisor of elections in Lafourche, Marcelin Ledet, initially announced that several of the polling booths were to be located within plantation boundaries. White Democrats were furious at this assumption of the power 'to go into men's plantations and to establish polls in or about sugar houses, most of which were at work'. The local Democratic paper reported that 'determined opposition' brought 'these usurpers to terms and to a little common sense in 24 hours after the notice had been published'. Under duress, Ledet seems to have acceded to announcing that the polling place would be a warehouse on the public road that fronted the R.H. Allen Plantation, a mile and a half from the quarters. At 3 a.m. on 7 November, however, the poll was apparently opened inside the sugarhouse, whereupon 'eighty-six negroes ... voted the Republican ticket', choosing the Republican state senatorial candidate and former slave Thomas A. Cage over the Democratic candidate, Isaiah D. Moore, Esq.[53]

The image of this early-morning gathering is a telling one. In this, the last election in which African-American voters in Louisiana would have any hope of voting freely for many years to come, collective action in the sugarhouse was the final line of electoral defence. To retain the ability to vote, sugar workers had to exercise solidarity and perhaps a degree of stealth. Democrats, with their own long history of attempting to monopolize ballot boxes, quickly cried foul and labelled the election of Thomas Cage fraudulent.

The 1887 Strikes

With these images and antecedents in mind, one can return to the year 1887. But this time it may be best to begin at the start of the year rather than focus immediately on the huge strike of November. Knights of Labor organizers had begun to move into the sugar regions in late 1886, though they may or may not have been the instigators of the first work stoppages. They were particularly active in the towns in St. Mary Parish, which came to hold twelve local assemblies of the Knights. Their members included farm hands, labourers, railroad employees, clothing workers, and building trade's workers; white and black, men and women.[54]

In the adjacent parish of Lafourche, court records show that already on 19 January 17 black men were apparently trying to halt work on the Mary Plantation. Jordan Brannon, Briscoe Wheeler, Johnny Phillips, William Pearson, Peter Young and James Lagarde were charged with unlawful disturbance and riotous assembly. In that same month, Clay Williams, Adam Elles and Israel Lucust were charged with trespassing on the Upper Ten Plantation, while Numa Gautreaux was charged with trespass on the plantation of Delphin Babin. In the case of Adam Elles, the charge was more specific: he was said to have prevented one Nelson Christian from working on the plantation.[55]

Testimony in the cases of Peter Young and Amos Johnson casts a bit more light on these events. Mary Plantation covered 1800 acres of land valued at $20,000.[56] The owner, Richard Foret, recalled that on 19 January 1887 he had come up from his estate to the town of Raceland to take 'the cars' to Thibodaux to do some business: 'On my way I met a crowd of colored men going down the bayou on the levee ... When I got to the depot Mr Sevin told me the crowd were going down to stop my hands from working ... as a matter of fact my hands stopped working at 12 M that day.' The clerk from Raceland whom Foret sent down to warn the overseer of the impending arrival of 'strikers' recalled, 'I told the boys on Mary Plantation to keep on working but they said no the men who had been there had said if they didn't stop they would come back and run them out of the field'. A resident of Mary Plantation, Lewis Anderson, recalled that the crowd of strikers had specified that they would not work for 60 cents a day, and that 'the Foret hands agreed at once to stop. They didn't make any threats they didn't have time to make any threats because the others were willing to stop.' The testimony of Wiley Jackson in the case of Peter Young conveys something of the atmosphere on the levee at Raceland that morning, as folks milled around and waited to see what would happen: 'All I know when the crowd went down Peter Young was on the levee and when they came back Peter Young was there yet. He didn't go down. I stayed around there, on the levee at the store, sometimes at the depot and down at the little boat.'[57] One has a sense here of the levee as the site of a tense political promenade with participants, spectators, surrogates and bystanders involved in a debate on the question of whether a man or a woman should work in the fields for 60 cents a day. (Indeed, even those 60 cents often came in the form of a credit slip at the company store.) Although individual workers may have had prior contact with Knights of Labor organizers, their strike actions seem not to have been formally called by the Knights.

By late October 1887 much of the sense of improvisation was gone. District Assembly 194 of the Knights of Labor met in Morgan City in St. Mary Parish on 19 October to try to set a rate of wages for sugar workers in St. Mary, Terrebonne, Lafourche, Iberia, and St. Martin parishes, together accounting for a large percentage of the state's sugar output. The demands were by now familiar: better wages, no payment in scrip, extra pay for night watches. The call from Morgan City was followed in Lafourche by a letter to sugar planters, reiterating the demands, signed by J.H. Bailey, president of the joint local executive board, Knights of Labor, and several others. An experienced schoolteacher, Junius Bailey took a courteous but forceful tone: 'should this demand be considered exorbitant by the sugar planters ... we ask them to submit such information with reason therewith to this board not later than Saturday, Oct. 29 inst. or appoint a special committee to confer with this board on said date'.[58]

Planters refused to negotiate, one noting smugly that 'it is impossible for the negroes to succeed in a strike for the reason that they are dependent on the planters for their living'. Work stopped on 1 November, and on 2 November the press in New Orleans estimated the number of strikers at 10,000. Militia were promptly deployed to the region. The *Daily Picayune* noted uneasily that 'the negroes generally are stubborn and disposed to stand their ground'.[59] As in earlier years, the links between town and country were crucial. The commander of the militia reported on the movement of workers back and forth to town, though he tended to interpret it as aimless: 'I noticed at Schreiver a very large body of negroes lounging around the depot, and at Thibodeaux, the streets were full of them. They would leave the surrounding plantations and walk into the towns, where they would loiter all day and return to their cabins on the farms at night.'[60]

To intimidate strikers and make room for strike-breakers, planters and the militia evicted families of workers from the quarters. Belongings were soon 'scattered along the bayou on the public road', outside the boundary of the plantation.[61] The local press reported during November on the exodus from the plantations to the town of Thibodaux, 'Every vacant room in town tonight is filled with families of penniless and ragged negroes. All day long a long stream of black humanity poured in ... bringing all their earthly possessions, which never amounted to more than a frontyard full of babies, dogs, and ragged bedclothing.'[62] Conflict flared on plantations in Lafourche Parish, and Richard Foret was said to have been wounded on 4 November by 'a negro striker' named Moses Pugh. According to press reports, when a deputy sheriff attempted to arrest Pugh 'about 150 negroes surrounded the murderer and defied the authorities'. The deputy sheriff returned with a detail of militia and completed the arrest. Foret turned out to be only slightly injured.[63]

Although the plantations were the scenes of scattered violence during the strike, it was in Thibodaux that the defining moment took shape. As in the days of the 1874 drills by Benjamin Lewis's militia, black men and women had come to Thibodaux from the surrounding countryside, but this time they came as evicted strikers. A Gatling gun now stood on the steps of the courthouse, deployed by the all-white militia under the command of a brigadier general from New Orleans. It was never fired, however. Instead, Brigadier General Pierce declared on November 20 that the major estates were back at work, and the militia no longer needed. He withdrew all but one of his units, a crew from Shreveport who had been dismissed but had not yet headed home. Pierce had earlier noted that the Shreveport militia was not in uniform, and that their officer had experienced difficulty 'preventing a collision between his men and the strikers'.[64]

That Sunday, 20 November, a meeting of Thibodaux's 'best citizens irrespective of trade' formed a Peace and Order committee and, with the assistance of local townspeople and perhaps the Shreveport militia, established pickets around the town of Thibodaux to prevent the entry or departure of any black men or women. Mary Pugh, the widow of a wealthy Democratic planter, later recounted events from her vantage point in town. Her sons, back at home, had been devoting themselves to pouring lead into moulds to make bullets. Early Wednesday morning someone fired at one of the pickets, she reported, and 'the ball began'. The scene was stark: 'they began then hunting up the [strike] leaders and every one that was found or any suspicious character was shot. Before Allen got back the rifles on St. Charles Street sounded like a battle.' She witnessed the capture of one hidden striker: 'they brought them by our side gate. I thought [they] were taking them to jail instead they walked with one over to the lumber yard where they told him to 'run for his life' [and] gave the order to fire. All raised their rifles and shot him dead. This was the worst sight I saw but I tell you we have had a horrible three days & Wednesday excelled any thing I ever saw even during the war.'[65]

Shooting seems to have gone on for hours. There is no way to estimate accurately the number of deaths. Officially, eight or nine people were killed. Mary Pugh herself dismissed the newspaper reports and guessed that fifty black people had died. Many more may have been injured.[66] Covington Hall, whose uncle lived nearby, recalled that 'Newly made graves were reported found in the woods around Thibodaux for weeks afterward', and the body of a dead man appeared in the yard of his uncle's place two miles south of Thibodaux.[67] The strike ended; many Knights of Labor organizers fled the region; and the harvest was brought in. Mary Pugh reflected on the events she had seen, and framed them not in terms of wages or labour, but in a language of race war and political dominion: 'I am sick with the horror of it. but I know it had to be else we would all have been murdered before a great while. I think this will settle the question of who is to rule the nigger or the white man? for the next 50 years but it has been *well done* & I hope all trouble is ended. The niggers are as humble as pie today. Very different from last week.'[68]

Conclusion

This examination of social geography, mobilization, and repression suggests several observations about the dimensions of freedom and the exercise of political voice in the Louisiana sugar parishes. The first rests on a renewed appreciation of the role of militia in Reconstruction and post-Reconstruction collective action. The presence of a visible and active militia led by men of colour in Lafourche and Terrebonne Parishes challenged the very structure of white domination – including the monopoly of access to the public space in front of the courthouse, and of the right to bear arms. For at least three years, the exercise of political voice at the ballot box by former slaves was accompanied by public displays of solidarity encompassing women as well as men. Sugar workers in town on the weekends in the early 1870s are unlikely to have forgotten the sight of Company C drilling in front of the courthouse. Some may also have attended Lewis's well-run school in the Second Ward in Terrebonne, or voted at the polling places where he served as commissioner. By 1887, however, militia service was again monopolized by those who counted themselves white. Indeed, 20 members of the local assemblies of the Knights of Labor in Morgan City also served in the now all-white local militia, fracturing cross-racial solidarity within the Knights as the conflict escalated.[69] The presence in Thibodaux of the restless Shreveport militia seems to have hastened the onset of direct repression, in which several different groups of white citizens then participated.

The second observation emerges from the examination of court records and the geography of the region. The spatial organization of the world of cane initially facilitated the mobilization of sugar workers, but later made efficient repression possible. Work stoppages were built and spread by flying squadrons of labourers moving along the bayou on the levee, on foot or on horseback, armed or just assertive in their numbers. If they were arrested for riotous assembly and arraigned at the courthouse in Houma or Thibodaux, their allies in town could in some instances post bond. Even a decade after the formal end of Reconstruction there were still black Masons, schoolteachers, and former officeholders active in town and able to lend a hand.[70] But once planters, both high-tariff Republicans and White-Line Democrats, were faced with a full-scale strike and evidence of collective determination among strikers' families, they closed ranks, spread rumours of violence, and set out to control the key spaces. The state militia took control of the railway line, and made its way up and down the levee, moving into the quarters, evicting strikers and their families from their cabins. Workers took the familiar roads to Thibodaux, but the town that had earlier served as a refuge and source of alliances had now became a dangerous cul-de-sac. When the white vigilante forces circled the town of Thibodaux they boxed in the evicted strikers, and by the time the rifles began firing on St. Charles Street, there was nowhere to go.

In retrospect, the risks taken by the strikers seem immense, and the weight of the repression that fell upon them seems foreseeable. At the time, however, the prior experiences of public mobilization of black men and women in conjunction with Lewis's and Peney's militia were still relatively near at hand. The power of collective work stoppages in an industry entirely dependent on wage labour had been tested in wildcat strikes, and might be expected to exact concessions from planters on the eve of the harvest, as deadly frosts approached. It was just barely possible to imagine collective action that would challenge both the hegemony of planters and the suffocating consequences of the White Line strategy of intimidation in electoral politics.[71]

The elite of Lafourche Parish was taken aback by the magnitude of the strike, and by the inability of the militia to bring it to an end. The *Thibodaux Sentinel* had in the past amused its readers with stories of streetcorner quarrels in which 'the colored people took to flight at the sight of a drawn pistol'.[72] Now the newspaper had to acknowledge a situation in which intimidation seemed not to be working. William Murrell, Jr., an African-American legislator from the more northerly cotton parish of Madison, had some years earlier recounted to a Congressional Committee the antecedents of the arrival in his parish of vigilante groups of white 'bulldozers': 'whenever these men got ready to come you can always tell – they put out what we call "a feeler"; the white people began to talk this way; they say "The negroes are going to burn the white folks' gin-houses; a massacre will come; the negroes are getting ready to burn our gin-houses". And wherever you hear that kind of talk our people understand and know very well that they are fixing to come.'[73] It was precisely such predictions of black violence that signalled the imminence of white violence in Thibodaux, as the Peace and Order Committee circled the town. The *Thibodaux Sentinel* claimed in retrospect that 'The negroes were in motion and rumors of contemplated violence on their part multiplied faster than mosquitoes on a sultry summer day. Their women boasted that they were ready to fire the town.'[74]

Once the repression began, the goals of planters and the vigilante units seem to have gone far beyond breaking the last of the strike and intimidating the Knights of Labor. They sought to force on both black workers and labour organizers an attitude of 'humility', by which they hoped to stop further mobilization, while creating the illusion that former slaves and their descendants were willing to accept a definition of freedom that declared them subordinated wage labourers, not citizens entitled to engage in collective action. But this exemplary violence was so stark, and contained so much of what Mary Pugh herself called 'horror', that it could in the end be spoken of only in private.

Just a few days after the killings, a letter to the French-language pages of the Thibodaux *Sentinel* reflected on the events and remarked that 'mieux vaut pour tous déchirer cette page de notre histoire que de chercher à l'expliquer' ('Better for all concerned that this page be torn out of our history rather than try to explain it.').[75] White citizens in Louisiana nearly succeeded in silencing the events that could easily have been called the 'Thibodaux massacre'. Evidence that would permit an accurate reconstruction of the dimensions of the killing does seem now to be beyond reach. But the events that preceded it can be reconstructed. Cane workers and their families, strikers and their allies left significant traces in the court records, on the land, and in a variety of manuscript documents. The story of their actions, in the end, is a page that was not successfully torn out from Louisiana's history.

Though Louisiana's white elite preferred to trace Redemption to the glorious 'Battle' of Canal Street initiated by the White League in New Orleans in 1874, and to the withdrawal of federal troops in 1877, it may be that for the sugar parishes the denouement came only with the massacre in Thibodaux more than a decade later. By extending our focus, then, to encompass the entire period between Union occupation in 1862–63 and the events in the sugar parishes in 1887, we can begin to see the dynamics of a quarter century of mobilization among workers in the bayou country, encompassing multiple and repeated assertions by a people 'stubborn and disposed to hold their ground'.

NOTES

I would like to express my gratitude to Larry Powell for his many insights and continuing encouragement, and to Aims McGuinness and Paul Eiss for their valuable and imaginative research assistance and editorial advice. I am also indebted to Elsa Barkely Brown, Richard Cándida Smith, Sueann Caulfield, Michael Foret, Sylvia Frey, Eric Foner, Jeffrey Gould, Robin

Kelley, Paul Leslie, Joe Logsdon, Leslie Parr, Rick Pildes, Peter Railton, Joseph Reidy, John Shy, J. Mills Thornton and Dan Usner for their generosity and counsel. I thank the staff of the Louisiana and Lower Mississippi Valley Collections at Louisiana State University, Baton Rouge; of the Library at Jackson Barracks, New Orleans; and of the office of the Clerk of the Court, Parish of Terrebonne, in Houma. I also appreciate the assistance of Barbara Lee at the Office of the Clerk of the Court, Parish of Lafourche, in Thibodaux; of Carol Matthias, Emily Pitre, and Clifford Theriot of the Allen J. Ellender Archives, Ellender Memorial Library, Nicholls State University, Thibodaux, Louisiana; of Judy Smith at the Louisiana State Library in Baton Rouge; and of Wayne Everard at the New Orleans Public Library.

1. *Report of Brig.-Gen. William Pierce Commanding State Troops in the Field in District from Berwick's Bay to New Orleans to General G. T. Beauregard, Adjutant General of the State of Louisiana. November 28th, 1887* (Baton Rouge, Louisiana, Leon Jastremski, State Printer, 1887), p.11.
2. Various primary sources on the strike are cited below. The best published secondary accounts are Jeffrey Gould, 'The Strike of 1887: Louisiana Sugar War', *Southern Exposure*, Vol.12 (November–December 1984), pp.45–55, and William Ivy Hair, *Bourbonism and Agrarian Protest: Louisiana Politics, 1877–1900* (Baton Rouge: LSU Press, 1969), Ch.8.
3. See Melton Alonza McLaurin, *The Knights of Labor in the South* (Westport, CT, Greenwood Press, 1978), pp.74–6, 131–48.
4. Gould, 'The Strike of 1887'.
5. Hair, *Bourbonism and Agrarian Protest*, Ch.8. On 'silk-stocking vigilantism', see the essay by Lawrence Powell in this volume. The Louisiana experience can also be examined in the context of other post-emancipation societies. For some thoughts in this direction, see Frederick Cooper, Thomas Holt and Rebecca Scott, *Beyond Slavery: Explorations on Race, Labor, and Citizenship* (University of North Carolina Press, forthcoming).
6. See Paul K. Eiss, 'A Share in the Land. The Production of Politics on Government Plantations, Terrebonne and Lafourche Parishes, Louisiana, 1863–1865', *Slavery and Abolition*, Vol.19, No.1 (April 1998).
7. See George S. Denison to Hon. S.P. Chase, 23 Oct. 1863, and other wartime reports reproduced in Ira Berlin, Thavolia Glymph, Steven J. Miller, Joseph P. Reidy, Leslie S. Rowland, and Julie Saville, *Freedom: A Documentary History of Emancipation, 1861–1867*, Series I, Vol. III, *The Wartime Genesis of Free Labor: The Lower South* (Cambridge, Cambridge University Press, 1990), pp.471–3.
8. Evidence on these arrangements comes from Records of the Assistant Commissioner, Louisiana, RG 105, Records of the Bureau of Refugees, Freedmen, and Abandoned Lands, reproduced in U. S. National Archives Microfilm Publication M1027 (hereafter M1027). On Orange Grove, see Monthly Report of 1st Lieut. J.S. Wadsworth, Asst. Inspr. Freedmen, for the Parish of Terrebonne, for the month ending 30 April 1866, M1027, Reel 28; and Monthly Report of George A. Ludlow, Asst. Inspr. Freedmen, for the Parish of Terrebonne, La., for the Month ending 31 July 1866, M1027, Reel 29. On a few estates in Lafourche Parish freedpeople still worked under rental arrangements and grew corn rather than sugar in 1868. See Monthly Report of John. H. Van Antwerp, Asst. Insp.Freedmen, Parish of Lafourche, La., for the month ending 30 September 1868, M1027, Reel 31.
9. On the reluctance to lease, see Monthly Report of Capt. C.E. Wilcox, Asst. Inspr. Freedmen, Parish of Lafourche, La., for the month ending 31 January 1866; and Hqtrs BRFAL, State of Louisiana, Inspection Report for Jan., Feb., March, 1866, both in M1027, Reel 28.
10. Wm. Dougherty, Provost Marshal and Asst. Inspt. of Freedmen, Inspection Report of Plantations, freedmen, &c. in the parishes Jefferson and Orleans, Right Bank, January 1866, M1027, Roll 28.
11. See Henry S. Wadsworth to Col. J.I. Grigg, Inspector General, 31 January 1866, in M1027, Reel 28.
12. See Monthly Report of Wm. Woods for the Parish of Terrebonne, La., for the month ending 30 April 1868. M1027, Reel 30.
13. The predominance of black and mulatto workers among plantation laborers in Terrebonne

Parish can be seen in the manuscript schedules of the 1870 census.

14. Noel Deerr, *The History of Sugar* (London, Chapman and Hall, 1949), Vol.1, p.250.

15. The events in Terrebonne can be followed in the *Daily Picayune* (New Orleans), 14 January to 20 January, 1874. John Rodrigue, in 'Raising Cane: From Slavery to Free Labor in Louisiana's Sugar Parishes, 1862–1880' (PhD, Emory University, 1993), sees the demand for leaseholds as a desperate response to falling wages (chap.5). Paul K. Eiss, in 'A Share in the Land', sees it as a continuation of the spirit of the labour companies.

16. See 'Our Future', *The Weekly Thibodaux Sentinel*, 14 February 1874.

17. See Ralph Shlomowitz, '"Bound" or "Free"? Black Labor in Cotton and Sugarcane Farming, 1865–1880', *The Journal of Southern History*, Vol.50 (November 1984), pp.569–96; John Rodrigue, 'Raising Cane', pp.504–32. In the summer of 1887 a labourer in Lafourche Parish might expect to earn 60 or 65 cents a day cultivating cane. See *The Weekly Pelican* (New Orleans) 13 August 1887, and the discussion of the strike below.

18. Rodrigue, 'Raising Cane', pp.551–2.

19. On Union recruiting in Southern Louisiana, see Ira Berlin, Joseph P. Reidy and Leslie S. Rowland (eds.), *Freedom. A Documentary History of Emancipation, 1861–1867*, Series II, *The Black Military Experience* (Cambridge, Cambridge University Press, 1982), pp.116–22. The testimony of Octave Johnson appears in Ira Berlin, Barbara J. Fields, Thavolia Glymph, Joseph P. Reidy and Leslie Rowland (eds.), *Freedom. A Documentary History of Emancipation*, Series I, Vol. I, *The Destruction of Slavery* (Cambridge, Cambridge University Press, 1985), p.217. See also James G. Hollandsworth, Jr., *The Louisiana Native Guards: The Black Military Experience during the Civil War* (Baton Rouge, Louisiana State University Press, 1995).

20. On the number of federal soldiers in Louisiana, see Joseph G. Dawson III, *Army Generals and Reconstruction: Louisiana, 1862–1877* (Baton Rouge, Louisiana State University Press, 1982), Appendix III.21. Wm. Dougherty, Provost Marshal and Asst. Inspt. of Freedmen, Inspection Report of Plantations, freedmen, &c. in the parishes Jefferson and Orleans, Right Bank, January 1866, in USNA, M1027, Roll 28.

22. Evidence on St. Mary comes from John J. Moore, in House Misc. Doc. No. 154, 41st Cong., 2nd Sess., 'Testimony taken by the Sub-Committee of Elections in Louisiana', [1870], pp.634–42. Moore described himself as 'a radical republican, as near as I can come at it'. His testimony is also cited and discussed in Nell Irwin Painter, *Exodusters: Black Migration to Kansas after Reconstruction* (New York, Alfred A. Knopf, 1977), p.11. For a brilliant discussion of comparable grassroots mobilization in South Carolina, see Julie Saville, *The Work of Reconstruction: From Slave to Wage Laborer in South Carolina, 1860–1870* (New York, Cambridge University Press, 1994), Ch.5. See also Michael W. Fitzgerald, *The Union League Movement in the Deep South: Politics and Agricultural Change During Reconstruction* (Baton Rouge, Louisiana State University Press, 1989), pp.32, 238.

23. See the entries for Thomas Cage, Ulgar Dupart, William H. Keyes, Frederick Marie, and Frederick R. Wright of Terrebonne Parish; Arthur Antoine, John B. Esnard, John J. Moore, and Isaac Sutton, of St. Mary Parish; and Oscar Crozier, William Murrell, and John Nelson of Lafourche Parish, in Eric Foner, *Freedom's Lawmakers: A Directory of Black Officeholders during Reconstruction* (New York, Oxford University Press, 1993). See also Charles Vincent, *Black Legislators in Louisiana during Reconstruction* (Baton Rouge, Louisiana State University Press, 1976).

24. On black militia in Louisiana, which dated back to 1870, see Otis Singletary, *Negro Militia and Reconstruction* (Austin, University of Texas Press, 1957), pp.13–14, 66–80. Singletary is mistaken in his view that African American militia activity in Louisiana was confined to New Orleans 'and never spread to the provinces' (p.80).

25. See William Garrett Piston, *Lee's Tarnished Lieutenant: James Longstreet and his Place in Southern History* (Athens, University of Georgia Press, 1987), p.120.

26. See Ted Tunnell, *Crucible of Reconstruction: War, Radicalism and Race in Louisiana, 1862–1877* (Baton Rouge, Louisiana State University Press, 1984), pp.151–72; Dawson, *Army Generals*, Ch.6 and 7; and Joe Gray Taylor, *Louisiana Reconstructed, 1863–1877* (Baton Rouge, Louisiana State University Press, 1974).

27. 'The Fight in Grant Parish', *Weekly Thibodaux Sentinel*, 19 April 1873.

28. 'Usurpation on the Rampage!!!', *Weekly Thibodaux Sentinel*, 24 May 1873.

29. 'La Ville et la Campagne', *Weekly Thibodaux Sentinel* (French section), 31 May 1873.

30. Peney was assisted by First Lieutenant James Madison and Second Lieutenant Scott Brown. See *Annual Report of the Adjutant General of the State of Louisiana For the Year ending December 31st, 1874* (New Orleans, The Republican Office, 1875), pp.24, 27, and 47 of the WPA typescript of this document, held at the Library, Jackson Barracks, Louisiana.

31. See *The Times Democrat* (New Orleans), 3 October 1887, transcribed in *Historical Military Data on Louisiana Militia July –Dec. 31, 1878*, Library, Jackson Barracks, New Orleans.

32. Ibid.

33. Singletary, *Negro Militia*, p.15.

34. See Vol.7, Louisiana, Ninth Census of the United States, 1870. Benjamin Lewis appears in household number 135, Third Ward, Parish of Lafourche, Post Office: Raceland. (These schedules are reproduced on Roll 516, U.S. National Archives Microfilm Publication 593.)

35. The supervisor's judgment appears in *Annual Report of the State Superintendent of Public Education, William G. Brown, to the General Assembly of Louisiana for the Year 1875* (New Orleans, The Republican, 1876), p.262. In the 1871 report, Lewis appears as a teacher in the Second Ward of Terrebonne Parish, along with Charles Preston and Mary A. Clay. In the 1872 report, 75 male and 41 female children were said to be enrolled in the Second Ward school, where they were taught by Benj. H. Lewis and Mary Ann Clay. See *Annual Report of the State Superintendent of Public Education, Thomas Conway, to the General Assembly of Louisiana, for the Year 1871* (New Orleans, The Republican, 1872), and Annual *Report of the State Superintendent of Public Education, William G. Brown, to the General Assembly of Louisiana, for the Year 1872* (New Orleans, The Republican, 1873).

36. William Murrell was President of the School Board in Thibodaux, commissioned in April of 1873, and Nelson Taylor was a member for Lafourche. See *Annual Report of the State Superintendent of Public Education, William G. Brown, to the General Assembly of Louisiana for the Year 1873* (New Orleans, The Republican, 1874).

37. See the W.P.A. transcriptions of the Policy Jury Minutes for Terrebonne Parish, 1868–1882 and 1882–1894, Box 183, Louisiana and Lower Mississippi Valley Collections, Louisiana State University, Baton Rouge (hereafter LLMVC). On the role of Keys and Kennedy in the sugar strike, see *Daily Picayune* (New Orleans), 16 January 1874 and 20 January 1874.

38. 'Communication' (in the French-language section), *Weekly Thibodaux Sentinel*, 22 October 1887.

39. For a dated but detailed account, see Paul Leland Haworth, *The Hayes-Tilden Presidential Election of 1876* (Cleveland, The Burrows Brothers Company, 1906).

40. *Historical Military Data ... 1878*, pp.87–94.

41. See Sheet 38, First Ward, Terrebonne Parish, Vol.16, Louisiana, Tenth Census of the United States, 1880. (Reproduced on Roll 472, Microfilm Publication T9, U.S. National Archives.) B. H. Lewis, mulatto, age 42, born in Maine, is listed along with his wife Ester, mulatto, born in Louisiana, and their children Ann Mary (age 5) and Ben Philip (age 2).

42. The names of black residents of Lafourche Parish appeared on the 1878 rolls of men eligible for the militia, though by then it was highly unlikely that they would be chosen. (These rolls can be found, uncatalogued, in the records of the Clerk of the Court, Lafourche Parish, Thibodaux, Louisiana.) For the text of the 30 March 1878 law reconstituting the militia, and the identification of the officers of the Special Military Force of the Second Military District, see *Annual Report of the Adjutant General of the State of Louisiana, for the Year Ending December 31, 1880* (New Orleans: The Democrat, 1881).

43. *Weekly Pelican* (New Orleans), 23 July 1887. Emphasis in original. For a subtle discussion of dancing, excursions, and public space, see Elsa Barkley Brown and Gregg D. Kimball, 'Mapping the Terrain of Black Richmond', *Journal of Urban History*, Vol.21 (March 1995), pp.296–346.

44. A Democratic leader recalled that in 1876 'The Majority of the armed men [lived] in all directions out in the country...', *The Times Democrat* (New Orleans), 3 October 1887, transcribed in *Historical Military Data ... 1878*.

45. Most of the information on Junius Bailey's career comes from A.E. Perkins, *Who's Who in Colored Louisiana* (Baton Rouge, Douglas Loan Company, 1930), p.109. For Bailey's place

of employment in 1887 I have drawn on Jeffrey Gould, '"Heroic and Vigorous Action": An Analysis of the Sugar Cane Workers' Strike in Lafourche Parish, November, 1887', ms.

46. On Kennedy, see the *Daily Picayune*, 20 January 1874.

47. I would like to thank Jerry McGee, the manager of Laurel Valley, for sharing his knowledge of the history and geography of the estate with me during my visit to the estate in 1996. See also J. Paul Leslie, 'Laurel Valley Plantation, 1831–1926', in Philip D. Uzee (ed.), *The Lafourche Country: The People and the Land* (Lafayette, Center for Louisiana Studies, University of Southwestern Louisiana, 1985), pp.206–24; Sam B. Hilliard, 'Site Characteristics and Spatial Stability of the Louisiana Sugarcane Industry', *Agricultural History*, Vol.53 (January 1979), pp.254–69; and John B. Rehder, 'Sugar Plantation Settlements of Southern Louisiana: A Cultural Geography' (PhD thesis, Louisiana State University, 1971).

48. See, for example, the letter of Frank H. Peck, Officer of the Day at Camp Parapet, 15 June 1862, in Berlin *et al.*, *The Destruction of Slavery*, pp.209–10. As avenues of communication, the rivers and bayous were complemented by the railway, which cut south-west from New Orleans toward Berwick Bay. The watercolor referred to is by Alfred Waud and is held in the Historic New Orleans Collection, New Orleans, Louisiana, catalogued 1965–21, O.C. Waud 13.

49. Paul Leslie, of Nicholls State University, called the expanding role of Acadian wage laborers to my attention. See also Carl A. Brasseaux, *Acadian to Cajun. Transformation of a People, 1803–1877* (Jackson, University Press of Mississippi, 1992). On Canary Islanders around Bayou Lafourche, see Gilbert C. Din, *The Canary Islanders of Louisiana* (Baton Rouge, Louisiana State University Press, 1988), especially p.135.

50. See Berlin *et al.*, *Destruction*, p.217.

51. See in particular Ernest J. Gaines, *Bloodline* (New York, W.W. Norton, 1976), and the criminal records in the office of the Clerk of the Court, Lafourche Parish. See also Richard C. Plater Jr., 'Acadia Plantation around 1900', Mss-0, Item 17, Allen Ellender Archives, Ellender Library, Nicholls State University, Thibodaux, Louisiana.

52. An exceptional collection of photographs from Evan Hall Plantation in the Bayou Lafourche region is held by the Historic New Orleans Collection, New Orleans, Louisiana. See, for example, the photographs taken in 1888 and catalogued as 1978.26.15, 1978.26.58, 1978.26.60, 1978.26.62. I have borrowed the phrase 'factory in the field' from Sidney Mintz.

53. See *Weekly Thibodaux Sentinel*, 11 November 1876, and *Report of the Senate Committee on Privileges and Elections in the Case of Moore vs. Cage to the Senate, State of Louisiana, Session 1878* (New Orleans: The Democrat, 1878), pp.34, 39. One cannot, of course, be certain of the details of this account, since portions of the evidence were generated by a dispute over alleged election fraud. As George Rable has noted, such testimony often 'reeks of perjury'. (George C. Rable, *But There Was No Peace: The Role of Violence in the Politics of Reconstruction* [Athens, University of Georgia Press, 1984], p.141.) Checking the various Democratic charges against each other, however, helps to fill in the story. It is the contemporary Democratic newspaper account, for example, that inadvertently discredits the later Democratic implication that the Poll #17 had been originally announced as the warehouse on the public road.

54. Hair, *Bourbonism*, p.177. Jonathan Garlock, *Guide to the Local Assemblies of the Knights of Labor* (Westport, CT, Greenwood Press, 1982), p.165.

55. The first case is to be found in the Volume labelled 'Criminal Cases, Vol. A, District Court, Parish of Lafourche', pages 384, 385. The second is found among the loose documents titled Criminal Cases, 1887. All are in the Records of the Clerk of the Court of Lafourche Parish, in the annex to the Courthouse, Thibodaux, Louisiana (abbreviated hereafter as CCLP). I thank Barbara Lee and other staff members of the office of the Clerk of the Court for their assistance in locating these materials.

56. See the entry 1913, Assessment Roll, Lafourche Parish, 1887. In CCLP.

57. The State of Louisiana vs. Peter Young and The State of Louisiana vs. Amos Johnson, Criminal Cases, 1887, CCLP.

58. *Daily Picayune* (New Orleans), 30 October 1887.

59. See *Daily Picayune* (New Orleans) 30 October 1887 and 2 November 1887.

60. Pierce, *Report*, p.4.
61. See Pierce, *Report*, p.9.
62. Cited in Covington Hall, 'Labor Struggles in the Deep South', ms., Part 2, p.7. Labadie Collection, Harlan Hatcher Library, University of Michigan.
63. *Weekly Capitolian Advocate* (Baton Rouge) 12 November 1887, transcribed in *Historical Military Data on Louisiana Militia, 1887*, in the Library, Jackson Barracks, New Orleans, Louisiana. Pierce, *Report*, p.10.
64. Pierce, *Report*, p.21, pp.27–34. For a vivid day-by-day description of events, see Gould, 'The Strike of 1887'.
65. Letter, Mary W. Pugh to Edward F. Pugh, Nov. 25, Folder 1, Mary W. Pugh Papers, LLMVC.
66. Hair, *Bourbonism*, pp.181–2.
67. Hall, 'Labor Struggles', Part 2, p.11.
68. Letter, Mary W. Pugh to Edward F. Pugh, Nov. 25, Folder 1, Mary W. Pugh Papers, LLMVC.
69. Gould, 'Heroic and Vigorous Action', n.38.
70. For a list of those who posted bond in the case of alleged assault on the deputy who arrested Moses Pugh, see p.402, Vol.A, Criminal Cases, District Court, Parish of Lafourche, CCLP.
71. On aspects of the White Line strategy, see Singletary, *Negro Militia*, Ch.9. It may also be well to recall an observation made by Albert Hirschman, who suggests that sometimes men and women make commitments in part because even if the goal turns out to be unattainable, they want to have been part of a principled and collective effort to achieve it. Albert O. Hirschman, *Shifting Involvements: Private Interest and Public Action* (Princeton, Princeton University Press, 1982), Ch.5.
72. *Weekly Thibodaux Sentinel*, 1 September 1883.
73. Testimony of William Murrell [Jr.], 2 April 1880, in Senate Reports, Vol.8, No.693, pt. 2, 46th Cong., 2nd sess., 'Negro Exodus from Southern States', pp.512–37.
74. See Thibodaux *Sentinel*, French section, 5 November 1887; English section, 26 November 1887.
75. 'Nouvelles Locales', *Weekly Thibodaux Sentinel*, 3 December 1887.

Reinventing Tradition: Liberty Place, Historical Memory, and Silk-stocking Vigilantism in New Orleans Politics

LAWRENCE N. POWELL

In September 1891 veterans of a Reconstruction-era conflict once known simply as the Battle of September Fourteenth erected a limestone obelisk near the foot of Canal Street in downtown New Orleans to honour the memory of the engagement and to provide a setting for annual commemorations.[1] The veterans had served together in an extralegal militia called the Crescent City White League, which, following a brief battle on 14 September 1874, had momentarily toppled the then New Orleans-based Republican State government. In recent years the 20-foot-high Liberty Place Monument, as it is now known, has been moved to an inconspicuous location behind the Aquarium of the Americas, tucked away on a grassy knoll just where an access road bends toward a parking garage. The white supremacy monument has become an embarrassment in a now black-majority city, and even modern-day descendants of the white elite who waged the battle more than a century ago have grown indifferent to its historical memory. 'No one in my social circle has the slightest knowledge of what the Battle of Liberty Place was, or gives a damn', says George Denegre, a senior partner in one of the city's oldest and most prestigious law firms and a former member of the Tulane governing board. 'The monument is gone and it ought to stay gone'.[2] But his blasé attitude was not always the rule. There used to be a time when the mere mention of September Fourteenth in polite circles was tantamount to a call to arms.

Something of this sort happened during the so-called 'Mafia Riots' on 14 March 1891, only five months prior to the monument's formal dedication. 'Riot' is an odd name for the lynching of 11 Sicilian defendants acquitted the day before of charges they had carried out a Mafia-ordered assassination of the city police chief. Walter Denegre, the present-day lawyer's great uncle, was one of the instigators. His speech at the base of the Henry Clay Statue, then sited on Canal Street, helped galvanize a mob composed and led by gentlemen of property and standing like himself. Their fathers had gathered at the same location 17 years earlier just prior to breaking open their secret arms cache. 'Not since the 14th day of

September, 1874, have we seen such a determined looking set of men assembled around this statue', declared Denegre. 'Then you assembled to assert your manhood. I want to know whether or not you will assert your manhood on the 14th day of March?' To the voices of 'shoot them' and 'lynch them', the city's frock-coated respectability marched on the city lock-up and murdered all 11 prisoners. While triggering a diplomatic crisis between the American and Italian governments, the lynching gave a much-needed boost to a stalled local fundraising campaign to complete work on the Liberty Place Monument.[3]

There is a misconception that the memory of September Fourteenth symbolized white solidarity within the political framework of a one-party South.[4] The fiction is partly based on the fact that every white political faction, certainly inside New Orleans, from time to time tried to wrap itself in the mantle of Liberty Place. But the fact remains, this particular tradition of 'good government' vigilantism was largely the symbolic property of the silk-stocking classes. For three generations it pervaded the politics of Uptown New Orleans, the exclusive residential area upriver from Canal Street where most of the city's white elite have lived since the 1830s. The memory of the Fourteenth has spawned mock battles and bar-room brawls, provoked armed insurgencies and ballot box showdowns. The banana republic tumult during the era of Huey Long boiled up from these angry waters. One is hard put to think of better examples of long memory. The September Fourteenth tradition enjoys nearly a hundred years of platitude. How did this tradition of elite violence become embedded in collective memory? More importantly, how did it get replenished – indeed, reinvented – generation after generation? It is helpful to bear in mind that generations, as Karl Mannheim argued long ago, are not defined by biology but history – social and political events that imprint themselves on consciousness at the 'critical period' when young people begin to learn about the larger society.[5] Generations become self-conscious when recollections of large public events are invested with the rich personal meanings of participatory experience.[6] The generation of the 1960s was formed by shared memories of President Kennedy's assassination, the Civil Rights movement, and the Vietnam War; their parent's generation, by the Great Depression and the Second World War. And the generational identity of the young white elites who came of age in Reconstruction New Orleans was shaped mainly by one stirring event: the Battle of September. But what about their sons and grandsons, indeed, great-grandsons? How did their autobiographical memory become fused with ancestral history? For collective memory to retain the power to produce social action, the remembrance has to be personal. Karl Mannheim explained it thus in his seminal work on 'generations': 'I only really possess those "memories" which I have created directly for myself, only that "knowledge" I have personally gained in real situations. This is the only sort of knowledge which really "sticks" and it alone has the real binding power.'[7]

So, how were succeeding generations of young white gentlemen in New Orleans able to personalize the historical experiences of their ancestors and appropriate them as their own? The explanation lies in the character of politics in post-Civil War New Orleans, where elections resembled soccer riots and voting was done in protective gear. Invariably, young gentlemen from the Garden District, Uptown's most exclusive neighbourhood, were in the forefront of the action, validating their manhood and asserting class prerogatives. It was as if every election offered them new opportunity to invest the Liberty Place tradition with autobiographical meaning, renewing a usable past for fresh abuse by the next generation.

The afternoon Battle of September Fourteenth actually commenced with a morning mass meeting. A call had gone out for white men to assemble at the aforementioned Henry Clay Statue to protest against the seizure by Republican State authorities of a secret shipload of Winchester rifles earmarked for the Crescent City White League. Truth to tell, the protest had been several years in the making. The immediate backdrop was the disputed gubernatorial election of 1872, which Democrats had filched at the polls only to see Republicans steal back in the recount. The dispute led to dual governments and a protracted succession crisis, played out in the courts and congressional hearing rooms. Soon, northern public opinion and the Grant administration began wearying of what Grant's Attorney General would come to call 'autumnal outbreaks' in the South. All the while, the US Supreme Court was actively abetting a retreat from Reconstruction that would eventually culminate in the 1896 *Plessy v. Ferguson* decision. The unmistakable signs of compassion fatigue were emboldening unreconstructed southern Democrats in every state in the old Confederacy where Reconstruction state regimes still functioned to seize the nettle of armed resistance. The Battle of September Fourteenth was one of the more spectacular manifestations of this regional backlash.[8]

Because of its ostensible origins in a mass meeting, the myth still persists that the battle burst forth from a spontaneous uprising of outraged citizens. But nothing could be further from the truth. The armed insurrection was actually the result of a brilliant conspiracy by arch conservatives within the Uptown establishment to reverse a drift toward racial accommodation on the part of the 'let's-get-on-with-business' segment of the city's older elite. The year before a bi-racial initiative known as the 'Unification Movement' had mobilized an influential segment of the business community behind a fifty-fifty power-sharing arrangement between blacks and whites. But the pro-compromise spirit foundered on the shoals of mutual suspicion. Still, the arch-conservatives, the so-called 'white liners' because of their determination to draw racial lines in the dust, remained wary of moderation. For this reason the white paramilitary group that gave battle on September Fourteenth chose to fight under the eponymous banner of racist defiance. 'The name White League was assumed as a protest against the unification humbug', one old battle veteran frankly admitted.[9]

The heart of the White League conspiracy consisted of the organization of young gentlemen and upwardly mobile clerks (usually merchant sons) into neighbourhood vigilance committees and ward clubs, because the real struggle was not merely for political supremacy but the hearts and minds of the next generation of white leadership. Many of these young men lived in the fashionable Garden District and, like their fathers before them, used to meet at Pope's drug store on the corner of Jackson Avenue and Prytania Street.[10] Eventually their ward organizations were folded into a secret organization called the Crescent City Democratic Club (CCDC), formed in 1868 by an ex-Confederate officer named Fred Ogden.[11] Meanwhile, in the pages of the New Orleans *Bulletin*, which had been created in March 1874, a parallel ideological mobilization had got underway to enforce white unity. From the *Bulletin* came a steady fusillade of crime stories.[12] There were sensational reports about white women being assaulted in broad daylight on the streets of the Garden District.[13] There were column inches about a detachment of black soldiers on their way back from a graveside decoration ceremony for the Union dead at Chalmette field who sought service in a whites-only soda fountain in the lower Garden District.[14] The *Bulletin* even ran a Caucasian job placement service in its classified section.[15] The stories, editorials, letters to the editor all had one aim in mind: legitimizing the cause of establishment violence. One letter echoed the familiar language of other upper-class Committees of Vigilance in antebellum San Francisco and New Orleans: 'If concert of action be deemed conspiracy, or an organized body to redress wrongs be considered unlawful, we say then *mobs* are the safety valve of a republic'.[16]

In late June 1874 the entire CCDC reconstituted itself as the Crescent City White League, a military regiment of 11 companies and 900-plus officers and men. At night they drilled secretly in places like Leeds Foundry. During daylight hours they wore white ribbons in their lapels.[17] Better educated than the white population at large, they were an elite group by any measurement.[18] Indeed, the Crescent City White League roster reads like a veritable who's who of New Orleans respectability: the Wisdoms, the Phelps, the Denegres, the Eustises, the Trufants, the Flowerses, the Griswolds, the Ogdens, the LeGardeurs. E.B. Kruttschnitt, the nephew of former US Senator and Confederate statesman Judah P. Benjamin, was a sergeant in Company B. He would later serve as President of Louisiana's

1898 disfranchisement convention. Edward Douglass White, who sat on the same US Supreme Court that handed down *Plessy v. Ferguson*, likewise saw action in 1874, albeit in one of the reserve units.[19]

There is a striking overlap between the membership of the city's exclusive gentlemen clubs, carnival krewes, and the Crescent City White League. 'Many members of the Boston and Pickwick Clubs joined the White League', writes the official historian of both the Battle of Liberty Place and the Boston Club, New Orleans's most exclusive gentleman's establishment. 'The call to arms and the strategy of the Battle of Liberty Place were planned by a committee which met at the Boston Club'.[20]

No doubt the deep enmeshment of White League leadership in New Orleans carnival explains why the battle resembles theatre as much as combat. The military engagement itself lasted less than 20 minutes, as approximately 8,400 Democratic White Leaguers easily routed a racially mixed force of 3,600 metropolitan policemen and State militia units. Casualties were slight: 32 deaths, 79 wounded. What was striking about the battle were its set-piece characteristics. New Orleans is a performance culture *par excellence*, and the Battle of September Fourteenth was nothing if not a performance. Thousands of spectators thronged balconies, rooftops, and the decks of steamboats to watch the contestants slug it out in the liquid heat of a late summer afternoon. The order of battle even resembled a New Orleans Mardi Gras parade, in which the social order is exemplified, not inverted, as is the case in Europe. Thus, the front lines were manned by the same Garden District youngbloods who filled the ranks of the Crescent City White League, while regiments comprising volunteers from different sections and social strata cooled their heels in reserve positions several blocks away. The Battle of September Fourteenth, in other words, was no mere struggle for home rule. It was a dramaturgical assertion of the right of the white upper class to rule at home.[21]

It is easy to understand why these stirring events, so masterfully stage-managed by a court of once-and-future carnival kings, imprinted themselves on the consciousness of the White League rank-and-file. Averaging between 16 and 25 years of age, the young fighters were at that stage of life when lasting political values are formed, when 'a distinctive personal outlook on politics emerge'.[22] Simply put, it was a textbook example of the intersection of history and autobiography. No wonder the veterans of September Fourteenth always thought of themselves forever after as 'the men of 1874'.

Self-conscious about their baptism under fire, not long after Reconstruction the veterans of September Fourteenth devised a civic ritual that extolled racial solidarity and upper-class civic reform. The organizers were the same men who had commanded the White League, Fred N. Ogden and his staff, and their efforts paralleled those of embattled elites elsewhere likewise confronting the breakdown of social order. In Europe and America alike, the period stretching from 1870 through the First World War was, to quote English historian Eric Hobsbawm, 'the heyday of "invented tradition", a time when old ceremonials were staged with an expertise and appeal which had been lacking before, and when new rituals were self-consciously invented to accentuate this development'.[23] The 1880s witnessed Victorian England's confection of its anachronistic and highly elaborate coronation ceremonials. The years immediately following 1875 saw Bismarck's newly unified Germany make a civil fetish of the Arminius Monument in the Teutoburg Forest. And the American Gilded Age saw the mass-production of those Civil War statuaries that anchor the courthouse squares and village greens of the country's civil landscape. A shared interest in restoring the social solidarity shattered by class conflict and the advent of mass politics lay behind these proliferating 'traditions'. Deferential authority had crumbled. To offset their waning political power, old elites thus tried to foster consensus, stability and continuity by exploiting traditional imagery and symbology – in effect, by interjecting 'irrational elements' into public discourse.[24]

The civic ritual devised by New Orleans elites to consecrate September Fourteenth had similar ends in view. Although themselves largely Protestant, the stage managers were shrewd in choosing to mix Catholic liturgy with military display. In a city famous for deep ethnic differences it was important to reaffirm upper-class unity across religious lines. But braided into that localistic concern was the same impulse that led similarly situated elites to make their own history serve as synecdoche for the collective memory of the whole community. For the 'men of 1874' knew full well that those who controlled the past also controlled the present.

From 1877 until 1882, the annual September Fourteenth ritual went as follows: the anniversary day would begin with an 8.00 a.m. requiem mass in St. Louis Cathedral, in Jackson Square, the traditional site for solemnizing the valour of New Orleans's previous military saviours. At midday General Ogden and his staff would make a pilgrimage to the gravesides of the White League dead, decorating them with evergreen wreaths bound with white satin ribbon bearing the legend, '14th of September, 1874', plus the initials of the deceased. The highpoint of the anniversary was the military pageantry performed by units of the State militia, which by now was simply the White League in official garb. Assembling at 3.00 p.m. for a march that traced the route of the soldiers of '74, the parade would always end up near the river for a 21-gun salute. These early celebrations often brought the city to a standstill. Businesses closed early. Crowds surged through balconied streets festooned with banners and bunting. Whether celebrants later in the evening danced to the strains of 'The White League Waltz' or the 'People Rights Quick Step' was not recorded. But they probably did. Sheet music versions of those tunes, along with the 'Ku Klux Klan Polka' and 'March of the Louisiana Banditti', saw steady sales in 1870s New Orleans.[25]

In 1877 the New Orleans *Picayune* marvelled at how the city's populace seemed to be moved by 'one common impulse' on this hallowed day, how men of opposite politics met each other on the streets in friendly greeting, 'utterly forgetting the differences of the past'.[26] But these public anniversary festivities began to ebb within a decade of their creation. By 1882 the military pomp surrounding September Fourteenth had died out completely. Ten years after that the focus of the annual commemoration had shrivelled to an increasingly subdued wreath-laying ceremony at the newly installed Liberty Place Monument on Canal Street.

This was not an unusual fate for the 'invented traditions' of the late nineteenth century. Most of them disappeared shortly after their invention due to the transparent class interests they sought to serve. 'Successful festivals', explains George Mosse, 'must embody transcendent ideals symbolized by the nation or the movement'.[27] Public rituals cannot artificially create communal unity where unity does not exist. And that was why the September Fourteenth liturgy was so frail: it lacked civic solidarity. The city's African-American community, which retained the elective franchise until 1898, rejected the assertions of entitlement embodied in the ceremony. This 'pompous military display', declared the *Weekly Louisianian*, then the city's only black newspaper, betrayed a deep hostility to black liberties. 'It is for this reason the 14th of September must always be a red flag shaken in our faces'.[28] But even a substantial segment of the white population spurned Ogden's 'invented tradition' by rebuffing the leadership of men like himself: the self-styled 'better classes'. For most of the post-Reconstruction period, the city's immigrant working classes supported the city 'ring', an Irish-dominated political organization with secure anchorage in the city's wards and neighbourhoods. The machine ran municipal affairs with a firm grip, and even enjoyed decisive leverage in state politics thanks to careful alliances with upstate rural bosses.[29] 'Louisiana is not governed to-day by men who inspired or who made that contest', fretted the New Orleans *Picayune* during the 1882 celebration of the Battle of Canal Street. Nor would this situation be remedied, the paper continued, until the veterans of 1874 'redeemed their own state from bad government'.[30] It is a measure of how much the memory of the Fourteenth had misted over with time that the aldermanic council in 1882 absentmindedly enacted an ordinance creating a park on ground regarded as hallowed by old White Leaguers. Three days later, under pressure from veterans of September Fourteenth, the council superseded the park ordinance with a new one consecrating the same site as 'Liberty Place', the name by which it became known for the next one hundred years.[31]

If parades and pageants lacked the power to perpetuate White League tradition, there were other means of engraving it into autobiographical memory: through 'virtual' battle re-enactments at the city's notorious hurly-burly polling places. Much of the voting in nineteenth-century New Orleans took place in bars and saloons. The belligerents were the 'ring' and a protean succession of good government reform groups that sprang Phoenix-like from the Garden District and the city's various 'exchanges' – the Cotton Exchange, the Sugar Exchange, the Produce Exchange, the Board of Trade. The *modus operandi* involved militarizing the 'young men' and future prominents of the city. And the vocabulary of mobilization was more or less constant – a call for a 'rising of the people' through appeals to the memory of September Fourteenth, coupled with challenges to the rising generation to emulate the gallantry of the heroes of '74. Even the organizing tactics owed something to the past. Young gentlemen and socially ambitious clerks were mustered into vigilance committees and ward clubs, and then armed, drilled, and marched to the polls. These were not merely elections; they were not merely colourful instances of the democratic class struggle. They were militaristic displays of 'manhood', to use a term much in vogue among the city's silk-stocking classes at the time.

Elections for mayor and aldermen took place in April (bi-annually until 1884; quadrennially thereafter). In these contests the 'ring' usually prevailed despite losing an occasional mayoralty election, largely because of its ability to elect the officials who controlled the city's patronage-rich administrative departments. Of these the police department was the most highly prized trophy of war. This was so not merely because every detective and patrolman was a political appointee. The police force were essential foot soldiers in the struggle for municipal supremacy. After the dissolution of the Reconstruction-era Metropolitan Police, which, according to a recent history, 'constituted a stronger and more nearly professional organization than any of the police forces that had previously seen service in New Orleans', the city's constabulary slid back into 'the morass of partisan politics from which it had partially emerged during Reconstruction'.[32] In every campaign from 1880 onward, regular patrolmen and 'special deputies' appointed for the occasion would converge on strategic polling places and, in the name of law and order, allow thugs and hoodlums to intimidate supporters of opposition candidates. (This was before the introduction of secret ballots. Voters merely deposited paper ballots that were easily identifiable on sight.) The 'ring' deployed 'linesters' – rough-looking men who would throng the lines queuing up to the ballot box to keep supporters of rival candidates from casting votes. It used 'strikers' to start election scuffles calculated to scare away the genteel. 'At every election', writes Joy Jackson, the historian of Gilded Age New Orleans, 'the newspapers reported fist fights, the discharging of guns, drunkenness'. This was putting it mildly. Left out of her account was mention of numerous knifings and the widespread use of brass knuckles, New Orleans's gift to gangland America.[33]

Good government reformers won three elections in post-Reconstruction New Orleans – 1880, 1888, and 1896 – usually because they were able to marshal superior force. The election of 1888 set the pattern. The immediate background was alleged electoral fraud that had helped defeat White League veterans Fred Ogden and William J. Behan in their 1884 campaigns for Governor and Mayor, respectively. 'Let the people rise in their might', thundered the New Orleans *Picayune*.[34] The 'spontaneous' uprising, however, took three years to materialize. In 1885 there emerged the Committee of One Hundred (just like past and future committees of 50, 70, 100 or 200, to list just a few of these protean groups) to purge the registration books. The following year saw the organization of the Law and Order League, presumably to co-ordinate the various vigilance committees that had been functioning since 1880 as private police in the city's exclusive neighbourhoods. Finally the 'young men' themselves stepped onto the stage in the summer of 1887 when they chartered a 'Young Men's Democratic Association' (the YMDA).[35] The association, according to its participant-historian, was 'not composed entirely of young men, nor of members of what is called the Democratic party'.[36] Still, it was dominated by rising leaders in business, law, and Uptown politics – men like John M. Parker, Jr., a future Progressive governor; Ashton Phelps; and Dr Henry Dickson Bruns. Each one of their fathers had fought in the ranks of the Crescent City White League on September Fourteenth. The average age of the founding group was 25. The president, a 30-year-old local businessman and lawyer named William S. Parkerson, was the group's greybeard.[37]

The YMDA founders tirelessly worked the exchanges, the law offices, and the counting rooms. To preclude co-optation by professional politicians, and ensure that only voters of 'good moral character' were let in, the identity of the membership committee was as secretive as the rolls of an elite carnival krewe.[38] The young reformers built their movement from the neighbourhood up. 'As soon as ten men from any one ward should join the association they were authorized to form central [or mother] ward clubs', read a clause of the constitution. Ten was about the size of a functional rifle squad. By early February 1888 the YMDA was able to fill Washington Artillery Hall with over 1,000 supporters, who adopted, with 'a perfect roar of affirmative votes' and 'an outburst of enthusiasm', a resolution declaring that 'municipal government in this city was more a business than a party question'.[39]

By election eve in mid-April the movement's organizers were staging massive rallies. One meeting in Congo Square (now Armstrong Park) drew a reported 5,000 spectators. 'A spontaneous and unmistakable uprising of the people', intoned the New Orleans *States* while describing how the platform was filled with 'prominent leaders in business and the professions'.[40] Young Dr Henry Bruns, whose physician father had written the 1874 appeal to the 'Citizens of New Orleans' that triggered the Reconstruction battle, gave a keynote address vowing that on election day the YMDA would put an army of 4,000 'special policemen' on the streets to guard the polls. They would 'sweep from the face of the earth' any ring hoodlums who interfered with balloting.[41] Another speaker challenged the assembled virility of the city's upper-class youth: 'The ring has triumphed heretofore largely through the cowardice of the silk stocking element'. There were cries of '"That's so" and cheers'. It remained for the YMDA's mayoralty candidate, Joseph Shakspeare, who had carried the good government reformers to victory in 1880, to draw the inevitable comparisons to the Battle of Canal Street. 'He had not witnessed such a crowd with such a spirit since the days which culminated in the triumph of the 14th of September', he told the crowd. 'And he was inclined to think we were in much the same fix as then. We were being led to salvation again by the descendants of the men who had redeemed their city on that day.'[42]

The final pre-election rally held on 14 April in Lafayette Square, in full view of city hall, was drenched in ancestral memory. A crowd estimated at 30,000 jammed in front of four platforms positioned on each side of the square. From one of them the young attorney Walter Denegre predicted that two days hence 'the citizens of New Orleans would accomplish by a fair ballot and free count what on the 14th of September 1884 [*sic*] they were forced to carry out by violence and bloodshed'. From another platform candidate Shakspeare exulted: 'At last the manhood of New Orleans has asserted itself'. But it was the military pageantry, the smart stepping ward clubs who 'poured into Lafayette Square like the mobilization of one of Napoleon's armies preparatory to crushing out an enemy', that gave the event its feeling of *déjà vu*. For all the world the scene resembled the filial-pietistic acting out of war stories as told by the fathers. Here is how a reporter for the New Orleans *Times-Democrat* described the setting: 'The sights, the music, the glare of lights, the rockets crossing the sky in all directions, the heads of columns marching north, south, east and west, all concentrating upon one given space and wheeling into position in perfect order and precision, presented a scene never to be forgotten'.[43]

The election two days later unfolded like a set-piece battle. The YMDA set up headquarters at the Continental Guards Armory, where 1,000 Winchester rifles and 500 revolvers had been stored.[44] It posted 'resolute' poll watchers backed by armed squads of 25–80 men. At YMDA headquarters reserve forces stood at the ready to travel by wagon to election trouble spots. Tensions mounted at day's end when the polls closed and the real election began: the counting of the vote. It was then, according to contemporary news reports, that 'knots of hoodlums began to gather around some of the polls and betrayed a disposition to be ugly and start a row'. And it was then that YMDA president W.S. Parkerson issued his famous call: 'Merchants, if you care for the prosperity of this city send us your clerks. Let me have them all and we'll see that the vote is counted at once ... The emergency is great. No man who has any manhood can fail to come.'[45] Swiftly the Continental Guards Armory swelled with 'stalwart young men' clamouring to join the armed squads being dispatched to embattled precincts. At three in the morning an armed force was sent post-haste to poll #1, First Ward, when intelligence reached headquarters that 'ring strikers' were gathering nearby. At poll #3, in the Second Ward, 40 YMDA men carrying rifles stood tense vigilance against a gang from St. Mary's Market. A captain of the 'YMDA Specials' guarding one of the precincts in the Eleventh Ward, put out an emergency call for reinforcements after discovering he was shorthanded. A dozen neighbourhood volunteers immediately converged on his salient, forming themselves on the spot into the 'Eleventh Ward Rangers', and electing their own officers and non-commissioned officers. They stayed at their posts throughout the night. At one polling place near the edge of the French Quarter a YMDA squad leader, more than a little jumpy over boasts by a local ward heeler 'to chase into the river with a toothpick' any YMDA man who 'showed his mug' in his precinct, threw out pickets around the perimeter of his duty post and placed the body of his force so as to be able 'to enfilade any party approaching from that direction'.[46]

Meanwhile, young John M. Parker, Jr. – who, like another patrician advocate of the manly virtues, Theodore Roosevelt, was weak and sickly as a child – earned his campaign ribbons by commanding 'a squad of thirty-six gallant men' against the 'shotgun brigade' mustered by the ring to recapture his electoral battle post. Meanwhile, armed patrols formed up to escort the ballot boxes to the sheriff's office. The procession from precinct #2 in the Second Ward was heralded by 'a band of music and followed by forty picked men, ten of whom were armed with Winchesters'. And so it went as young gentlemen from the Garden District faced down such notorious ring 'strikers' and 'linesters' as 'Tug Wilson, the slugger' or 'Bowlegged Donovan'.[47]

Then came the marathon canvassing. YMDA President Parkerson followed in the footsteps of the gallant Fred Ogden by refusing to desert his duty post until victory had been secured. 'I showed up at Odd Fellow's Hall at four o'clock Tuesday morning and never closed my eyes, took off my clothes, or went to bed until two o'clock Friday morning, when the last box was brought in', he told his son, in an autobiographical letter meant to instruct.[48]

The YMDA won the election. Miraculously, despite an atmosphere thick with tension, there were no 'fatalistic exhibitions of violence', only 'a few shooting affrays' and the usual 'fistic encounters'.[49] 'It was a bloodless Fourteenth of September', intoned the *Times-Democrat*, 'one whose result was just as great and equally as necessary to the substantial prosperity not only of the Crescent City, but likewise to the cause of reform and good government'.[50]

Here, in a word, was how the tradition of the Fourteenth became assimilated into the political life and collective memory of generations of Uptown gentlemen: through a repetition of militaristic mobilizations and armed electoral showdowns between young swells and the police forces of an immigrant-based, working-class political machine. The re-enactments engraved into autobiographical memory the overarching themes of Liberty Place – the assertions of upper-class political entitlement; the assumptions of class and racial supremacy; the vindication of masculine virility; and, most of all, the legitimization of establishment violence in the name of good government – so that, in the end, historical consciousness became more than mindless homage to patriarchal pieties. It became the medium through which political memories of late adolescence and young adulthood were generationally imprinted and an activist tradition of six decades standing continually rejuvenated.[51]

Thus, the mayoralty election of 1888 was reprised eight years later for yet another generation of young gentlemen. This time a 'Citizen's League' sprang up headed by a local banker and recent king of carnival. It, too, grasped the baton handed it to it by a predecessor good government group, the Citizen's Protective Association, which in 1894 impeached its long-time nemesis, Mayor John Fitzpatrick – on September Fourteenth, naturally.[52] As a run-up to the April 1896 mayoralty contest, the Citizen's League – which commingled young and old, and included thirty White League veterans among its charter members[53] – staged mass rallies at the Liberty Place Monument, where the sacred memory of 'those gallant young men' of 1874 was invoked again and again.[54] Three days later a huge procession stepped off from Lee Circle to the monument at the foot of Canal Street. It was like a carnival night, one reporter said. Thousands of torches and gasoline lights backlit the scene. There were bands. There was the obligatory military parade: 'The clubs came from all directions amid a blaze of fireworks and the avenue was lit up as bright as day'. The martial display was not for the entertainment of adulatory crowds who lined the streets. It was to send a message to 'the St. Mary Market toughs, the Brewster heelers, and other foaming-at-the-mouth beer guzzlers who glared at the omnipotence of the *people* with a sort of mad frenzy as they read the doom of the heelers' business for at least four years' [emphasis added].[55] This time the show of force succeeded in pressuring representatives of the ring to send a delegation to a peace parley in the home of White League veteran and past president of the Boston Club, E.B. Kruttschnitt, where a truce was hammered out and bloodshed averted. The silk-stocking reformers carried the day, electing as mayor Walter Flower, the son of a White League veteran.[56] 'It is not often that a local holiday is celebrated for twenty odd years – nearly a lifetime – but it is well that it should be so', editorialized the *Times-Democrat* on the occasion of that year's twenty-second anniversary celebration. 'Nothing has done more to direct New Orleans in the path towards good government than the memory of this day. It satisfied the people that they were the power.'[57]

Eight years later, in 1904, the 'people' were threatening to exercise their prerogatives yet again. This time it was under the banner of 'Home Rule' and the leadership of the old YMDA head, W.S. Parkerson. And this time the *cause célèbre* was reformer demands that the 'bosses' replace nominating conventions with the white primary. There were more rallies at the Liberty Place Monument. There were pointed challenges to the city's young gentlemen: 'Is that monument which yonder rears its head ... to be a constant reminder of the shame of their sons? (Cries of "No, no".)'[58] There were efforts to post armed guards of ten men at each polling place. There were clashes with the city police.[59] There was the same verbal swagger and over-stylized assertions of 'manhood'. But this time a newly reorganized machine won the election, eliciting cries of fraud from the good government camp and threats of violence. 'Old men and young men climbed into Home Rule headquarters, begged that a leader might be found, and promised that New Orleans might yet be redeemed'.[60]

As rhetoric, the September Fourteenth tradition persisted well into the latter half of the twentieth century, energized by the challenge of civil rights. But its activist component – the capacity to elicit violence from the Uptown elite – waned sharply following the assassination of Huey Long. Just prior to Long's stormy emergence into politics, a semblance of electoral peace reigned over the polling places of New Orleans. The cessation of armed warfare was partly the result of black disfranchisement, since the poll tax and property test measures used to slash black registration also led to a dramatic fall off in voter turnout by low-status whites as well. But the metamorphosis of the city machine also helped drive the silk-stocking vigilante tradition into semi-hibernation. After its reconstitution in 1896 as the 'Old Regulars', or 'Choctaws', the machine jettisoned its pro-labour stance in favour of an alliance with New Orleans utility, traction, and financial interests, becoming, in the words of T. Harry Williams, 'one of the most business-oriented machines in the country'.[61] So far had the 'Old Regulars' drifted from working-class moorings that their titular head in 1934 was a blue blooded banker's son by the name of T. Semmes Walmsley, then mayor of the city.[62] Just prior to the 1932 anniversary Walmsley had created a new Board of Commissioners of Liberty Place. 'The city has been derelict in its duty in not having a larger celebration of this anniversary of the Battle of September 14', Walmsley told the audience.[63] The ceremony concluded with the unveiling of a new inscription (since sandblasted off) for the monument's granite plinth: 'United States troops took over the state government and reinstated the usurpers but the national election in November 1876 recognized *white supremacy* and gave us our state' [emphasis added].

In the past whenever they felt their interests under attack the New Orleans establishment had instinctively hoisted the banner of racial solidarity, and that feeling was stealing over them again. By 1934 Huey Long's split with the Old Regulars had widened into a canyon. The rift arose mainly from his attacks on the machine's financial allies. In February of that year, over nationwide radio, the 'Kingfish' had announced the formation of his Share Our Wealth Society, with its catchy slogan 'Every Man a King'. That summer Senator Long returned from Washington to prod the State legislature into enacting a bevy of new taxes – on personal income, utilities, chain stores, newspaper advertising receipts, Cotton Exchange transactions – to pay for an expansion of the Longite social programme. Just as the 'Kingfish' was stepping up his assaults on financial privilege, he set about wrecking the Old Regulars' vote-producing machinery by abolishing the poll tax. While depressing turnout among the poor, the levy had allowed the New Orleans machine to pad its own majorities by paying the poll taxes of poor people who agreed to sell their votes.

Most threatening of all, in July, under pressure from Huey, State lawmakers passed a bill transferring authority over the New Orleans Police Department to a gubernatorially appointed State board. The measure promised to neutralize the police as a tool for controlling elections, which of course had been one of the department's unofficial functions since Reconstruction. Mayor Walmsley and the city had secured a court injunction suspending the law's enforcement. It was only a matter of time before the State Supreme Court decided the issue.

The 'Choctaw' machine was starting to come apart under Huey's sledgehammer blows. Already he had succeeded in breaking loose the city's large Italian vote from the 'Old Regular' coalition. But what must have seemed even more threatening to the machine and the New Orleans upper classes was Huey's overtures to the heretofore quiescent African-American community – notwithstanding his frequent resort crude to crude white supremacist rhetoric.[64] The last Share Our Wealth circular penned by the 'Kingfish' used language not uttered by white Louisianians since Reconstruction: 'The movement to free the black man reached a strength impossible to overcome in 1860 to 1865. This is the fight to liberate white and black.' No wonder the custodians of the September Fourteenth tradition saw fit to inscribe white supremacist shibboleths to the plinth of the Liberty Place Monument. Huey was assassinated before the broadside was printed, however.[65]

By August 1934 the rupture between the 'Choctaws' and the Long machine had reached a crisis stage. Indeed, for more than six weeks prior to the sixtieth anniversary celebration the Crescent City had been teetering on the brink of armed warfare. On 30 July the Kingfish, intent on controlling the September elections for the State Supreme Court and US Congress, ordered his puppet governor to have the National Guard seize the voter registration office in downtown New Orleans. Shortly before midnight a detachment of 50 Guardsmen broke the lock and took possession of the building. 'To resist Long's illegal invasion', Mayor Walmsley augmented the city police force with 400 'special deputies'. 'Go out and arm yourselves', Police Superintendent George Reyer told the new officers at their swearing in. 'I don't care what sort of firearms you get, so long as they can shoot'. Meanwhile, he announced that the city had just received a large shipment of machine guns, tear gas, and arsenic bombs.[66] A few weeks later a citizens' committee composed of 100 prominent business and professional men sprang into action, just like similar groups had done during every political crisis as far back as the Know-Nothing troubles of the 1850s. The *ad hoc* 'good government' group issued a 'Call to Civic Duty' adjuring volunteers to step forward to make 'a determined stand for a fair and honest election and count', and thereby to 'prove before the nation their own willingness to assert and defend their own rights'.[67]

Only a narrow street separated City Hall and the Registration Office. Day after day armed special deputies and state guardsmen glared at one another along machine-gun barrels. Low comedy alternated with high drama. During one special legislative session, where bills were read, engrossed, reported out of committee, and passed within 24 hours, the Kingfish arranged for legislative hearings into the Walmsley administration's alleged involvement with New Orleans vice interests. Huey had himself appointed special counsel for the joint investigating committee and the hearings were broadcast from a makeshift radio studio atop a local New Orleans bank building. The investigation focused mainly on police payoffs made by brothel-keepers and handbook operators, an old New

Orleans tradition. At one point Huey hauled Police Superintendent Reyer into the studio. 'Take off your coat, Chief', Long bellowed. 'You look like it's getting hot in here'.[68]

Throughout the emergency the Kingfish and the mayor used the airwaves to trade barnyard expletives. 'Turkeyhead' Walmsley, Huey jeered at the tall, balding, angular-faced mayor. 'Screech owl', hooted the mayor over his own radio hookup, adding for good measure that the Senator was a gangster, a moral leper, and a madman.[69] The crisis reached boiling point one week before the September Fourteenth anniversary celebration, when Walmsley summoned to his office the legendary former police chief and soldier of fortune, Guy 'Machine Gun' Molony.[70] Molony, a native New Orleanian who had begun his mercenary career in the Boer War, mastering the machine gun in the Philippines during the Spanish–American conflict, had come by his reputation training and commanding the private armies of American banana companies against recalcitrant regimes in Central America. Police Superintendent Reyer himself had served in one of these armies. Among a generation of Uptown gentlemen Molony had long enjoyed iconic status by virtue of having instructed the elite Washington Artillery in the use of modern firearms during both the Mexican Revolution and the First World War. 'Those boys were mostly college boys', Molony, who had attained the rank of Lieutenant Colonel in the famed unit, told an interviewer shortly before his death. 'Of course, I could give them the rough end of the game. I don't think I improved their college education, but I could tell them how to soldier.'[71]

News that Molony had arrived in town from Honduras set Huey's nerves on edge. A few weeks earlier five rifle shots were fired from a speeding car into Long's New Orleans home on Audubon Boulevard, raising the Kingfish's mounting fears of assassination. For years Long had been openly feuding with Molony's old patron Sam Zemurray, owner of United Fruit Company. It was from Zemurray's private yacht that Colonel Molony and another legendary New Orleans gun-for-hire, Lee Christmas, had staged the 1911 invasion installing a pro-American regime in Honduras.[72] During his 1930 race for US Senate, Huey accused Zemurray of coming to the 'Old Regulars's' assistance by pouring 'barrels of gold' into the campaign coffers of the incumbent senator Long was about to unseat.[73] After arriving in Washington, the Kingfish went on a crusade to block US troop deployment in Latin America to protect the interests of Sam Zemurray, 'the banana peddler'.[74]

Once Long learned Molony was in town, he summoned him before his vice commission, to verify reports Molony had commanded an armed force of 25 men stationed in the St. Charles Hotel, then the city's grandest, during the last election. The colonel confirmed the rumours. Did he plan similar measures for the election on Thursday, Huey asked, and did 'the expert in guerrilla warfare [have] a machine gun nest planted in the city'?

> 'It is not true,' Molony said over the radio in a quiet but firm voice, adding quickly, 'but I will be glad to' in the event of trouble.
> 'Try and do it,' shouted Long.
> 'Watch us,' replied the Colonel.[75]

Huey then ordered Governor O.K. Allen to dispatch practically the entire State militia of 2,000 men to Jackson Barracks outside New Orleans.

Long ultimately won this six-week war of billingsgate and ballots, just as he did most of his confrontations with the Uptown elite. All of his candidates won by comfortable margins on 11 September.[76] But though bloodshed had been averted, the air remained humid with portents of banana coups and generalissimos, like the atmospherics in some Gabriel García Marquez novel.

The sixtieth anniversary ceremony of September Fourteenth took place in the evening. That afternoon the temperature had reached a muggy 87 degrees. Light winds out of the Gulf brought scant relief. Twenty surviving veterans of the 1874 engagement were assigned places of honour. There was a reading of the roll of the 16 White Leaguers who had fallen in battle. A local boyscout troop carried chrysantheum wreaths to the monument through a path cleared by a police guard, while buglers sounded taps.[77] The featured speaker that evening was a professional patriot and Tulane historian named George Kernion, and he rehearsed the whole hackneyed history, beginning with the central myth of Reconstruction: 'Former slaves now posed as the Political masters of the proud white citizenry of the South!' He blasted away at the corruption (of which there had been plenty), the widespread white disfranchisement (of which there had been little), 'the black-and-tan Neros' in the legislature (which was a myth). He bemoaned the subversion of free and fair elections. He denounced the military's encroachment on civil authority. Some of his claims were half-truths; most bordered on historical libel. But in 1934 there were enough parallels between past and present to give Kernion's overheated rhetoric the feel of real relevance. For then as now Louisiana was in the grip of highly centralized state regimes that did not scruple to dominate the election machinery and undermine local control of city police. And then as now the political air was filled with accusations of illegitimacy and usurpation.[78]

The marrow of Kernion's peroration, however, was its call to duty. Twice he adverted to 'the real Red-Blooded Men in Louisiana' who were 'unafraid even of Death when their Honor and their Freedom were at stake!' Once he pointedly admonished the audience 'to take up the burden which they [the heroes of 1874] have thrown upon our shoulders ... even though, in so doing, some of us may have to sleep as some of them did that day, upon a glorious field!' And he concluded with a none-too-oblique equating of Huey with the carpetbaggers: 'We have the Demagogue always with us'.[79] The remarks stirred one surviving White League veteran sitting near the podium to volunteer 'to get his ancient musket and fight once more'.[80]

For all of its spread-eagle oratory, Kernion's rhetorical effort to provide historical license for establishment violence was nothing new. Huey's more outspoken enemies had been proclaiming the same openly for years. There was a 'wildness in the air', as one of Long's opponents said famously in an interview years later.[81] At a huge anti-Long rally at the State Capitol earlier in the summer, one man yelled out: 'The glorious pages of Louisiana's history are written in blood.'[82] 'Big' Hodding Carter, then publishing a paper in Hammond, Louisiana, across the lake, declared that only 'ancient methods' were capable of curbing Longism, and he hoped to God that 'Louisiana men [would] awake to these wrongs and to the sole remaining method of righting them'. This kind of rough talk was commonplace in the elite circles of New Orleans, as well. Immediately after the seizure of the Registrar's Office Mayor Walmsley shouted: 'I warn you, Huey Long, you cringing coward, that if a life is spent in the defence of this city and its right of self-government, you shall pay the penalty as other carpetbaggers have done before you'.[83] A few years earlier, before Long gave up the governor's mansion to take up lodging in Washington, Colonel Robert Ewing – the New Orleans *States* publisher tagged by Huey with the nickname 'Bow Wow' – predicted that the 'valiant heroes' who had expelled the carpetbaggers 'would know how to deal with the "little chineapin-headed misfit now in the governor's chair"'.[84] It was as though the armed mobilization of the city's young gentlemen had awakened in all their ferocity the ancestral memories of September Fourteenth, with its themes silk-stocking vigilantism and manly virtue.

There is absolutely no evidence of Uptown complicity in Huey's assassination on 7 September 1935, a mere week before the sixty-first Liberty Place anniversary celebration. But some of the city's most prominent blue bloods as much as prophesied the event, and the feeling will not go away that they shaped the violent-filled atmosphere as well. The old YMDA'er John M. Parker, Jr., in a 1933 letter to Vice-President John Nash Garner, called then US Senator Huey P. Long 'a dangerous paranoic' and advised the US Senate to have him permanently committed to a criminal insane hospital in Washington 'to save certain trouble and probable future killing'.[85]

Few tears were shed in Uptown parlours when the Kingfish died a few days after being shot in the skyscraper State capitol he had commissioned as a monument to his own power. Hilda Phelps Hammond had learned the

White League legend at her father's knee, just like her male counterparts.[86] 'I never tired of that story – how men drilled secretly night after night through the stifling summer months, how they pooled their money to buy the "chassepots" and "needle guns" of the Franco-Prussia War through New York brokers'. In the Phelps household September Fourteenth was a hallowed day. She and her father never visited Canal Street together without his pointing out 'the long, narrow white shaft which marks the spot where citizens fell fighting for free government'. Her father's political war stories helped lift her sights from that of 'a child of the Garden District' to those of 'a Louisianian' – and, as Pamela Tyler's book makes clear, those of a political activist in an aggressively masculine political world, as well.[87]

By 1935 Phelps had become one of Huey's most implacable opponents, issuing the following press statement after Long's death: 'Regrettable as bloodshed always is, thoughtful Americans while contemplating what has happened will remember that there is a human breaking point in the endurance of oppression by man, that he who lives by the sword perishes by the sword and that the State of Virginia bears upon its great seal the prophetic words "Sic Semper Tyrannis"'.[88] Those words could have been spoken at the time the Crescent City White League tried to drive the carpetbagger governor William Pitt Kellogg into the river.

NOTES

The author would like to thank Eric Foner, Sylvia Frey, Lance Hill, Joseph Logsdon, Patrick Maney, R. Plater Robinson, Howard Schuman, Rebecca Scott, and Betty Wood for their helpful comments.

1. Right after it was fought, the battle was called either the Battle of Canal Street or the Battle of September Fourteenth, or both. Beginning in the late nineteenth century, following the dedication of the Liberty Place Monument, the term Battle of Liberty Place came into increasingly wide usage. In this essay I sometimes use all three terms.
2. Interview with George Denegre, New Orleans, 7 February 1992.
3. New Orleans Times-Democrat, 15 March 1891. On the Mafia riots and the part played by the Uptown elite, see Joy Jackson, New Orleans in the Gilded Age: Politics and Urban Progress, 1880–1896 (Baton Rouge, Louisiana State University Press, 1969), pp.247–53; and Schott, 'John M. Parker of Louisiana', pp.27–36. On the fundraising campaign, see Lawrence N. Powell, 'A Concrete Symbol', Southern Exposure, Vol.18 (Spring 1990), p.41.
4. See, for example, Jackson, New Orleans in the Gilded Age, p.30; and Edward F. Haas, Political Leadership in a Southern City: New Orleans in the Progressive Era, 1896–1902 (Rushton, LA, McGinty Publications, 1988), p.56.
5. Quoted in Howard Schuman and Jacqueline Scott, 'Generations and Collective Memories', American Sociological Review, Vol.54 (June 1989), p.359.
6. I am following Maurice Halbwachs' famous dichotomy. See his On Collective Memory, edited, translated, and with an introduction by Lewis A. Coser (Chicago and London, University of Chicago Press, 1992), pp.23–4, 37–40.
7. Karl Mannheim, 'The Problem of Generations', in his Essays on the Sociology of

Knowledge, ed. Paul Kecskemeti (London, Routledge & Kegan Paul, 1952), p.296.

8. The best brief summaries of the battle are in Joe Gray Taylor, *Louisiana Reconstructed, 1863–1877* (Baton Rouge, Louisiana State University Press, 1974), pp.291–6; and Judith Schafer, 'The Battle of Liberty', *Cultural Vistas*, Vol.5 (Spring 1994), pp.8–17. The story is told in greater detail in Stuart O. Landry, *The Battle of Liberty Place* (New Orleans, Pelican Publishing Co., 1955), which is a 350-page white supremacist rant. For the national background see Eric Foner, *Reconstruction: America's Unfinished Revolution, 1863–1877* (New York, Harper & Row, 1988), esp. pp.524–86.

9. Walter L. Pritchard (ed.), 'Origins and Activities of the White League', *Louisiana Historical Quarterly*, Vol.23 (April 1940), p.534. For more on the Unification movement, see T. Harry Williams, 'Louisiana Unification Movement of 1873', *Journal of Southern History*, Vol.11 (August 1945), pp.348–69.

10. Joseph Roach, *Cities of the Dead: Circum-Atlantic Performance* (New York, Columbia University Press, 1996), p.257.

11. See the newspaper clippings on him in the Frederick N. Ogden Papers, Special Collections, Howard-Tilton Library, Tulane University.

12. See, for example, the New Orleans *Bulletin*, 14 April 1874, p.2 story about the Kellogg administration pardoning 57 convicts. 'In times gone by, when just such a state of affairs existed, what did the people of New Orleans do? ... they rose in their might and asserted their right to defend themselves, since crime was rampant and the law was powerless to protect them.' By early May, vigilance committees began forming. 'A Vigilance Committee Formed', ibid., 9 May 1874, p.1.

13. 'Lady Grossly Insulted on the Streets', ibid., 24 July 1874, p.3; 'Another Outrage. A Negro Insults a Young Lady in Daylight. The Terror in Coliseum Square', ibid., 29 July 1874, p.3.

14. 'Outrage by the Negro Militia', ibid., 2 June 1874, p.3.

15. See, for example, 'White vs. Black Labor', ibid., July 9, 1874, p.1.

16. 'Citizen Not Seeking for an Office', ibid., 24 May 1874. J. Dickson Bruns, the featured speaker at the first anniversary of the September 14th engagement, who, incidentally, had been in on the planning for the battle itself, said much the same thing, 'If the White League is a "mob", it is, at the worst, a mob of gentlemen'. 'Address of Dr. J. Dickson Bruns', in the clipping file of the Bruns Family papers, Special Collections, Howard-Tilton Memorial Library, Tulane University. On San Francisco, see Roger W. Lotchin, *San Francisco, 1846–1856: From Hamlet to City* (New York, Oxford University Press, 1974), pp.245–75; and Philip Ethington, *The Public City: The Political Construction of Urban Life in San Francisco, 1850–1900* (New York, Cambridge University Press, 1994), pp.86–169. On antebellum establishment violence in New Orleans see Leon C. Soule, *The Know Nothing Party in New Orleans: A Reappraisal* (Baton Rouge, Louisiana Historical Association, 1961).

17. George Washington Cable, 'The White League of New Orleans', *The Century Magazine*, Vol.39 (April 1890). Coincidentally, the 400 'special deputies' deputized by the Walmsley administration during the 1934 crisis were given ribbons to wear in their lapels. 'Reyer Swearing in 500 Officers', New Orleans *States*, 1 August 1939, p.3.

18. See the appendices in Jennifer Lawrence, 'Crescent City White League' (Tulane University Honors Thesis, 1992).

19. *The Roll of Honor: Roster of the Citizen Soldiery Who Saved Louisiana* (New Orleans, J. Curtis Waldo, [1877]).

20. Landry, *Battle of Liberty Place*, p.67. As Joseph Roach puts it: 'the officer corps of the White League (and a not insignificant number of its rank and file) formed an interlocking directorship with the secret membership of the exclusive Mardi Gras krewes and men's clubs, especially Comus-Pickwick'. Roach, *Cities of the Dead*, p.261.

21. On the performance rituals that permeate New Orleans culture, see Roach's penetrating *Cities of the Dead, passim*.

22. Quoted in Howard Schuman and Jacqueline Scott, 'Generations and Collective Memories', *American Sociological Review*, Vol.54 (June 1989), p.359. They were also too young to have seen service in the Civil War. For a demographic, residential, and socioeconomic profile of the Crescent City White League, see Lawrence, 'Crescent City White League'.

23. David Cannadine, 'The Context, Performance and Meaning of Ritual: The British Monarchy and the "Invention of Tradition"', in Eric Hobsbawm and Terence Ranger, (eds.), *The Invention of Tradition* (Cambridge and New York, Cambridge University Press, 1983), p.108.

24. Ibid., 101–64. See also Eric Hobsbawm's two essays, 'Introduction: Inventing Traditions', and 'Mass-Producing Traditions, 1870–1914', both in *The Invention of Tradition*, pp.1–14, 263–308; and Gaines Foster, *Ghosts of the Confederacy: Defeat, the Lost Cause, and the Emergence of the New South* (New York, Oxford University Press, 1987), pp.79–81. Regarding statuary Kirk Savage puts the matter thus: 'Public monuments do not arise as if by natural law to celebrate the deserving; they are built by people with sufficient power to marshal (or impose) public consent for their erection'. See his 'The Politics of Memory: Black Emancipation and the Civil War Monument', in *Commemorations: The Politics of National Identity* (Princeton, Princeton University Press, 1994), p.135. See also Sanford Levinson, 'They Whisper: Reflections of Flags, Monuments, and State Holidays, and the Construction of Social Meaning in a Multicultural Society', *Chicago-Kent Law Review*, Vol.70 (1995), pp.1080–1119.

25. See the sheet music illustrations between pp.180–1 in Landry, *Battle of Liberty Place*. See also the famous opinion by John Minor Wisdom knocking down Louisiana's Registration law: United *States v. State of Louisiana*. 225 F. Supp.353 (1963), 367n. Judge Wisdom's father fought with the White League.

26. Editorial, 'The Anniversary', New Orleans *Picayune*, 15 September 1877. See all the front-page coverage of the commemoration in the same issue, as well as in the issues of 15 September 1879, September 15, 1880; also the New Orleans *Times-Democrat*, 15 September 1882, p.1. The clippings file in the Fred N. Ogden papers in the Special Collections Division Tulane also contain material on the celebration.

27. See his 'Caesarism, Circuses, and Monuments', *Journal of Contemporary History*, Vol.6 (1971), pp.172–3.

28. 'The Day We Celebrate', [New Orleans] *Weekly Louisianian*, 20 September 1879, p.2.

29. Jackson, *New Orleans in the Gilded Age*, pp.55–110. A few other White Leaguers, chiefly from the auxiliary units, were also elected mayor, but they were under the control of the 'ring'.

30. 'Is There a Lesson in the 15th [*sic*!] of September?', New Orleans *Picayune*, 16 September 1882.

31. 'Wronging the Heroes of September 14th', New Orleans *Picayune*, 12 November 1882. See also the stories on the ordinance and its repeal in ibid., 15 November 1882, and 16 November 1882.

32. Dennis C. Rousey, 'The New Orleans Police, 1805–1889: A Social History' (unpublished PhD dissertation, Cornell University, 1978), pp.230, 268.

33. Jackson, *New Orleans in the Gilded Age*, p.32.

34. Quoted in John Smith Kendall, *History of New Orleans*, I (Chicago and New York: The Lewis Publishing Company, 1922), pp.450–1.

35. Ibid., pp.455–6; Jackson, *New Orleans in the Gilded Age*, 86–96. On private police forces see Rousey, 'The New Orleans Police', pp.291–4, particularly the activities of the secret 'Committee of Public Safety'.

36. William W. Howe, 'Municipal History of New Orleans', in *Johns Hopkins University Studies in Historical and Political Science*, Vol.7 (Baltimore, Johns Hopkins University Press, 1889), p.33.

37. For a list of the founding members see 'Y.M.D.A: A History of this Political Organization', New Orleans *Times-Democrat*, 22 April 1888, in 'Dr. Henry D. Bruns Scrapbook', New Orleans Public Library, hereinafter NOPL. The ages of members for whom information is available come from Haas, *Political Leadership in a Southern City*, pp.123–33. On Parkerson, see W.S. Parkerson to his son Emmett Parkerson, 8 January 1912, Parkerson papers.

38. 'The originators of the movement', explained one journalistic booster shortly after the election, 'desired that ... it should come from the people interested in the business welfare and commercial prosperity of this city'. Quoted in 'Y.M.D.A: A History'.

39. 'Y.M.D.A: A History'.
40. 'The People Speak', New Orleans *States*, 10 April 1888. Also in the Henry Bruns Scrapbook, NOPL.
41. 'A Great Meeting', New Orleans *Times-Democrat*, 10 April 1888, in Bruns scrapbook, NOPL. On Bruns' father, see Wisdom's decision *United States v. State of Louisiana*, 372n.
42. 'The People Speak'.
43. 'A Monster Meeting', New Orleans *Times-Democrat*, 15 April 1888, in Bruns Scrapbook, NOPL.
44. W.S. Parkerson to Emmett Parkerson, 8 January 1912, Parkerson papers. Parkerson says the YMDA's headquarters were in Odd Fellows Hall, but his memory must have been playing tricks on him. Contemporary sources indicate it was the Continental Guards Armory.
45. 'A Joyful Day', New Orleans *Times-Democrat*, 19 April 1888.
46. Ibid.
47. 'Glad Tidings', New Orleans *Times-Democrat*, 20 April 1888, in Bruns Scrapbook, NOPL. Also, Matthew James Schott, 'John M. Parker of Louisiana and the Varieties of American Progressivism' (PhD dissertation, Vanderbilt University, 1969), pp.17, 25–6, 32–3.
48. Parkerson to Emmett Parkerson, 12 January 1912, in Parkerson Papers.
49. 'The Ring Smashed'.
50. 'Glad Tidings'.
51. On the psychological tendency to filter historical events not personally experienced through the presentist lens of personal life events, see Lewis Coser's introduction to Halbwachs, *On Collective Memory*, pp.24–6; and Schuman and Scott, 'Generations and Collective Memories', pp.378–9.
52. 'The People's Anniversary', New Orleans *Picayune*, 14 September 1894; Jackson, *New Orleans in the Gilded Age*, p.142.
53. See the appendix in Haas, *Political Leadership in a Southern City*.
54. New Orleans *Picayune*, 15 April 1896, p.1.
55. Ibid., 18 April 1896, p.1.
56. Jackson, *New Orleans in the Gilded Age*, pp.312–16.
57. 'Louisiana's Independence Day', New Orleans *Times-Democrat*, 14 April 1896.
58. New Orleans *Times-Democrat*, 25 September 1904.
59. 'Better Ballots Now Than Force Later On', in ibid. 13 October 1904, p.1.
60. New Orleans *Times-Democrat*, 8 November 1904.
61. T. Harry Williams, *Huey Long* (New York, Alfred A. Knopf, 1969), pp.188–91; the quotation is on p.190.
62. Walmsley also descended from the former Confederate Senator Thomas J. Semmes. 'Thomas Semmes Walmsley', in Henry E. Chambers, *History of Louisiana*, III (Chicago and New York, The American Historical Society, 1925), pp.351–2.
63. New Orleans *Times-Picayune*, 15 September 1932, p.3.
64. Williams, *Huey Long*, pp.628–33; 692–706; 716–20. Also, Alan Brinkley, *Huey Long, Father Coughlin, and the Great Depression* (New York, Vintage Books, 1982), pp.36–81.
65. The typed circular is in the Huey P. Long Collection, UNO Archives, Earl Long Library, University of New Orleans. Thanks are due to Joseph Logsdon for drawing my attention to this important document.
66. 'Reyer Swearing in 500 Officers', New Orleans *States*, 1 August 1934; Williams, *Huey Long*, pp.722–3.
67. New Orleans *Times-Picayune*, 26, 27 August 1934, p.1.
68. Quoted in Williams, *Huey Long*, pp.724–30; the quotation is on p.730.
69. Ibid, pp.724–30.
70. Ibid., p.731.
71. Guy Molony interview, 11 November 1959, in the Herman Deutsch Collection, HTL, TU. See also, Lester D. Langley and Thomas Schoonover, *The Banana Men: American Mercenaries & Entrepreneurs in Central America, 1880–1930* (Lexington, The University Press of Kentucky, 1995), pp.99–100, 121–4, 160–3; *Washington Artillery Year Book, 1922* (New Orleans, 1922), p.22.
72. Langley and Schoonover, *The Banana Men*, pp.127–9.

73. Huey P. Long, *Every Man a King: The Autobiography of Huey P. Long*, with an introduction by T. Harry Williams (Chicago, Quadrangle Books, 1933 [1964]), pp.213–17.
74. Williams, *Huey Long*, p.468.
75. 'All State Troops Mobilized by Long', *New York Times*, 7 September 1934, p.19.
76. Williams, *Huey Long*, pp.732–6; William Ivy Hair, *The Kingfish and His Realm: The Life and Times of Huey P. Long* (Baton Rouge, Louisiana State University Press, 1991), p.282.
77. New Orleans *Times-Picayune*, 15 September 1934, p.1.
78. Williams, *Huey Long*, pp.182–4, 716; Taylor, *Louisiana Reconstructed*, pp.177–8. Huey once said that the only former Louisiana governor he ever respected was the roguish young carpetbagger, Henry Clay Warmoth. In his use of power politics, Long often paid Warmoth the compliment of imitation.
79. 'Address of the Hon. George C. H. Kernion at the Sixtieth Anniversary Celebration of the Fourteenth of September, 1874' (New Orleans: Board of Commissioners of Liberty Place, 1934), in New Orleans Collection Pamphlets, Special Collections, Howard-Tilton Library, Tulane University.
80. Quoted in Hair, *The Kingfish and His Realm*, p.280.
81. Quoted in Williams, *Huey Long*, p.841.
82. Quoted in ibid., p.717.
83. Quoted in Allan P. Sindler, *Huey Long's Louisiana* (Baltimore, Johns Hopkins University Press, 1956), p.91.
84. Quoted in Williams, *Huey Long*, p.449.
85. Quoted in Schott, 'John M. Parker of Louisiana', p.491.
86. See, for example, W.S. Parkerson to his son Emmett Parkerson, 8 January 1912, in the W.S. Parkerson papers, Pearl River Collection, Special Collections, HTL, TU.
87. Hilda Phelps Hammond, *Let Freedom Ring* (New York, Farrar & Rinehart, 1936), pp.19–21. Pamela Tyler, *Silk Stockings and Ballot Boxes. Women and Politics in New Orleans, 1920–1963* (Athens, University of Georgia Press, 1996).
88. Hammond, *Let Freedom Ring*, p.284.

The Slave Trade Remembered on the Former Gold and Slave Coasts

THERESA A. SINGLETON

Remembering the trans-Atlantic slave trade has abounded during the 1990s. From films such as Haile Gerima's *Sankofa* and Steven Spielberg's *Amistad* to museum exhibitions such as the Transatlantic Slave Gallery in Liverpool, England, this interest has taken shape in diverse contexts.[1] The UNESCO (United Nations Educational, Scientific and Cultural Organization) initiative entitled 'The Slave Route' is perhaps the most ambitious undertaking aimed toward the memorialization of the slave trade. The goal of the project is to foster historical research on the slave trade, the preservation and interpretation of sites and monuments connected with the slave trade, the promotion of cultural tourism connected with slavery, and the sponsoring of visual and performing arts in the countries of African diaspora.[2]

The individuals and institutions responsible for these projects are to be commended for setting the stage wherein the slave trade can be reflected upon and better understood. Yet, this renewed interest in trans-Atlantic slavery begs the questions: what are we trying to remember; how will remembering help us in the present; and can reconciliation result from competing legacies of trans-Atlantic slavery?[3]

This essay attempts to grapple with these questions, but is particularly concerned with the last one. It considers how trans-Atlantic slavery is remembered in West Africa using place memory as an analytical framework. Place memory refers to the 'persistence of place as a container of experiences ... an alert and alive memory connects spontaneously with place'.[4] Dolores Hayden comments that 'places trigger memories for insiders, who have shared a common past, and at the same time often can represent shared pasts, to outsiders who might be interested in knowing about them in the present'.[5] The most powerful places where the memory of slave trade resides in West Africa are in the castles, forts, and other sites where captured Africans were brought until they awaited the horrific Middle Passage across the Atlantic Ocean.[6]

My intention here, however, is not to interpret these sites simply as elements of African diasporic history, but rather to examine the multiple meanings of the memory embedded in these places. Objects often have multiple and sometimes contradictory meanings. Meaning also changes according to the context.[7] For example, the meaning of a goblet will vary according who is drinking from it, what is contained in it, and where the drinking is taking place. Similarly, the goblet's meaning changes if it was received as a gift, purchased, or recovered from an archaeologist's trowel. Its meanings to a connoisseur of fine beverages, an alcoholic, or an advocate of temperance may contradict each other. Thus, one object offers the possibility of revealing many stories associated with it.

Interpreting memory is a contemporary activity. It does not provide a lens into the past, rather it informs us about present phenomenon. In the case of Ghana (the former Gold Coast), reawakening the memory of slavery resulted in conflicts between Ghanaians and groups of African Americans. Whereas in the Republic of Benin (the former Slave Coast also later known as Dahomey), the Beninois have appropriated the memory of slavery to emphasize their historical cultural linkages with diaspora communities. Both cases poignantly illustrate the 'power of place', where memory and social identity are intertwined.

'Explore Your Heritage'

My inspiration for considering the multiple meanings of the European castles and forts – the tangible reminders of the Atlantic trade first in gold, and later in human cargoes – was a sign directing visitors to Elmina castle. It simply read 'EXPLORE YOUR HERITAGE' (Figure 1). A similar sign was placed at a comparable distance away from Cape Coast castle approximately ten kilometres from Elmina. This message raises questions as to whom is it directed? To all visitors? To tourists only? Ghanaians? Did it also include the residents in the towns of Elmina and Cape Coast? Whose heritage is contained in Elmina and Cape Coast castles? Who owns these castles?

Answering these questions is difficult because the histories associated with these structures are complex. Take Elmina castle, for example. The Portuguese reached coastal Ghana in the 1400s, and built *São Jorge da Mina* (St. George's of the Mine), their first and largest fortress in 1482. In time, both the castle and the African village near it became known as Elmina. Elmina castle served as the headquarters, living quarters, and storage facility for the Portuguese trade in gold. In 1637 the Dutch attacked Elmina and the Portuguese surrendered the castle to the Dutch. The Dutch traders remained in control of Elmina castle for the next 245 years during which time they were engaged in the trade of gold, humans, and other commodities. In the seventeenth and eighteenth centuries, several other

FIGURE 1

SIGN INDICATING LOCATION OF ELMINA CASTLE, GHANA

Source: Theresa Singleton.

European powers established trading centres along the 500-kilometre coastline of the Gold Coast (extending from Assine in the Ivory Coast to the Volta River in Ghana), including the British, Danes, French, Swedes, and Brandenburgers. In total, the Europeans built over 60 trade-posts there, more than any other part of the African continent. Declining profits due to increased competition from the British along with the desire to strengthen trade in the East Indies, the Dutch sold Elmina castle to the British in 1872. By this time, Britain was seeking sole territorial control of the Gold Coast. Leaders of the powerful Asante Kingdom, located further inland from the coast, successfully checked British advances at first, but in the end the British prevailed. In 1873 the Asante marched toward the coast to confront the British invaders. To stop the Asante and their allies – the Fante inhabitants of Elmina – the British bombarded the town of Elmina from the ramparts of Elmina castle and destroyed it. The part of the town immediately adjacent to the fortress was never rebuilt, and has been the focus of archaeological research since 1985.[8]

The castles, however, speak to more than the power struggles among Europeans in their pursuit of African resources; they also played a role in shaping social identities within the African towns adjacent to them. One example of this is seen in the formation of *asafo* companies among the Fante – the dominant ethno-linguistic group of Ghana's central coast both historically and today. *Asafo* companies are military associations organized in villages, towns, and traditional states of southern Ghana in which membership is usually inherited patrilineally, but outsiders can sometimes be initiated into them. These associations perform important civic works by balancing the powers of the chief. Fante *asafos* are highly developed, and are known for their animated processions, colourful uniforms, flags embroidered with different motifs, and cement shrines. Fante towns typically have from two to fourteen separate Asfao companies.[9]

Asafo or a similar system of military organizations appears to be an indigenous African institution that was in place when the Portuguese arrived in the 1400s.[10] However, at least two *asafo* companies clearly emerged from European contact: the company of 'castle slaves' *Brofomba* or *Brofumba*, and the company of mulattos, *Akrampa*. In all of the castles, the Europeans brought in enslaved people usually from elsewhere in West Africa to work in the castles.[11] An oral tradition of Cape Coast suggests that the 'castle slaves' were the builders of the castle, originally called Carolusburg under the Swedes, but finally took the name Cape Coast under the English in 1664. These African labourers received training in the castle as carpenters, bricklayers, coopers, sawyers, and stonemasons. They were assigned land near the castle, and eventually formed their own separated company – the *Brofumba* (white men's children) *or Brofunkua* (white men's slaves).[12] The 'castle slaves' of Elmina also formed their own *asafo* company. Unlike many of the slaves in the Americas, however, castle slaves earned wages, owned property, and had definite rights.[13]

A small community of mulattos emerged from the relationships between the European men in forts and castles and African women. Members of this Afro-European community often rose to prominence, and took advantage of economic opportunities the trans-Atlantic commerce afforded them. In fact, many Afro-Europeans were slaveholders.[14] That mulattos constituted their own *asafo* company – the *Akrampa* (mulattos) – indicates that they were well integrated into the sociopolitical structure of the Gold Coast.[15] *Asafo* companies of mulattos were in place in both Elmina and Cape Coast by the mid-nineteenth century.[16] Both the *Brofumba* and the *Akrampa* are active *asafo* companies among the Fante today.

In addition to *asafo* companies, residents of Elmina and Cape Coast have historically occupied a privileged position because of their association with the castles. This relationship was particularly evident in the town of Elmina, where for most of its history, the town functioned as a separate polity. Eliminians prospered from the Atlantic trade of which the slave trade was only one dimension. Archaeological investigations of the pre-colonial town of Elmina revealed that imported ceramics, glass, metal objects, and trade beads vastly outnumbered locally produced artefacts.[17] This suggests that Elminians could afford, and possibly preferred, European imported goods to locally produced goods.[18] The use of imported goods among Eliminians was far greater than that of other coastal states excavated thus far along the lower Guinea Coast.[19]

Since the pre-colonial trade, the castles and forts have served many purposes. In recent years they have been used as administrative offices, museums, prisons, training schools, and post offices. Christiansborg Castle in Accra functions as the seat for presidential headquarters of the Republic of Ghana. Twenty-five of the extant forts and castles were designated National Monuments in 1972. As national monuments they are protected by law under the stewardship of the Ghana Museums and Monuments Board (GMMB). This means that GMMB is responsible for their care and oversees how they are used. In addition to being national monuments, the castles and some of the forts are listed as World Heritage Sites by UNESCO.[20]

No indigenous Ghanaian site either archaeological or architectural has received national monument status. This privileging of the castle and forts has produced an unfortunate disparity in the preservation of Ghana's rich archaeological and architectural heritage. The European-associated sites have always attracted and received considerably more funding than indigenous Ghanaian sites.[21] In retrospect, designating the castles and forts national monuments while excluding indigenous sites was misguided;

however, the rationale for this decision lies in the perception that the castles and forts are of interest, not only to Ghanaians, but to an international audience who would be interested in making the long, expensive journey to visit these places. For this reason these historical sites have been granted this special status.

FIGURE 2
INTERIOR OF ELMINA CASTLE, SHOWING ENTRANCE TO SLAVE
DUNGEON FOR FEMALES

Source: Theresa Singleton.

This concern in attracting international visitors is also evident in the public interpretation of the castles. Most tours are directed toward the interests of the outsiders. Although tours vary, they emphasize the architectural history and the uses of the castles in the trans-Atlantic trade. Details of the slave trade are interpreted in the slave dungeons (Figure 2). Visitors are particularly moved on entering the slave dungeons in Cape Coast castle where the stench of human excrement and decaying flesh still lingers today. The tours, however, provide virtually no information on the history and culture of the area or on the relationship between the Europeans in the castle and the people of the adjacent towns.[22]

The Struggle over Meaning and Ownership

A shift toward interpreting the castles from an African perspective began taking shape in the early 1990s. The United States Agency for International Development (USAID) launched a project to restore totally both Cape Coast and Elmina castles as well as the former Dutch fort, Saint Yago in Elmina. This restoration effort was part of a larger, five-year developmental scheme to promote tourism in Ghana's Central Region which involved collaborating organizations in Ghana and in the United States.[23] Cape Coast Castle had partially functioned as a museum, known as the West African Historical Museum since the mid-1970s. Through this new effort, however, the castle, under its new name – Cape Coast Castle Museum – would be entirely restored with new exhibits, storage, and conservation facilities, and would serve as the museum for the entire Central Region of Ghana. Elmina castle would be an adjunct to the Cape Coast Castle Museum serving as local museum and training facility.[24] In December 1994 the inaugural exhibition 'Crossroads of People, Crossroads of Trade' opened at the Cape Coast Castle Museum which covers the past 500 years of Ghana's history, and places the forts and castles within this socio-economic and historical context. This exhibition, however, has been criticized for its overemphasis on the African diaspora in North America.[25]

As the restoration efforts received publicity, a small but vocal African-American community in Ghana reacted strongly against restoration of the castles. They referred to the restoration of the castles as the 'whitewashing' of the history associated with the slave trade.[26] Their protests were reinforced by groups of visiting blacks from other countries in the Americas, who were appalled to learn that the ramparts above the slave dungeons were often used as a staging area for concerts, plays, and other public events. They were also annoyed to see a restaurant and bar directly above the slave dungeon for males. The restaurant and bar are now closed, and only appropriate musical performances and religious services are permitted in the monuments.[27]

The African Americans opposed the restoration because they see the castles solely as memorials to the slave trade – the sacred ground where their ancestors forcibly departed from Africa, and where many others ended their lives in the dungeons. The African Americans want to preserve the appearances and smells that evoke feelings of fear, hopelessness, dread – emotions undoubtedly experienced by those enslaved within the castle walls. Restoration would erase these images, and 'cleanse' buildings associated with a tragic past.

The museum personnel of Cape Coast Museum (as well as many Ghanaians) see the slave trade as only one chapter in the complex histories of the castles, and of Ghana as a whole. At present, the castles house museums, and their staffs desire to have updated facilities that would make these museums first-rate institutions. Moreover, routine maintenance and stabilization of the castles and forts are necessary to counteract the corrosive effects of the coastal salt air in order to preserve them for the future. Finally, the sentiment of many Ghanaians is most likely summed up in the comments conveyed to me by a member of the museum staff of the Cape Coast Castle Museum: 'We inherited these buildings and would like to use them to tell our stories'.[28]

The conflict between museum professionals at the castles and African-American residents and visitors over the meaning and interpretation of the castles received a significant amount of media attention in the United States.[29] It is apparent from these articles that the African Americans involved in this protest want atonement from those whose ancestors complied in the slave trade. While acknowledging the tragedy of the slave trade, the Ghanaians interviewed feel that they have no reason to apologize for activities for which they were not responsible. Another sentiment expressed by the director of the Cape Coast Castle Museum was that African Americans are unwilling to contribute financially to the preservation of the castles: 'they [African Americans] don't want to contribute anything to what we're doing. Then they want a big say in what we do.' In the same article, an African-American resident of Ghana responded saying that through their enslavement 'the ancestors of African Americans paid the highest price already'.[30]

Absent from the debate over the castle restoration are the voices of local residents and their interests.[31] The traditional council of chiefs claims the land on which the castles were built, but this claim has not entitled the chiefs or their constituents to any special access to the castles. When the chief of Elmina died in 1993, the council of chiefs sought permission from GMMB to place his body in Elmina castle for viewing. GMMB denied the request on the grounds that the funeral would draw too many people to the area around the castle.[32] Since the renovation of the building, Elminians find themselves increasingly separated from their castle. There was a market with sellers and foodstuffs which has since been relocated from the castle. Additionally, signs are posted in the immediate area of the castle, 'THIS AREA IS RESTRICTED TO ALL PERSONS EXCEPT TOURISTS'. By far the greatest insult is that Elminians are expected to pay the same fee as tourists to enter the castle, although most do not.[33]

Analysing the struggle over the meaning of Cape Coast and Elmina castles brings to mind Pierre Nora's characterization of memory: 'Memory is life, always embodied in living societies and as such in permanent evolution, subject to the dialectic of remembering and forgetting, unconscious of the distortions to which it is subject, vulnerable in various ways to appropriation and manipulation, capable of lying dormant for long periods only to be suddenly reawakened'.[34] Prior to the USAID project, the memory of slavery contained in the castles laid dormant – forgotten by most Ghanaians and only conscious to the few African-American and other non-Ghanaian visitors to the castles. The international attention on the conflicts surrounding the castle restoration reawaken the world to the historical role the castles played in the slave trade. Albeit this reawakening has been controversial, but Ghanaians have responded by remembering those who were enslaved in two ceremonies.[35]

Yet, reawakening the memory of the slave trade has distorted the other stories associated with these structures. Elmina castle is being memorialized as a slave castle, but it was built for the gold and spice trades that preceded the slave trade. The overemphasis on the African diaspora in the exhibition at Cape Coast Castle Museum reduces the vibrant history and culture of Ghana's Central Region to a singular theme. Referring to routine stabilization necessary for the preservation of the castles as 'whitewashing history' ignores the structural histories of these buildings, and assumes that they have remained unchanged for all of these many years.

Today, both castles function as museums. In the United States, museums are trying to develop collecting, exhibition, and educational programmes that are directed to their multiple constituencies. Despite the fact that the castles are World Heritage Sites, the vast majority of the visitors to the castles are Ghanaian, yet the emphasis of the interpretation of these buildings continues to be directed to outsiders. It is unfortunate that the USAID consultants did not encourage the Ghanaians to develop public programmes that would address the interests of their varied audiences, but not at the cost of ignoring their primary audience. The castles are containers of the shared pasts of Ghanaians, African diaspora communities, and Europeans. The public interpretation of these monuments' programmes should invite each of these groups to explore their heritages.

Place Memory on the Slave Coast

The memory of slavery in the Republic of Benin (the Slave Coast) contrasts sharply with that of Ghana in two essential ways: first, the 'memory frame – the setting within which specific content is presented to us' differs between the two nations.[36] In Ghana, the castles and forts, particularly the slave dungeons, provide the memory frame for the slave trade. Whereas the memory of slavery is alive in a variety of modern monuments and memorials rather than in slave dungeons.[37] The second difference is seen in the consciousness of this memory. The Ghanaians had either forgotten or were uncomfortable with the memory of slavery. The Beninois, on the other hand, openly acknowledge their historical role in the slave trade and have apparently come to terms with this legacy. These differences raise questions used here to structure the following the discussion on Benin: if not in slave dungeons, where does the memory of slavery reside in Benin; and why are the Beninois very conscious of this memory?

The absence of slave dungeons in Benin is the result of several factors related to the operation of the trans-Atlantic trade along the Slave Coast (an area of approximately 322 kilometres extending eastward from the Volta River in Ghana to the Lagos lagoon in, the corner of south-western Nigeria).[38] These conditions include: the initial refusal of African leaders to permit the building forts; the use of impermanent or other ephemeral materials such as mud in the building of lodges or factories (warehouses used to house enslaved people); the possible use of floating barracoons; and the destruction of many lodges during local wars and other seizes.

The African rulers of the Slave Coast did not want Europeans to build fortresses as they had done along the Gold Coast. In 1670, when the French asked the King of Allada permission to construct their trading lodge in the European fashion (presumably in brick or stone, rather than mud), he refused. He reasoned that the French might install a cannon, turn it into a fortress, and become the masters of his kingdom as the Dutch had done in Elmina.[39] Similarly, the Whydah king not only prohibited the Europeans from fortifying their trading lodges, but he required them to be adjacent to the king's palace in the capital town of Savi. The Whydah king also assumed responsibility for the construction and upkeep of the lodges, building them in the local vernacular tradition. This action denied the Europeans the opportunity to employ European-styled buildings to distinguish themselves from each European nation and from their Africans hosts.[40]

An alternative to lodge was the 'floating barracoon' – a hull permanently anchored in a creek or estuary to house enslaved people.[41] In 1638 the Dutch West India Company considered establishing a slave lodge in this fashion:

'in the event no permanent lodge was established on-shore in Allada, the trade being conducted instead from a ship moored permanently off the coast'.[42] Whether or not the Dutch employed this kind of lodge is not clear; the Dutch built several lodges on land, most of which were short-lived. The lodge constructed in 1660 at Offra (the port for the Allada kingdom) persisted for over 30 years until it was destroyed in a local war.[43]

In the eighteenth century, English, French and Portuguese traders received permission to build forts in Glenhue (modern Ouidah) to protect their lodges. These forts had very limited military power because they laid over 3 km from the ocean and could not be used as landing places for their own supplies. This location, however, facilitated African control of European activities which made the forts vulnerable to direct assaults.[44] For example, the Dahomian armies occupied and burned the Portuguese fort on two occasions in 1727 and again in 1743.[45] Nonetheless, these forts serviced the slave trade throughout the eighteenth century until they were abandoned in the respective order: the French in 1797, the Portuguese in 1805, and the British in 1812.[46] Francisco Felix de Souza, a Brazilian merchant, who continued the trade there until his death in 1849, revived slave trading at the Portuguese fort. From other points along the coast, later Brazilians – including former enslaved returnees from Bahia – were engaged in the slave trade for the Brazilian and Cuban markets until it finally ended in the 1860s.[47]

Of the former European forts, only the Portuguese fort now serves as a memorial to the slave trade. The Historical Museum of Ouidah was established in what remained of the fort after it was vacated and set afire by its last Portuguese residents in 1961.[48] The museum contains artefact collections, photographs, and drawings that depict the slave trade. It also has exhibits that illustrate the similarities in religion practices of Beninois and those of diaspora communities in Brazil, Haiti, and Cuba – areas where most people enslaved from Slave Coast were transported.

Another museum, known simply as the 'Brazil House', the former residence of a prominent Afro-Brazilian family in Ouidah, features displays of objects and clothing used in Afro-Brazilian rituals in Bahia, Brazil and in Benin. As the name of the museum implies, its collections focus on the contributions of Afro-Brazilians to the art and architecture of Ouidah and other places where they settled.[49] Particularly notable are objects known as *asen* – metal altars used in ceremonies that honour deceased relatives. These objects represent the spread of African beliefs and ideas to the Americas and their later reintroduction in Ouidah by Brazilian returnees. Afro-Brazilian-influenced *asen* are larger, more elaborately decorated, and embellished with polychrome pigments than those that predate the Afro-Brazilian return to Benin.[50] Brazil House has a collection of *asen*, and photographs illustrating their ritual usages.

The most provocative memory place of the slave trade in Ouidah is the re-creation of the road leading from Ouidah to the ocean, known as the 'slave route'. In the 1860s a visitor noted that the town of Whydah was 'separated from the shore by a broad leek-green swamp, by a narrow lagoon, and a high sandbank'.[51] Enslaved people were taken from the lodges in town and herded like cattle along this former track of swamp and sand to board ships destined for the Americas. Today, the road has been improved with culverts and a short bridge crosses over the lagoon. Sculptures of human-like and allegorical figures adorn various points along the path. These figures allude to the human suffering endured by those forced into slavery. The slave route is also used for vodun ceremonies. A monument in Zoungbodji, a village off the slave route, commemorates the First International Festival of Vodun Art and Culture held in Ouidah in February 1993. This monument also memorializes the slave trade. On one side of the monument, a mural made in mosaic depicts human figures images chained together walking toward a slave ship (Figure 3).

The memory of slavery was not only alive in museums, modern-day monuments, and the re-creation of the slave route, but also in my conversations with the people there as well. A principal voodun priest told me that he had maintained close ties with practitioners of vodun in the Americas and had travelled to Haiti, Brazil, and other places where large communities of practitioners now live. In doing this he was breaking away from the tradition wherein the principal priest seldom travelled beyond his local environs.

Even in more informal conversations, the Beninois are aware of the memory of slavery. At times, they appeared to be a bit embarrassed by this history, but they were not apologetic of it either. They appeared genuinely interested in learning about those who are the descendants of those enslaved. Why was memory of slavery so evident in Ouidah? Was this consciousness simply the result of tourism geared toward memorializing the slave trade? Or was the memory of slavery being used to serve other purposes. The answers to these questions began to unfold in Allada.

'Toussaint Louverture, he is our hero, too!'

In the town of Allada, located approximately 35 km north of Ouidah, a bust in the image of Toussaint Louverture overlooks a clearing (Figure 4). Why is there a monument in Benin dedicated to the famous leader of the most successful slave rebellion in the Americas? According to one of Toussaint's sons, Gaou Guinon – the father of Toussaint – was a descendant of an Ardra [Allada] king.[52] While many Americanists have regarded the information about Toussaint's African heritage with scepticism, the people of Allada, if

FIGURE 3
A MOSAIC BY F. BANDEIRA (A BENINOIS ARTIST LIVING IN COTONOU)
AFFIXED TO A MEMORIAL TO THE FIRST INTERNATIONAL FESTIVAL OF
VODUN ART AND CULTURE, FEBRUARY 1993

Source: Theresa Singleton.

FIGURE 4
MEMORIAL TO TOUSSAINT LOUVERTURE, ALLADA,
REPUBLIC OF BENIN

Source: Theresa Singleton.

not all Beninois, have accepted it and have claimed him as their native son. What is the likelihood that Toussaint was a descendant of Ardra royalty?

Allada or the Ardra was the most powerful kingdom along the Slave Coast, when the Portuguese began trading there in the 1560's. At its peak, the kingdom of Allada was believed to control most, if not all, of the region that became known as the Slave Coast. Allada enjoyed a monopoly on the European trade until Whydah [Hueda] challenged her authority and emerged as a separate state in 1670. From 1670 to 1724, Allada competed with Whydah for the European trade. In 1724, Dahomian troops marched against Allada burning its capital and taking over 8000 prisoners. About 3,000 refugees from the Allada fled to Whydah where they were either sold into slavery to European traders or died of starvation.[53] A section of the royal dynasty of Allada established a new independent kingdom of Allada known under its European name as Porto-Novo. In 1730, Agaja, the Dahomian king who conquered Allada established his residence on present site of Allada located approximately three kilometres west from the old site of the capital known today as Togudo-Awute.[54]

In the Americas, enslaved people traded from Allada, and sometimes from the Slave Coast in general, were referred to as *Araras* or *Aradas*. The Aradas were one of the dominant nations on Saint Domingue (Haiti) particularly in the first half of the eighteenth century.[55] In fact, the owner of the Bréda Plantation, where Toussaint was born in 1744, preferred Aradas to Africans of some of the other nations, because 'they submitted silently to plantation discipline and worked well'.[56] That Toussaint was of Arada parentage is highly possible, but to establish that he was of royal heritage is a more difficult task. Enslaved people sold through Allada and Whydah were drawn from a large area. They were usually prisoners of war and less likely to be drawn from within the kingdom conducting the sale. Of course, there were exceptions: debtors, enemies, or persons committing other offences within the kingdom were also sold.[57] It is possible that Toussaint's father was a refugee from Dahomian conquest in 1724 or some other local war or internal conflict.

Whether or not Toussaint is of royal Ardra or even of Ardra heritage, another, arguably, more important reason the Beninois claim him is that he successfully fought against France to obtain independence for his fellow countrymen and countrywomen. The slave rebellion in Saint Domingue that culminated into an independent Haiti is comparable to the Beninois anti-colonial struggle against France. Thus, Toussaint is as much a symbol of Beninois independence – their post-colonial identity – as he was presumably a descendant of the Ardra kingdom.[58]

By claiming Toussaint as one of their own and establishing religious and other cultural linkages with African diaspora communities, the Beninois have constructed a memory of slavery that celebrates the common ancestry Beninois shared with these communities. It is understandable that the Beninois would choose a celebratory memory of the slave trade rather than one that dwells on its tragedies. Dubbed the infamous 'slave coast', Benin, particularly under the hegemony of the Dahomey Kingdom, became notorious for the its militarism, brutal slave raids, and severe depopulation that left an indelible imprint on the landscape.[59] These tragedies, however, have not been forgotten, but are remembered in the art, exhibitions, and re-creation of the slave route – all subtle, but effective ways of saying 'never again will we let these things happen'.

Conclusions

Remembering the slave trade is important and necessary. It is a major theme of modern history that spans almost four centuries. Yet, amazingly, this important theme has often been reduced to a mere footnote or totally ignored in the public histories of Africa, the Americas, and Europe. Only in the past decade have concerted efforts been undertaken to reawaken the world to this history. The history of trans-Atlantic slavery is complex and multi-dimensional, and it is doubtful that it will ever be fully understood. Consequently, there is no *one* narrative of the slave trade, but multiple narratives and multiple memories. Places associated with the slave trade help to root these memories and provide tangible links in the present with the past, whether these places are former slave dungeons, modern re-creations, or other memorials. The slave trade is a very emotionally charged subject that is bound to result in potential conflicts between those who are the descendants of the enslaved and those who are the descendants of the enslavers. It may be helpful to heed the words of Nana Kwesi Tandoh, who is reported saying at the ceremony in which those sold into slavery were mourned in Elmina, 'Africans can only forge ahead if they make an objective analysis of the mistakes of their past'.[60] While it doubtful that an objective analysis of the past is truly possible, it is necessary for Africans and people of the African diaspora to forge ahead, and not blame those in the present for the mistakes made in the past.

NOTES

I wish to acknowledge the many people who contributed to making this essay possible and made my trip to Ghana and Benin one of the most delightful and rewarding experiences of my life. A special thanks goes to following individuals: Christopher DeCorse, Francis Duah, Raymond Agbo, Bosman Murray, Sallars Awortwi, Constance Dobge, Alexis Adande and Joseph Adande. I am particularly grateful to the Adande family for inviting me to stay at their home, and taking me on several excursions throughout Benin.

1. Exhibitions have been a very important medium used to remember slavery. Exhibitions such as *Before freedom Came* have examined the everyday lives of enslaved men and women, see Campbell and Rice (eds.), *Before Freedom Came: African-American Life in the Antebellum South* (Charlottesville, University Press of Virginia, 1991). Exhibitions that have specifically addressed the trans-Atlantic slave trade include: 'Les Anneaux de la Mémoire' (Chains of Memory), see *Les Anneaux de la mémoire* (CIM, Coderie Royale, France, 1992); 'Transatlantic Slavery: Against all Human Dignity', see Anthony Tibbles (ed.), *Transatlantic Slavery: Against Human Dignity* (London, HMSO, 1994); and 'A Slave Ship Speaks: The Wreck of the Henrietta Marie', see Madeleine H. Burnside (ed.), *A Slave Ship Speaks: The Wreck of the Henrietta Marie* (Key West, Mel Fisher Maritime Heritage Society, 1995).

2. UNESCO has hosted conferences and funded research and restoration projects through the Slave Route Initiative.

3. I raise these questions rhetorically in much the same way Andreas Huyssen discusses the proliferation of Holocaust museums, monuments, and general media attention directed toward this subject at the end of this century. Andreas Huyssen, *Twilight Memories: Marking Time in a Culture of Amnesia* (New York, Routledge, 1995).

4. Edward S. Casey, *Remembering: A Phenomenological Study* (Bloomington, Indiana University Press, 1987), p.186.

5. Dolores Hayden, *Power of Place: Urban Landscapes as Public History* (Cambridge, MA, MIT Press, 1995), p.46.

6. I visited these places in both Ghana and Benin in Fall 1993. I spent most of my time in Ghana where I was undertaking an archaeological project with Christopher DeCorse of Syracuse University. After my work was completed in Ghana, I went to Benin, met Beninois colleagues and visited several archaeological and historical sites, some of which are discussed herein. Although I have not returned to either Ghana or Benin, I have kept up with more recent developments that are related to these sites. Other sources that have considered this topic as it pertains to Ghana include Edward Bruner, 'Tourism in Ghana: The Representation of Slavery and the Return of the Black Diaspora', *American Anthropologist*, Vol.98, No.2 (1996), pp.290–304; Christine Mullen Kreamer, Contested Terrain: Cultural Negotiation and Ghana's Cape Coast Castle Exhibition, 'Crossroads of People, Crossroads of Trade', paper presented at Symposium on Memory and Slavery, University of Chicago, 23–25 May 1997; Enid Schildrout, 'The Kingdom of Gold', *Natural History*, Vol.105, No.2 (1996), pp.36–47. I am not aware other sources on this topic for Benin.

7. Christopher Tilley, 'Interpreting Material Culture', in Ian Hodder (ed.), *The Meaning of Things* (London, 1989), p.191.

8. Pre-colonial histories of the Gold Coast include: Kwame Daaku, *Trade and Politics on the Gold Coast: A Study of the African Reaction to European Trade* (Oxford, Clarendon Press, 1970); John. K. Flynn, *Asante and Its Neighbours, 1700–1807* (Evanston, Northwestern University Press); Ray Kea, *Settlements, Trade and Polities in the Seventeenth-century Gold Coast* (Baltimore, Johns Hopkins University Press, 1982); Larry Yarak, *Asante and the Dutch, 1744–1873* (Oxford, Oxford University Press, 1990). For discussion of the histories of the forts and castles of the Gold Coast, see A.W. Lawrence, *Trade Castles and Forts of West Africa* (London, Jonathan Cape, 1963); Albert Van Dantzig, *Forts and Castles of Ghana* (Accra, Sedco, 1980). For discussion of the archaeological research at Elmina, see Christopher DeCorse, 'An Archaeological Study of Elmina, Ghana: Trade and Culture Change on the Gold Coast between the Fifteenth and Nineteenth Centuries' (PhD diss., University of California at Los Angeles, 1989); 'Culture Contact, Continuity, and Change on the Gold Coast, AD 1400–1900', *African Archeological Review*, Vol.10 (1992), pp.163–96; and *Under the Castle Cannon: An Archaeological View of African-European interaction on the Gold Coast* (Washington, DC, Smithsonian Institution Press, forthcoming).

9. Sources on Fante *asafos* consulted here include: Peter Alder and Nicholas Barnard, *Asafo! African Flags of the Fante* (London, Thames and Hudson, 1992), pp.39–47; I. Chukwukere, 'Perspectives on the *Asafo* Institution in Southern Ghana', *Journal of African Studies*, Vol.7, No.1 (1980), pp.38–47; Ansu K. Datta and R. Porter, 'The *Asafo* System in Historical Perspective', *Journal of African History*, Vol.12, No.2 (1971), pp.279–97; Arthur Ffoulkes, 'The Company System in Cape Coast Castle, *Journal of the African Society*, Vol.7

(1907–1908), pp.262–77.

10. Authors have debated whether the *asafo* was indigenous to the Fante or a product of European contact, see discussions in Chukwukere and Datta and Porter. Alder and Barnard (pp.9–10) suggest that *asafo* was an indigenous concept, but that certain aspects of European military traditions were adopted such as performing musketry salutes, marching in processions, and the use of flags and numbering of companies.

11. Datta and Porter, p.286.

12. Ffoulkes, p.262.

13. Datta and Porter, pp.286–7.

14. For slaveholding among Afro-Europeans in the Gold Coast see, Adam Jones, 'Female Slave-owner on the Gold Coast', in Stephan Palmié (ed.), *Slave Cultures and the Cultures of Slavery* (Knoxville, University Press of Tennessee), pp.101–11; Larry W. Yarak, 'West African Coastal Slavery in the Nineteenth Century: The Case of the Afro-European Slaveholders of Elmina', *Ethnohistory*, Vol.36, No.1 (Winter 1989), pp.44–60.

15. Yarak, 'West African Coastal Society', p.47.

16. Datta and Porter, pp.286–7.

17. DeCorse, 'Culture Contact, Continuity, and Change', p.182.

18. DeCorse cautions readers that the consumption of European goods by Elminians should not be interpreted as their acculturation to European ways of life (archaeologists have traditionally interpreted the presence of European goods at the sites of non-Europeans as acculturation). DeCorse amply demonstrates that although their material culture changed, Elminians maintained many African cultural practices, namely in the use of domestic space, foodways, and mortuary patterns. DeCorse, 'Culture Contact, Continuity, Change', pp.182–90.

19. Although only a few sites of coastal states have been archaeologically tested or excavated along the Lower Guinea Coast (Ivory Coast, Ghana, Togo, Benin, and Nigeria), none has yielded the quantities of European goods that were recovered from Elimina. DeCorse, personal communication.

20. Benjamin W. Kankpeyeng, 'Archaeological Resources Management in Ghana' (MA paper, Syracuse University, 1996), pp.16–17.

21. Kankpeyeng, p.45.

22. This is my impression of the tours in 1993, and I have since asked other individuals who have visited them, and they agree with my interpretation.

23. The Central Region is a political unit of Ghana comparable to a province or a state. In 1989 a team of Ghanaians developed a project to promote tourism in the Central Region and approached institutions in the United States for funding and technical support, Preparatory Committee on Tourism and Development Scheme for the Central Region, 'Executive Summary: Pre-Feasibility Study Report on Tourism Development Scheme for the Central Region' (Cape Coast, Ghana, 1989 mimeograph), 48 pp. USAID provided the bulk of the funding to supplement funds provided by the Government of Ghana, the United Nations Development Project, and donations from the Ghana branch of Shell Oil. The collaborating organizations included Conservation International, the Consortium of Midwestern Universities, US branch of the International Council of Monuments and Sites, and the Smithsonian Institution. These organizations worked with several Ghanaian institutions, including GMMB, University of Ghana, Wildlife Department, and Tourist Board to improve and expand hotel and tourist facilities, to develop Kakum National Park, to stabilize and preserve the Elmina and Cape castles, and Fort St. Jago, and to provide technical assistance and staff training for exhibits at the both castles and Kakum National Park.

24. Preparatory Committee on Tourism, p.8. Not all of the proposals in this document have been implemented.

25. Although I did not see the exhibition, I have read a brochure about it. The brochure, however, is apparently deceptive of the exhibition's actual contents. It suggests that the diaspora is a small part of the exhibition's total story-line, but according to those who have seen it the exhibit devotes considerable attention and space to the diaspora in North America. See Schildkrout, p.38, and Kreamer.

26. 'Whitewashing' the castles refers to application of a lime mixture to their exterior walls in

order to stabilize them from the corrosive effects of the salt air. GMMB is required by the National Museum Regulations, 1973 to paint or whitewash the national monuments periodically (see Kankpeyeng, pp.67–8). The castles and forts have received this treatment at least since the mid-1970s, and most likely much earlier.

27. Bruner, p.294.

28. Given the acrimonious nature of this debate I prefer to keep the name of the individual confidential. Schidkrout reports a similar attitude from Ghanaian museum professionals who feel that 'since these are the first museums [in Ghana] to attract major international funding, the exhibitions should showcase Ghanaian culture', p.38.

29. There were articles in the *New York Times, Chicago Tribune* and *Washington Post*, among others. Stephen Buckley, 'U.S., African Blacks Differ on Turning Slave Dungeons Into Tourist Attractions', *Washington Post*, 17 April 1995; Eric Ransdell, 'Africa's Cleaned-Up Slave Castle', U.S. *News and World Report*, 18 September 1995, p.33; Liz Sly, 'Ghana Still Hears Rattle of Slave's Chain', *Chicago Tribune*, 2 April 1995.

30. Buckley, *Washington Post*, A-10.

31. Bruner did interview some of the local residents of Elmina. Brunner, pp.297–300.

32. Personal communications, Sallars Awortwi, Raymond Agbo and Francis Duah, November 1993. The funeral for the chief of Elmina took place in December 1993, during that time renovations of Elmina castle were in full swing. GMMB possibly denied the request of the council to prevent those attending the funeral from potential injury. This safety issue, however, was not mentioned in any of the conversations to which I was privy.

33. Brunner, p.298.

34. Pierre Nora, 'Between Memory and History', in Pierre Nora (ed.), Arthur Goldhammer (trans.), *Realms of Memory* (New York, Columbia University Press), p.3.

35. The first event remembering those enslaved was held in December 1994 by a group of Ghanaian chiefs for a group of visiting African Americans. The ceremony was for the atonement for their ancestors' role in slavery, see Liz Sly. The other event was held in August 1997 at the opening ceremony for the third Pan-African Historical Theatre Festival (PANAFEST), where the chiefs and local communities dressed in mourning clothes to remember those who were sold into slavery, victims of anti-colonial struggles, and departed African leaders, see: Janet Quainoo, 'Elmina Mourns Slaves', *Daily Graphic* (Accra, Ghana), 30 August 1997.

36. Casey, p.68.

37. Of the European forts only the Portuguese fort once known as Fort Saint-Jean Baptiste Ajuda still stands in Ouidah. Its dungeons are partially intact, but over the years these spaces have obviously been altered and used for other purposes. They do not evoke the memory of the slave trade as the castle dungeons do in Ghana.

38. Robin Law, *The Slave Coast of West Africa, 1550–1750: The Impact of the Atlantic Slave Trade on an African Society* (Oxford, Clarendon Press, 1991), p.13. This discussion focuses on the memory of the slave trade in two places of the former Slave Coast: first, the present-day city of Ouidah, originally known as Glehoue, served as the port of the Hueda Kingdom (also known historically as Whydah (English), Fida (Dutch), Juda (Portuguese). Formerly dominated by Allada, Hueda existed as a separate state from 1670 until the Dahomian army conquered it in 1727. The second place is Allada, which refers to the kingdom (also known as Ardra kingdom), its capital (Great Allada, or Zima) and the present-day town by that name. Dahomey conquered the kingdom of Allada in 1724; see, Law, Ch.1, 4, 6, and 7. I discuss these places in the order in which I visited them not in the chronological order of their histories.

39. Law, *Slave Coast*, p.151.

40. Kenneth G. Kelly, 'The archaeology of African-European interaction: investigating the social roles of trade, traders, and the use of space in the seventeenth- and eighteenth-century *Hueda* Kingdom, Republic of Benin', *World Archaeology*, Vol.28, No.3 (1997), p.358.

41. Basil Davidson, *The African Slave Trade*, revised and expanded edition (Boston, 1980), p.105. Davidson cites as an example of a floating barracoon off Dahomey in 1739 serving as a fortress and trading station for an English company. I only found references, however, to onshore slave lodges and factories in the secondary literature of the Slave Coast.

42. Law, *Slave Coast*, p.122.
43. Ibid.
44. Ibid., p.151 and Kelly, pp.358–9.
45. Law, *Slave Coast*, p.151.
46. A. Akinjokin, *Dahomey and its Neighbours, 1708–1818* (Cambridge, Cambridge University Press, 1967), pp.3–198 and appendix 2, pp.216–19. All these forts were later reoccupied for the illegal slave trade, the palm oil trade, or missionary activities. Richard Burton, *A Mission to Gelele, King of Dahomey* (London, Tinsley Brothers, 1864), pp.64–76, 84–92, 108–14; Pierre Verger, *Flux et reflux de la traite des negrès entre le golfe de Benin et Bahia de todos os santos du dix-septième au dix-neuvième siècle* (Paris, Mouton, 1968), p.564.
47. Patrick Manning, *Slavery, Colonialism and Economic Growth in Dahomey, 1640–1960* (Cambridge, Cambridge University Press, 1982), pp.46–50.
48. In 1865 the Portuguese reoccupied the fort in 1865 which was used alternately for Catholic and Protestant missionary activities, see Manning, p.56. It was finally abandoned on 31 July 1961, a year after Dahomey became independent from the French. In an effort to destroy the fort, the Portuguese set fire to the main building. Samuel DeCalo, *Historical Dictionary of Benin* (Landham, MD, Scarecrow Press, 1995), pp.269–70.
49. Afro-Brazilians settled in several coastal cities and towns in addition to Ouidah, including Agoué, Porto Novo, and Lagos, see Verger, pp.559–63, and plates 36–46.
50. *Asen* is used for both singular and plural forms. Bryna Freyer, 'Asen: Iron Altars from Ouidah, Republic of Benin', 17 December 1993–24 April 1994 (exhibition brochure) National Museum of African Art, Smithsonian Institution, pp.1–3.
51. Burton, p.58
52. The source of this information is a document in the Bibliothèque Nationale, Paris. Toussaint's son made this claim about his father's heritage after Toussaint's death, so the information is suspect. David Geggus, 'Toussaint Louverture and the Slaves of Bréda Plantations', *Journal of Caribbean History*, Vol.20 (1985–86) pp.31, 32, 45 n.8. The name of Toussaint's father is given in Martin Ros, *Night of Fire: The Black Napoleon and the Battle for Haiti* (New York, Sarpendon, 1994), p.8.
53. Law, *Slave Coast*, p.279.
54. Personal communication, Alexis Adande, Université Nationale du Benin, December 1993. Adande has undertaken archaeological investigations at Togudo-Awute, see: Alexis Adande, 'Togudo-Awute, capitale de l'ancien royaume d'Allada, étude d'une cité précoloniale d'après les sources orales, écrites et les données de l'archéologie' (Université de Paris I Panthéon-Sorbonne, Paris, 1984).
55. Carolyn E. Fick, *The Making of Haiti: The Saint Domingue Revolution from Below* (Knoxville, University Press of Tennessee, 1990), p.281 n.59.
56. Geggus, p.38.
57. Law, *Slave Coast*, pp.184–5.
58. This is my interpretation based on later conversations with Beninois students who felt that it did not matter to them whether or not Toussaint was from Allada, he was their hero because he fought against the French, as they had done to win their independence.
59. See Law, *Slave Coast*, pp.345–50, and Manning, for further discussion of the points.
60. Quainoo, 'Elmina Mourns Slaves', Nana Kwesi Tandoh, acting president of the district which includes Elmina, gave the welcoming address at the opening of PANFEST, see note 35 above.

Notes on Contributors

Rosanne Marion Adderley is Assistant Professor of History at Tulane University. Her publications include 'Orisha Worship and "Jesus Time": Rethinking African Religious Conversion in the Nineteenth-century Caribbean', *Pennsylvania History* [Special Issue] (1997).

Sylvia R. Frey is Professor of History at Tulane University. Among her publications are *Water from the Rock. Black Resistance in a Revolutionary Age* (Princeton, Princeton University Press, 1991) and (with Betty Wood) *Come Shouting to Zion. African American Protestantism in the American South and British Caribbean to 1830* (Chapel Hill, University of North Carolina Press, 1998).

Linda Heywood is Associate Professor in the Department of History at Howard University, Washington, DC.

Lawrence N. Powell is Professor of History at Tulane University. His publications include *New Masters: Northern Planters during the Civil War and Reconstruction* (New Haven, Yale University Press, 1980).

Julie Saville is Associate Professor of History at the University of Chicago. She is the author of *The Work of Reconstruction: From Slave to Wage Laborers in South Carolina, 1860–1870* (New York, Cambridge University Press, 1994).

Rebecca J. Scott is Professor of History at the University of Michigan. Her publications include *Slave Emancipation in Cuba: The Transition to Free Labor, 1860–1899* (Princeton, Princeton University Press, 1985) and 'Defining the Boundaries of Freedom in the World of Cane: Cuba, Brazil, and Louisiana after Emancipation', *American Historical Review* (1994).

Theresa A. Singleton is a historical archaeologist and is curator at the National Museum of Natural History, the Smithsonian Institution, Washington, DC and a member of the Department of Anthropology at Syracuse University. Her publications include *The Archaeology of Slavery and Plantation Life* (Orlando, 1985) and 'An Archaeological Framework for Slavery and Emancipation, 1740–1880', in Mark P. Leone and Parker B. Potter (eds.), *The Recovery of Meaning: Historical Archaeology in the Eastern United States* (Washington, DC and London, 1988).

Mary Turner is attached to the Institute of Commonwealth Studies at the University of London. She is the author of *Slaves and Missionaries: The Disintegration of Jamaican Slave Society, 1787–1834* (University of Illinois Press, 1982); 'Chattel Slaves into Wage Slaves: A Jamaican Case Study', in M. Cross and G. Heuman (eds.), *Labour in the Caribbean: From Emancipation to Independence* (London, 1988), and edited *From Chattel Slavery to Wage Slavery* (London, Bloomington and Indianapolis, 1995).

Daniel H. Usner Jr. is Professor in the Department of History at Cornell University. He is the author of *Indians, Settlers and Slaves in a Frontier Economy: The Lower Mississippi Valley before 1783* (Chapel Hill, University of North Carolina Press, 1992).

Betty Wood is Lecturer in the Faculty of History at the University of Cambridge. Her books include *Slavery in Colonial Georgia, 1730–1775* (Athens, 1985); *Women's Work, Men's Work. The Informal Slave Economies of Lowcountry Georgia, 1750–1830* (Athens, 1996); *The Origins of American Slavery: The English Colonies to 1700* (New York, 1997) and (with Sylvia R. Frey), *Come Shouting to Zion. African American Protestantism in the American South and British Caribbean to 1830* (Chapel Hill, University of North Carolina Press, 1998).

Index